THE SANCHEZ FAMILY

THE SANCHEZ FAMILY

Mexican American High School and Collegiate Wrestlers from Cheyenne, Wyoming

Jorge Iber

UNIVERSITY OF WYOMING PRESS
Laramie

Published by University of Wyoming Press
An imprint of University Press of Colorado
1580 North Logan Street, Suite 660
PMB 39883
Denver, Colorado 80203-1942

Printed in the United States of America

The University Press of Colorado is a proud member of Association of University Presses.

The University Press of Colorado is a cooperative publishing enterprise supported, in part, by Adams State University, Colorado School of Mines, Colorado State University, Fort Lewis College, Metropolitan State University of Denver, University of Alaska Fairbanks, University of Colorado, University of Northern Colorado, University of Wyoming, Utah State University, and Western Colorado University.

∞ This paper meets the requirements of the ANSI/NISO Z39.48-1992 (Permanence of Paper).

ISBN: 978-1-64642-751-2 (hardcover)
ISBN: 978-1-64642-752-9 (ebook)
https://doi.org/10.5876/9781646427529

Cataloging-in-Publication data for this title is available online at the Library of Congress

For more about the Sanchez family, visit https://sanchezwrestlinghistory.weebly.com.

Cover photo courtesy of the Sanchez family.

As always, this book is dedicated to my wonderful wife, Raquel, and also to our son, Matthew. Additionally, I would like to thank Jim Sanchez and the other members of his family for all their assistance in helping to make this project possible.

Contents

Introduction 3

1. The Sanchez Family Arrives and Settles in Cheyenne: 1915–1956 17
2. Athletics/Sports as a Part of the Latino/a Historical Literature 44
3. The Sanchez Name Begins to Stand Out in State Wrestling Circles: 1956–1967 59
4. Ray Sanchez Has a Brilliant Future: 1962–1981 80
5. The Next Generation of Sanchezes as Wrestlers and Coaches: 1979–2023 95

Conclusion: The Most Recent Generation of Sanchezes on the Mat and the Significance of Sport in Latino/Hispanic History and Life 129

Notes 141

Bibliography 169

Index 179

About the Author 187

THE SANCHEZ FAMILY

Introduction

IN LATE APRIL 1965, a boisterous crowd of more than 250 locals gathered at the Cheyenne Regional Airport and awaited the return of a conquering hometown hero. Was it University of Wyoming legend Kenny Sailors, perhaps, arriving in town on his way to his old stomping grounds in Laramie?[1] Was it former Cheyenne High School star and Green Bay receiver Boyd Dowler (the 1959 NFL Rookie of the Year), who, by this time, was already a two-time NFL champion (and would go on to be part of five Packer title teams)?[2] Was it Richard Babka, who earned a silver medal in the discus in the 1960 Olympics?[3] No, it was none of those august names from Wyoming's sporting history. Instead, the locals were there to welcome an unlikely champion who had brought national recognition to his birthplace.

There were two major differences between the subject of this story and the likes of Sailors, Dowler, and Babka. Although hoop legend Sailors was not particularly tall (even by Basketball Association of America and National Basketball Association standards of that time), standing 5′10″

https://doi.org/10.5876/9781646427529.c000

and weighing around 175 lbs., this title holder was even smaller in stature. Our subject was certainly a lilliputian in comparison to Dowler, who stood 6′5″ and weighed 220 lbs. and Babka, who was as tall as Dowler and carried a frame of 267 lbs. In contrast, this new hero was around 5′5″ and tipped the scales at less than 120 lbs. In what sport could such a diminutive person participate and triumph? That sport was wrestling.

An even more critical distinction was that the new luminary was not part of the majority population of the state. He was, rather, a member of a group that has often endured difficult and discriminatory circumstances: a Mexican American. As this work will detail, this population was often relegated to "the poor side of town" and toiled in menial, manual labor such as working for the railroads or in agriculture for a majority of the state's history. Indeed, it was common to see signs in parts of Wyoming that stated: "No dogs or Mexicans allowed." A recent article on a Mexican American couple in Lovell documents such improprieties, as the interviewee, Milton Ontiveros (who has lived in the state since the 1940s), noted that while his clan followed the beet crop, "We use to stop in towns hungry to go buy something to eat, but we couldn't eat at (the) restaurants. They had signs—no Mexicans or Negroes allowed. Just like a dog, you see."[4]

In April 1965, however, here was someone special, an individual who even merited mention in the "Faces in the Crowd" column of *Sports Illustrated* after claiming his eighty-first consecutive mat triumph, over Wright Fujikawa of Worland.[5] The name of this competitor was Ray Sanchez, and given the positive press to Cheyenne, might this Mexican American be seen differently than his fellow Spanish-surnamed Wyomingites? What impact would that have on his family and, indeed, on persons of Mexican descent living in the state?

The reason for all this revelry was that Ray had returned with a championship title in Freestyle wrestling from Nationals in San Francisco.[6] That was not his only accomplishment, however, as Sanchez eventually completed a legendary, undefeated high school career for the Cheyenne High School (CHS) Indians, finishing with a mark of 98–0 and four state titles (at three different weight classifications: 103, 115, and 120 lbs.). Although he had achieved tremendous success, Ray felt a bit intimidated as he traveled with his coach, Joe Dowler, to the Golden State to participate in a tournament that not only included the best high school grapplers in the country but also featured collegiate competitors as well. As he recounted to his nephew Jim (a high school and collegiate wrestler himself) many years later, "It was a little scary going to the Nationals while still in high school. . . . Really, I went to the meet just for the experience."[7] Still, Ray proved himself at this elite level of competition, and earned the applause and admiration of fellow Wyomingites.

In addition to his performance as an athlete, Coach Dowler portrayed Ray to the community as a typical "All-American" youth. Even before Ray headed to Nationals, Sanchez's mentor noted that this athlete was "not only a great wrestler, but he exemplifies high school athletics at its best. He trains hard, learns well and fast, and above all possesses the outstanding ability to compete." He also did well in the classroom, carrying a high B average. Would Ray continue his wrestling career at the University of Wyoming and bring further athletic glory to his home state?[8] Such positive acclamations were not a particularly common occurrence for Spanish-surnamed individuals in this state at that time.

Ray was the youngest of a family of wrestlers (brothers Gilbert, David, and Arthur) who made their mark on the mat (and other sports as well) during the late 1950s and into the early 1960s. All of these youths, save one, would go on to have collegiate careers. More important, this particular generation (born between 1938 and 1946) utilized sport as a mechanism to radically alter the Sanchez clan's economic and social standing into the 1960s and beyond. Through the use of athletics, this first generation created opportunities almost unheard of for Mexican Americans in Wyoming: the occasion to go to college and earn middle-class standing and income. Subsequent generations of this family followed their fathers and uncles on to mats at various institutions and earned degrees, entering professional occupations. Indeed, it is not misleading to contend that wrestling became the family's "business"—a mechanism by which it extricated itself from the working class of Cheyenne and moved on to economic progress and improved social standing.

This work will follow the Sanchezes from their arrival in the Equality State in the early decades of the twentieth century through the lives and careers of three generations.[9] What issues did this family confront upon arriving in Wyoming? How were their experiences similar to or different from those of other Latinos/as in this state? Most significant, how did sport help them change their social/economic trajectory? There are two main goals for this project: First it aims to add to the overall history of Latinos in the state of Wyoming. Second, it seeks to utilize this family's historical experiences to demonstrate that athletic participation (in this case, wrestling) has been (and still is) a valuable tool that Mexican Americans (and other Latinos) have utilized to challenge their current status and how the broader/majority population perceives them. To the surprise of many readers, there is a growing academic literature on this topic, which will also be briefly discussed in this work.

Given these changes, do subsequent generations of this family continue the tradition of wrestling, or did the changes brought about by participating in athletics in earlier decades make it possible to have a broader number of choices (sporting, educational, and occupational), including no longer continuing in what, for many years, was considered to be the "family tradition?" The topic of sporting participation and its impact upon individuals, families, and communities has become an area of research for scholars of the Mexican American (and other Latinos/as as well) experience in recent years.[10]

Before proceeding to an overview of the various chapters that follow, it is necessary to proffer a brief discussion of two key theoretical underpinnings that guided this research. A crucial first line of inquiry was to examine the way that the majority population (in Wyoming and nationwide) perceived Mexican Americans as a specific group. In other words, when a "typical" citizen of the United States in the years before World War II (in a historical and daily life context) envisaged the cultural, physical, and intellectual traits of people from Mexico (or their descendants), what did they visualize? Two works by Natalia Molina, *Fit to Be Citizens? Public Health and Race in Los Angeles, 1879–1939* and *How Race Is Made in America: Immigration, Citizenship, and the Historical Power of Racial Scripts*, provide extensive coverage of this topic.[11]

Next, it was also crucial to envisage what Americans believed about Spanish-surnamed *atletas* (athletes) and their "limitations" (in regard to their intellectual and physical capabilities) during the first few decades of the past century. Given that sport, and acceptance of "American" games, was seen as a key element of how "foreigners" could become acculturated to life in the United States, how did Latinos (and, specifically, Mexican Americans) fit into the hierarchy of athletic competition?[12] In other words, did this group have the "smarts" and "capacity" to contend in the rugged world of American sport? I will examine this theoretical thread utilizing materials from a work by Jorge Iber, Samuel O. Regalado, José M. Alamillo, and Arnoldo De León entitled *Latinos in U.S. Sports: A History of Isolation, Cultural Identity, and Acceptance*. Therein, these authors scrutinized what academicians (and others) who focused on such topics had to say about Spanish-surnamed athletes.[13]

Molina's 2006 work *Fit to Be Citizens?* provides an overview of how of health officials perceived Mexicans within the diverse population and assumed racial hierarchy of Los Angeles. While, originally, there was a sense that this "race" would simply (like Native Americans) "fade away," starting in the 1910s (with the arrival of more Mexicans to fill manual labor needs) there commenced a shift in the bureaucrats' assessment. By the time of the Great Depression, the notion that this population was indeed inferior seemed clearly to be "indisputable."[14] From there, a plethora of hygiene-related and intellectual "problems" became affixed to them. Molina provides extensive coverage of an overabundance of assorted "maladies" and cultural traits that demonstrate their "backwardness." For example, they were disease carriers,[15] unsanitary and ignorant of proper hygiene,[16] avoided bathing,[17] had crude and primitive parenting skills,[18] were in need of uplift by whites,[19] were genetically flawed,[20] were less able bodied (particularly emphasized during the Great Depression),[21] and were feebleminded (to the point that a number merited sterilization).[22]

Molina's subsequent study *How Race Is Made* builds upon her previous research and examines the idea of "racial scripts" as a mechanism of oppression. Here, the author argues that the process of assigning negative traits, such as those noted above, to certain groups sets the stage for such assumptions to be acted upon by "a range of principals, from institutional actors to ordinary citizens."[23] Thus, if the broader society believes that a certain population is lazy and possesses limited intelligence, it acts accordingly toward them. Why, then, were the Spanish-surnamed people in Cheyenne and the rest of Wyoming overwhelmingly concentrated in menial positions over the years? Simply because society believed those were the limits of their intellectual/occupational capabilities. Why did they remain mired there in successive generations? Because they simply did not have the determination, motivation, and personal initiative to move up the economic and occupational ladder.

While the acceptance and utilization of racial scripts by whites could pigeonhole ethnic and racial groups, Molina also notes that there exists a tool often marshaled to fight against such assumptions: She designates these apparatuses as "counterscripts." These she describes as "practices of resistance, claims for dignity, and downright refusal to take it anymore," utilized to challenge the "dominant racial scripts." While researchers have focused on a variety of counterscripts, such as "protests or community organizing" (e.g., joining unions, working through religious organizations, joining political movements, and other models), these efforts do not have to be "organized." As Molina argues, they, instead, can be "encompassed in daily expressions of compassion and solidarity."[24] A recent work by George J. Sanchez on the Boyle Heights neighborhood in Los Angeles well articulates the overarching goals of counterscripts. Such tools, he argues, "allow us to understand how those racial and ethnic groups that were seen as disposable . . . would band together to proclaim their worth as Americans who belonged."[25] Until recently, the scholarship on Mexican Americans and Latinos did not include an examination of sport as an implement with which to present counterscripts. Examples of counterscripts are present throughout the lives of the various generations of Sanchezes in this study, both on the mat and in other parts of their lives.

In conjunction with the racial scripts applied to the bodies and intellect of Mexican Americans, there is also research specifically focused on their athletic "limitations," and the work of Iber et al., *Latinos in U.S. Sports* provides a summary of such endeavors. One of the contributors to this study, Arnoldo De León, in his magisterial work *They Called Them Greasers: Anglo Attitudes Toward Mexicans in Texas, 1836–1900*, not only confirms Molina's analysis but moves the time of such assumptions back to the early nineteenth century. Starting with Austin's "Old Three Hundred,"[26] Anglos coming into the territory made their postulations abundantly clear with statements such as that Mexicans were "descendants of a tradition of paganism, depravity, and primitivism . . . [their] habits clashed with American values, such as the work ethic." One of the most extreme utterances argued that the bodies of Mexicans were so foul that "not even worms or animals would consume their cadavers."[27]

Specifically concerning athletic ability (or, rather, inability) and the use of sport to "control/civilize" Mexican Americans, Iber and his coauthors unearthed a surfeit of material—primarily master's theses and doctoral dissertations from the early 1920s through the mid-1950s. A sampling of such research efforts is recapped in the following paragraphs.

In 1923, David Julian Chavez's master's thesis at the University of Texas, entitled "Civic Education of the Spanish-American," documented how educational leaders wanted/needed to utilize sport as a way to help make youths from this populace into "real" Americans. Learning to play according to "the rules," along with notions of self-control, reliability, and teamwork, would help in the "acquisition of requisite mental attitudes," and "if enough time is given . . . through physical exercise . . . there is every reason to believe that the Spanish-American will become as efficient a citizen as those of other nationalities."[28]

Two years later, at the same institution, Florrie S. Dupre's dissertation, entitled "Play as a Factor in the Education of Children," sought to encourage the government of the city of San Antonio to increase spending on parks and school recreational implements to "counteract negative trends among local youths." Of course, a substantial portion of the project focuses on arguing that the Mexican American youths were particularly in need of such investment, with them being overly (genetically?) prone to "idleness, in loafing, in wandering aimlessly about the streets and other undesirable districts." Hopefully, disbursements in these areas would help to straighten out what Dupre referred to as the "lower classes" or "greasers."[29]

While these first two items focused on how to use sporting activity to "improve" Mexican Americans to make them more "civil" (under the direction of whites, of course), the first series of articles these authors found which provided a direct scientific (supposedly) analysis of the athletic abilities of this group come from the journal *American Physical Education Review* in 1922. The author was Elmer D. Mitchell, who, in addition to an academic career (in the area of physical education), served as field general of the football team at Michigan State Normal School (now Eastern Michigan University) between 1915 and 1916 and as head basketball coach at that institution between 1915 and 1917, before moving on to Ann Arbor to coach the Wolverines in hoops from 1917–1919.[30] The essays, which appeared in three consecutive issues of the journal, all bore the same title—"Racial Traits in Athletics"—and sought to describe the physical characteristics and sporting temperament of various racial and ethnic groups (a total of fifteen). The clans were organized in what Mitchell considered to be descending order; thus, the first tier consisted of the most gifted, followed by those less endowed. In the first level, we find the American, English, Irish and German "races." These were depicted as the most vigorous, talented, and intellectually capable of participating in American sport.[31]

The second essay is where we discern the first discussion that bears upon Mexican Americans. Here, Mitchell listed the next-highest level of humanity in regard to athletics. This group included Scandinavians, Latins, Dutch, Poles, and "Negro." In regard to the "Latins," the author combined what he called the "Southern races" (the French, Italian and Spanish). He summarized the whole group by stating that sports were a problem because this group's "emotions, being more on the surface, make the Latin more lighthearted . . . and at the same time, more quickly aroused to temper and fickle in his ardor." Mitchell then proceeded to further break down the larger unit, with the French being the best of the bunch, since they, "being the northernmost of the Latin kin and having the larger share of Teuton blood, are naturally the most self-controlled." The Spaniard, on the other hand, is much more problematic, for they "tend to an indolent disposition. . . . He has less self-control than either the Frenchman or the Italian . . . [and he] is cruel, as shown by the bullfights in Mexico and Spain." Certainly, given such assumptions, this portion of the Mexican American's genetic makeup can only spell trouble on the field, the court, or the mat.[32]

In the final essay, Mitchell gets down to the bottom of the athletic barrel, and here is where we find the "South American" (along with Jews, "Indians," Greeks, "Orientals," Slavs, and Finns). Those who live below the Rio Grande, it appears, inherited the negative traits of both Spaniards and Native Americans. His quote on this topic is long, but it is worth citing in its entirety in order to make clear how educationalists and those involved in leadership of physical education thought of such individuals:

> The South American has not the physique, environment, or disposition which makes for a champion athlete. . . . In build he is of medium height and weight, and not rugged. The games he has borrowed from foreign countries are not conducive to leisurely play. . . . [He] has inherited an undisciplined nature. The Indian in him chafes at discipline and sustained effort, while the Spanish half is proud to a fault. . . . [His] disposition makes team play difficult. . . . [T]he steady grind and the competition involved in winning a place on the Varsity has no attraction for them. Their sensitiveness makes them rebel against the outspoken manner in which the American coach shouts out criticisms upon the coaching field.

Given these faults and limitations, how could Mexican Americans succeed in American sport? Still, not all was lost and, just as Chavez and Dupre assert earlier, proper training under the right leadership could help bring these folks along, leading them to become "Americanized in American games just as in everything else."[33]

Moving into the next decades, analogous observations continued in academic literature. In a 1936 thesis by Genevieve King, her conclusion was that the Mexican American students she worked with in San Antonio had little interest in exercise. In 1952, Albert Folsom Cobb reached a similar conclusion and summarized his research by stating that the Spanish-surnamed were "not as interested or eager to participate in physical education program[s], particularly in inter-school competition as are Anglo-American boys."[34]

While the consensus remained on the side of arguing that Latinos were poor athletes, there were some subtle changes in the analysis by the 1940s and later. For example, a 1942 study by Merrell E. Thompson and Claude C. Dove, which appeared in *Research Quarterly*, noted that the Mexican American ("Spanish American") youths they studied, when "equated according to age, health, and weight . . . were superior in all events tested and significantly superior in all but the shot-put." To what did Thompson and Dove attest the surprising results? It was due to lifestyle. (Could we take that to mean that these youths often worked in order to help support their families?) The authors summarized their findings by stating that "Spanish American children lead a more vigorous physical life than do the Anglos. This condition seems to produce . . . physical development and thereby superiority in the events . . . tested." Another researcher, Bruce

Walsh-Shaw, came to similar conclusions in his 1951 MA thesis at the University of Texas. More important, however, Walsh-Shaw also stipulated that success in athletic competition "did have a slightly positive impact on how Anglo children perceived their Mexican American counterparts." All told, the racial scripts tended to flow in one conventional direction: that Latinos would not succeed in athletic competition, and thus "whites in the United States were bombarded with negative images of the physical and intellectual capabilities of Spanish-surnamed people in their midst and most ultimately assumed that the sports of the American were too sophisticated, vigorous, and challenging for the feeble minds and bodies of Latinos."[35]

A much more recent example following the trends hinted at by Walsh-Shaw so many decades ago can be found in a 2017 work by Brett Thomas Olmsted entitled "Los Mexicanos de Michigan: Claiming Space and Creating Community Through Leisure and Labor, 1920–1970." Here, the author proffers an effectual instance of how success in athletics moderated the perception of Spanish speakers by the majority population.[36] The counterscripts presented by Olmsted in regard to organizing leagues, teams, and athletic events, while focused on Michigan (and not even mentioning the sport of wrestling), provide clear parallels between his research and aspects of the lives of the Cheyenne-based Sanchezes. For example, he argued that

> sports emphasized hard work and competitiveness that allowed Mexicans to contest their imputed position as weak and passive sojourners. . . . [P]laying fields constituted a vital social area allowing Mexicanos to engage in the civic arena, to defy segregation by claiming first class citizenship access to public space . . . [thus] this took on an important function . . . by providing positive publicity to the . . . population group.[37]

Olmsted also noted the significance of participating in sports to the small number of such athletes in Michigan-area high schools he researched. Success in the realm of the local institution changed the way the majority populace thought about such individuals, thus making "interethnic acceptance" all the more possible.[38] Last, victories on the gridiron, court, diamond, or, as in the case of the early generations of Sanchezes, the mat, generated positive press in newspapers, and that, in turn, "provided at least tacit acceptance of the Mexicano . . . as social athletic equals."[39]

Having made this argument via Olmsted, this author finds an important question to address at this point is whether success in sports does overcome racial misperceptions and antagonism. A recent article entitled "It's Worth a Shot: Can Sports Combat Racism in the United States?," by University of St. Thomas (MN) law professor David A. Grenardo, addresses this issue and acknowledges that while sports cannot eliminate all elements of racism, the author does contend that it can be a powerful tool to change perceptions and also to provide opportunities to minority individuals.[40]

How do sports accomplish this important task? Among other elements, Grenardo argues that athletic endeavors provide an opportunity for "whites and minorities to interact with each other to break down barriers (both conscious and unconscious)" while pitted as competitors or when participating as teammates. Further, in an interview with author Howard Bryant, Grenardo sheds light on another critical point: the opportunity for athletics to provide a chance to further one's education and get better jobs (not only in the realm of sports, such as coaches and management, but via collegiate degrees in professional fields). "One potential way, then, to confront racism is to provide opportunities and access to jobs for minorities." Next, Grenardo argues that "once minorities have more opportunity, then their lives improve and in turn society improves." Finally, the intellectual side of sport—the planning, the strategizing, and the coaching—helps make it possible for the majority population to see minorities as more than just "bodies meant to 'shut up and dribble,' their minds become more appreciated, and they are valued for all of the abilities and talents they possess."[41]

Another way that sports can combat racism is by presenting stories of athletes of color to a broader audience. In other words, as noted earlier in my discussion on Molina, these stories (told mostly in newspapers for the Sanchez family) are themselves counterscripts, mostly, if not exclusively, written or told by members of the majority population (particularly for the first two generations of Sanchez competitors). Each triumph, especially for a local high school or university, can make people in the majority population see minorities in a different light (even if only for selfish reasons). "Moreover, telling stories to people of different races can help create bonds and bridges while educating others about their own race and culture."[42] Ultimately, while Grenardo acknowledges that "some people will not change," that does not in his view diminish the power of sport, and the stories told about athletic competition, to challenge the way that a good number of those in the majority population view minorities. In summary, Grenardo concludes (by paraphrasing Wayne Gretzky) that "sports can have a positive impact with respect to combating racism, and thus any attempts that make such an impact are shots worth taking."[43] The story of the Sanchez family from Cheyenne will provide a clear example of these arguments.

Now that the theoretical underpinning of this work is imparted, the rest of this study will proceed over the following chapters. In chapter 1 the focus turns to the arrival of this particular Sanchez clan. Where in Mexico did they come from? What were circumstances like for them in "the old country"? What drew them north, and to Wyoming and Cheyenne in particular? Where their experiences similar or different from those of other Mexican Americans in the state at that moment in time? In order to better frame their story, interviews from the La Cultura Hispanic Heritage Oral History Project from the 1980s are utilized to provide context. These interviews featured adults born in the later years of the 1800s and early 1900s wherein subjects recalled what conditions were like for them in Wyoming during the first decades of the twentieth century. All of the interviewees discussed in this chapter were born prior to 1938, the year that the first Sanchez wrestler (Gilbert) was born.

Another set of oral history interviews vital to this work were conducted over a period of many months with numerous members of the various generations of the Sanchez family. Through their words, we see how wrestling provided opportunities rare to Latinos/as in the first half of twentieth-century Wyoming, such as the chance to travel nationally and internationally and perform at the highest levels of athletic endeavors; it afforded the opportunity to be mentored by, and compete against, legends of the sport of wrestling. As these interviews articulate, these contacts (and the efforts of the Sanchezes) helped move the competitors on the path toward success on the mat and in their subsequent careers. Through this evidence, readers will "hear" the voices of these individuals as they remember their life experiences recounting their athletic and academic agency that ultimately led to the family's improved circumstances. The words of the family members, along with the positive newspaper stories on their athletic feats, provide powerful counterscripts to the negative perception of the Spanish-surnamed that had existed for so long in the state.

In chapter 2, it is necessary to convey a summary of some of the relevant academic literature that details the role of sports in the lives of Latinos/as; specifically, how has this populace, now spread out over much of the nation and over an extended period of time, utilized athletic challenges (and successes therein) as a way to impugn negative perceptions about them. Participation in sport has not just been about simply "playing," "blowing off steam," or the enjoyment of competition, as Olmsted argued in his work. These scholarly materials detail how such endeavors have played a role in community, ethnic, and labor organizing. There already exists a fairly extensive narrative that encapsulates the efforts at "counterscripting" via athletic success, and the story of the Sanchezes will add to that literature.

Chapter 3 will spotlight how Gilbert, David, and Arthur, the majority of the first generation of Sanchezes to take to the mat (and other sports as well), exploited their sporting successes as a way to not only graduate from high school but to do something quite uncommon for Latinos of the generation born during the 1930s and 1940s: go on to college, graduate, and then move on to professional careers. Their many successes, as noted in Wyoming papers, provided early counterscripts to the negative narrative associated with Mexican Americans in the state, and made it possible for each of them to attend college and subsequently begin the family's upward social and economic trajectory.

Chapter 4 follows the career of Ray Sanchez, the fourth member of this first generation who won four state titles in Wyoming and completed his high school career with an unblemished record. The reaction by the crowd after his final match for Cheyenne High School presents a vivid counterscript to the way that most Latinos were perceived in this state in the first half of the twentieth century. Further, he then went on to don the colors of his state's leading collegiate institution, offering the possibility of bringing even more recognition to Wyoming. Ray's success on the mat presented him as a model "All-American boy" and made him a hero to wrestling fans all over the state. Given the more positive perception of Ray Sanchez by locals in the 1960s, how were circumstances changing for other members of this ethnic group by this decade? Once again, the La Cultura interviews provide a glimpse of a changing (albeit slowly) context for the Spanish-surnamed in Wyoming. The group of interviewees discussed in this chapter all were born at around the same time as the first generation of Sanchez wrestlers (from 1940 through the mid-1950s).

Chapter 5 examines the second generation of this family's competitors and brings the chronicle up to the present time. Here, the movement away from an emphasis on the mat but a continued focus on education provides different counterscripts from those available to the very first generation.

Finally, the conclusion examines (briefly) the third generation. Additionally, it mentions other Latino wrestlers from Wyoming who made their mark in this sport and also offered other examples of a minority group's athletic prowess. The conclusion also ties the story of the Sanchezes to academic literature in other fields (such as economics and education) as well as summarizing the significance of this family's history to the broader narrative of Latinos/as in sport.

1

The Sanchez Family Arrives and Settles in Cheyenne

1915–1956

The earliest members of the family to arrive in the state were the grandparents of the first generation of wrestling competitors. All four of these individuals were natives of the state of Guanajuato born in the latter part of the nineteenth century. On the paternal side was Elijio Sanchez (1897) and María Romo (1899). Both hailed from the community of Irapuato. The couple married in 1914 and arrived in Cheyenne in the late 1920s (with several stops along the way). The maternal grandparents were Manuel Guadian (1897) and Valina Bonilla (1899). They were born in Romita (which is about twenty-one miles north and west of Irapuato), married in 1915, and migrated to Wyoming shortly thereafter.

Before turning to a discussion of the two pair's progeny, it is necessary to quickly detail circumstances back in Mexico that motivated their migration, eventually to Wyoming. For that, it is required to briefly consult literature that discusses conditions nationwide, and in Guanajuato, in the years preceding and during the Mexican Revolution. A basic introduction to the state is presented by Peter Standish in his work entitled *The States*

https://doi.org/10.5876/9781646427529.c001

of Mexico: A Reference Guide to History and Culture.[1] Herein, the author notes that Guanajuato contains three distinct regions: El Bajío, the southern portion, which is primarily agricultural; the Sierra, a more centrally located area featuring cattle raising as its main industry; and finally, Los Llanos del Norte, which has been a hub for mining since the sixteenth century.[2]

For the common laborers of Guanajuato, key areas of employment centered around lower-skilled posts in these industries. At around the time of the birth of Elijio, María, Manuel, and Valina, the primary occupations in El Bajío were sharecropping (or peonage), with its inherent drawbacks and limitations for personal/familial progress. As Alan Knight noted in his magisterial work *The Mexican Revolution*, "Around León . . . virtually all of the corn produced on the eve of the Revolution was the work of sharecroppers. . . . it was reckoned that most . . . were in debt; some were forced to sacrifice their precarious independence and become peons or wage laborers."[3] Further north, increased industrialization in undertakings such as shoemaking and leatherwork damaged the local artisanal industry (a traditional sector in and around León), thus limiting employment possibilities even for more highly skilled laborers. A final possibility, mining, also featured low-paying, dangerous jobs.[4] In sum, the majority of employment in these fields failed to provide workers with realistic prospects for substantive social and economic improvement. In part, such trends made Guanajuato one of the principal states pushing people to the United States in the early 1900s.[5]

A quick way to examine the need to seek better economic circumstances in *el norte* is gleaned from a couple of works detailing wages and living standards in Mexico during the late nineteenth and early twentieth centuries. Jeffrey Bortz and Marcos Aguila's work, "Earning a Living: A History of Real Wage Studies in Twentieth Century Mexico," for example, provides a broad description of real wages and standard of living in the country. Therein, the authors cited a 1923 Mexican government report; it argued that "wages and salaries, with few exceptions, were in 1902 almost the same as in 1870." The essay further articulated some key misperceptions of the ruling class regarding daily life of the common folks during the Porfiriato. Citing an 1898 article (written by José de la Cruz and quoting Porfirio Díaz's foreign minister, Matías Romero), one would have thought that there would be no reason to leave a burgeoning economy to travel north. This elite argued that "the rate of wages keeps moving upwards. . . . [T]here is no sign that it has reached its limit. . . . [O]ur peons are not starving, and are, for the most part, a quiet and philosophic people . . . complaining very little, while a Patriotic government has their interests at heart." Even after the installation of the revolutionary 1917 Constitution, which mandated a minimum wage that would "be considered sufficient, attending to the conditions in each region, to satisfy the normal necessities of life of a worker, his education and his honest pleasures, considering him the head of the family," it was clear to many that greater chances for betterment existed outside of Mexico.[6] Clearly, by the time that national law codified this right, hundreds of thousands of young men such as Elijio Sanchez and Manuel Guadian had determined to take themselves, and their spouses, elsewhere.

A second study that documents the impact of economic issues upon the lives of Mexico's laboring class can be found in an article by Moramay Lopez-Alonso from 2007.[7] This work argues that while the process of industrialization during the Porfiriato benefited some, it did not generate a positive outcome among the laboring classes. According to the data presented, workers who were born during the period between 1850 and 1880 "were better off than their counterparts who were born in the last quarter of the nineteenth century," in other words, the very height of the Díaz regime. Lopez-Alonso's research succinctly summarizes the circumstances that Elijio and Manuel confronted as they married and sought to begin their families. The period of industrialization ultimately curtailed any hopes of improvement in economic standing for the Sanchezes and Guadians, as "living standards for laboring people then stagnated during the first part of the twentieth century . . . [and] in a long-term perspective, the economic growth fostered during the Díaz regime and the social and political transformation that resulted from the 1910 Revolution did not substantially improve . . . standards of living of the Mexican laboring class."[8]

As if the pre- and postrevolutionary commercial changes in Mexico were not sufficient to push people out of the country, another key element was the mayhem caused by the widespread fighting throughout the nation. Once again, we can turn briefly to the work of Knight, who provides glimpses of what this was like in Guanajuato. In the early stages of the revolt, "manufacturing cities of the Bajío were particularly prominent in the spate of riots which hit Mexican cities in the spring of 1911."[9] The political situation in the state was unstable and shifted between leadership that was loyal to the maintenance of a government that was interested in "honest, stable, constitutional government, which would respect rights, property and votes" (in other words, maintain a semblance of the status quo) to other interests who spearheaded who "a vigorous revolutionary movement." Some of the latter came from higher levels of society who had made what Knight referred to as "a tactical adhesion to the revolution itself; if they could not beat it, they would have to join it." Others, such as Cándido Navarro, led a group in Guanajuato that was "spoiling for a fight," and he was a man considered "a dedicated revolutionary with a strong popular following." Still others supported bandits, and their activities became "extensive and ingenious" in the area. In response to this element of banditry, by 1912, middle-class families in Irapuato recruited individuals to counter the lawlessness. In sum, it is possible to encapsulate the goings-on in this state by noting that "opportunist rebellions . . . represented local, defensive reactions to the revolutionary upheaval of 1911. And, since the upheaval continued into 1912 and 1913, such freelance activity continued, ultimately to reach its apogee in . . . 1916–1920."[10]

This is but a brief summary of what the young couples who would head to Wyoming endured/witnessed around them during the time of their courtships and marriages. It is no wonder that Guanajuato expelled so many individuals during the Porfiriato and the revolutionary period. By contrast, even a remote locale such as the Equality State held much greater promise. The question now is what type of jobs Elijio and Manuel would find in order to support themselves and their families upon arrival in this remote corner of *el norte*.

There is a significant amount of research that provides information on these occupational fields and how Mexicans and Mexican Americans fit into Wyoming's labor force, with many articles in the *Annals of Wyoming* and dissertations covering this topic. Not surprisingly, to those familiar with the literature on Mexican Americans and labor in the early twentieth century, the choices for work were limited mostly to low-remunerative and relatively low-skilled occupations. Many of these studies not only discuss circumstances on the job but also shed light upon daily life.

Trisha Venisa-Alicia Martínez's dissertation entitled "Living the Manito Trail: Maintaining Self, Culture, and Community" was completed in 2019 at the University of New Mexico. This scholar noted two of the key elements that helped bring Latinos/as to Wyoming: First, "Economic development related to the growth of agriculture, ranching and sheepherding led to an increasing need for permanent and seasonal workers"; Second, Manitos (the term used for self-reference by such persons from New Mexico and southern Colorado) "had relatively easy access to the villages of northern New Mexico and so they traveled back and forth between their homes and Wyoming."[11] In addition to recruitment efforts for sheepherding, there were also advertisements for "opportunities" in the beet fields in many local papers in the Land of Enchantment as well as visits by "the bosses themselves of labor contractors . . . to hire a crew for particular jobs." What made such prospects in Wyoming appealing, according to Martínez, was the fact that the "socio-economic conditions of early 1900s rural New Mexico became more devastating as Anglo business excursions infiltrated the territory."[12] In summary, Martínez argued that while there was some benefit to working in Wyoming, the trail often did not lead to enormous prosperity. "In a predominantly Anglo state, Manitos were marginalized and treated unfairly in all aspects of life, including work, school, living conditions, etc."[13]

Vanessa Fonseca's article, part of a special 2017 edition of *Annals of Wyoming*, provides further insight into the travel from New Mexico to Wyoming during the early decades of the twentieth century. Fonseca's use of census data revealed that while many individual men went north during this time period, "more families arrived in the 1920s and 1930s. Most individuals who arrived at Wyoming were born in New Mexico with both parents born in New Mexico. . . . [These people] were beginning to establish themselves . . . making their homes along the I-80 corridor where jobs were plentiful."[14] This same issue included an extensive essay by Virginia Sanchez that discussed the reason for movement from the Mora Valley to the Equality State:

> Due to generations and generations of settlement and farming, the once fertile . . . [Valley] could no longer sustain its growing population. By the 1940s, families on small farms found it more and more difficult to make

> ends meet. . . . Many found seasonal work as sheepherders and field laborers, leaving their wives and children to care for the family crops and livestock. After obtaining permanent work in Cheyenne, many uprooted their families . . . to earn wages and seek a better life for their children. . . . As consistent wage earners, these men were able to provide for their growing families in terms of opportunities for a better standard of living and education.[15]

Given that sheepherding was the earliest area of occupational concentration, Peg Arnold's 1997 essay "Wyoming's Hispanic Sheepherders" is important.[16] In this effort, the author noted that the men who worked as *borregueros* tended to make pilgrimages to the state that lasted for anywhere between six to ten months. Three different groups of Spanish-surnamed individuals comprised the bulk of this group. The largest, came from New Mexico and were "born in such towns as Taos, Mora, Valdez, Las Vegas, Arroyo Seco, and Costilla. . . . To a lesser degree . . . [some]were born in Mexico . . . [and] Finally, a third segment . . . moved north from their Colorado birthplaces, such as Denver and Florence."[17] Most tended to work around the vicinity of Rawlins, though others also toiled in areas from Cokeville to Douglas. Another important aspect of this life was that sheepherding "was often concentrated in families and, according to the owner and operator of a large enterprise, the Nelson Land and Livestock Company, these herders were very effective in their jobs, with losses always well below that of other groups who worked with this livestock." In contrast, Nelson recalled, non-Mexican herders incurred substantial damages. "Annual death losses due to predators and water hole drownings reached ten percent." This important field of endeavor was not particularly well remunerated, with average earnings during the 1950s of only around $270 per season. Still, *borregueros* managed to raise families and survived what Arnold called "the financial roller-coaster ride attached to the industry . . . [and] doubled as the labor supply for other industries vital to Wyoming's development and prosperity, namely agriculture and the railroad."[18]

A 2000 thesis by Camila Montoya at Michigan State University focused on the circumstances of Mexican migrants to Wyoming (and other states) working in the beet fields during the first three decades of the twentieth century. These individuals endured low pay, harsh living conditions, and devious practices by employers designed to limit their movement and ability to seek better employment opportunities. Indeed, so many persons of this background worked in this industry, that by the late 1920s, one sugar company administrator argued that "'in Kansas, Colorado, and Wyoming . . . beet work has come to be regarded as a Mexican's privilege and duty. . . .' Identifying beet farming with Mexican labor, employers confined the migrants to this most physically demanding, repetitive and low paying occupation." Given the demands of this type of work, the employment of entire *familias* in the fields was quite common. By this same time, many of these laborers were directly recruited from some of the midwestern communities (such as Chicago, Cleveland, Detroit, and Kansas City) that had already established Mexican populations.[19]

Once in Wyoming the sugar companies produced remarkably insidious mechanisms to keep their Spanish-surnamed workers tied to the land. For example, one particularly effective tool was to withhold $1 per acre harvested from the first and second payments for the season's work. The $2 would then be included "only at the completion of topping." Additionally, if a family earned a bonus (for production above an average quota set by the company), they would not collect this extra compensation if they moved on from their original work locale. This was due to these migrants finding "the postal card system very cumbersome and ineffective" as a way to receive such payments. This issue was quite common, as it was estimated that by the end of the fall, around two-thirds of such employees would leave the areas where they had worked. Last, another inducement was to offer a place to stay during the winter, with employers arguing that "those who remained in the area . . . had a better opportunity to become Americanized, accustomed to settled habits and had a better chance to educate their children."[20]

Given these conditions, there were some attempts to counter ill treatment, although options were limited. One of the most basic was simply to break off contractual agreements and move on to employers offering better terms. There were at least some efforts at unionization, with the establishment of La Sociedad de Obreros Libres (The Society of Free Laborers) in Gilcrest, Colorado, and the Alianza Hispano-America (The Hispano American Alliance) in both Brighton, Colorado, and Cheyenne in the 1920s. Still, these endeavors met with inadequate success, as Montoya noted that "obstacles to organization [were] posed by their migrant lives . . . [and] the record number of Mexicans that migrated to the United States in the decade of the 1920s probably constituted another obstacle . . . as surplus labor weakened the bargaining position of any farm workers' union that might have formed at that time."[21]

A second, and more personal discussion of life and labor in the beet fields of Wyoming comes from Alephonso García, who documented the experiences of his family in Wheatland during 1942 in a 2001 essay for *Annals of Wyoming*. The family, which came to the state from the El Paso area, signed on to work for nine months for a local farmer named Homer Cockran. Much of what this writer discusses is in line with the negative experiences detailed elsewhere in the literature. For example, the family of ten lived in "a run-down, two-room house with no foundation." The Garcías were able to go to school, but only for a period of time. They attended an institution known as Mule Shoe with the offspring of farmers, braceros, and other "local Mexican children." While Alephonso does not go into particular details about what he experienced within the school's walls, he does have one telling sentence about how he and other "Mexicans" were perceived. "As kids we all seem to know who we were and our place within the school." Additionally, he also mentions that he and his siblings were pulled out when it was "time to thin the sugar beets." Such workdays were always "from sunrise to sunset," and workweeks were Monday through Fridays with a half day on Saturday. Although others have noted discrimination in Wyoming communities, García mentions that he was able to attend the local movie theater with no problem. The backbreaking toil did pay off for this family, however, as the clan managed to pay off the monies owed on a 1937 International truck. After this one season in Wyoming, the Garcías headed back to El Paso.[22]

Other scholars have documented the work of Spanish-surnamed persons in other industries in Wyoming. Among these are projects by Ellen Schoening-Aiken (on mining), Miguel A. Rosales (on railroad work), William Hewitt and Jennifer Macias (on various occupational fields and daily life in the years of World War II and just after).[23]

The dissertation by Schoening-Aiken presents a slightly more positive discussion on work and race/ethnic relations than do most of the other studies presented so far. Starting with recognition of the United

Mine Workers of America (UMWA) by the Union Pacific (UP) in southern Wyoming in 1907, this scholar argued that this began a "halting, yet in the end genuine, commitment to racial and cultural inclusiveness." While the work was not easy, the union's efforts helped to emphasize "the ways in which race and ethnicity . . . interacted in specific settings to shape class sensibilities and influence collective action" in places in and around Rock Springs.[24] By the early part of the twentieth century, a small number of Mexicans and New Mexicans had "trickled into the coal towns [of Wyoming]," although "more of them worked as railroad section hands than as miners." A larger number of them would arrive during World War I. Still, as we saw with the sheepherders, the pattern of these workers' participation in mining included a back-and-forth movement to New Mexico. Schoening-Aikens mentioned one Manito who followed this pattern for fifteen years before his wife finally joined him in Rawlins. Such circumstances tended to hamper the acceptance of individuals into these communities.[25] Ultimately, the importance of this research for the Latino/a history of Wyoming can be summarized as showing that there were local- and period-based differences in the level of acceptance and day-to-day life experiences of Spanish speakers in the state. In some locales, there was greater tolerance at certain moments in time in the first decades of the 1900s.[26]

As just noted in the discussion on mining, the railroads were a much more significant component of the Latino/a work experience in Wyoming. Rosales's 2001 article in *Annals of Wyoming* documented the story of a family that has been connected to this field of endeavor since around 1920 and provides an excellent overview of how this populace interacted with this area of employment.[27]

The core of Rosales's project concerns another family with the Sanchez surname. In late 1992 Jesús and Guadalupe Sanchez and their descendants were recognized as the first "permanent Hispanic family to settle in the town of Laramie," and as with many other persons of Mexican descent in the American West, the clan's earliest arrivals found work in the field of transportation. What was the reason for this concentration in Wyoming (and elsewhere)? As Rosales noted, it was "the ability of Mexican labors [*sic*] to work in less-than-ideal conditions . . . and [that they] generally received lower pay than did other ethnic groups." Jesús, who hailed from the state of Michoacán, initially went to Chicago to seek work and eventually moved on to Ohio, California, and Texas. After a short time working for another railroad in the Lone Star State, he accepted a position with Union Pacific in Laramie. This would be the start of a multidecade career for this patriarch and eventually included six of his offspring toiling for the same company—including three of his daughters, who proudly claimed the mantle of Rosita la Remachadora (Rosie the Riveter) during their contributions in the years of World War II. Although the family members tended to remain in lower-paying positions over what proved to be long tenures, Rosales's summary of the Sanchezes experience does sound a positive note, not only for this group but for other Mexicans and Mexican Americans in the Equality State. These blue-collar jobs provided stability and at least some measure of economic progress for many of these Spanish-surnamed peoples and "hundreds, if not thousands . . . of families in Wyoming have similar experiences. . . . This is one story of many, and hopefully the telling of it will encourage . . . a better comprehension of the significant contributions Mexicans have had in the building of Wyoming's railroads and culture."[28]

An earlier essay, this one by William L. Hewitt in 1982, provides a bit more detail about circumstances in the railroad yards and is not quite as positive as the tale presented by Rosales.[29] In this work, the author noted that while Spanish-surnamed railroad workers did tend to earn more money than their fellow ethnics in agriculture (an average of $50 per week versus $19.20 for beet workers), the unions and companies worked simultaneously to limit their employment (and that of African Americans as well) to only the lowest-level occupations.[30]

Hewitt noted that as early as 1943, there were discrimination charges against multiple railroads and unions who had classified Mexican ethnics and African Americans as "nonpromotables." "Workers charged the union . . . at the train yards in Cheyenne" with such practices. The complainants argued that they were capable of performing satisfactorily in more demanding (read that to mean "better-paying") posts and that they were systematically excluded. The article provides summaries of the testimony by several such individuals before a Fair Employment Practices committee. It appears that the documentation was quite immense, as shortly after the presentation of such evidence the Union Pacific "hired or upgraded four men (presumably Mexicans or persons of Mexican descent), one as a boiler and three as helpers."[31]

A way to encapsulate not only railroad work but also the results of other fields of endeavor by Wyoming-based Latinos/as in the immediate post-war years appears in a recent article by Jennifer Macias entitled "The Years After World War II: Latinxs Families in Wyoming."[32] Herein, Macias discusses the relationship between what has been termed the "American Dream" and the realities of life for the Spanish-surnamed workers of Wyoming. Concisely, she argues that while some progress was made, the majority of this population realized that "the American Dream of the 1950s . . . did not fit their circumstances." This would lead to a redefinition of what such aspirations actually meant to this "non-white" group. They would seek to achieve this goal by focusing on civil rights, as well as economic and political progress. It was into this occupational milieu that the Sanchezes and the Guadian families entered and, as we will see, the first generation of wrestlers managed to begin grasping onto the "American Dream" due to their parents' diligence under trying circumstances as well as the educational opportunities provided by their sport.

The Sanchezes came to the United States shortly after their marriage, and their earliest stop was in Sanders, Arizona, where Elijio worked in mining. What attracted him to this area? Surely it was the promotion of opportunities presented by *enganchistas* (job recruiters) who, no doubt, touted a chance for better pay and the possibility of improving conditions for individuals and families. While there is not a specific discussion concerning Sanders in the literature, there is research from the 1970s that contextualizes the circumstances Elijio encountered in the Arizona mining industry.[33] A more recent study on this topic is a dissertation by Andrea Yvette Huginnie in 1991.[34]

The newer research focuses on differences in the treatment of white and Mexican workers (both those born in Mexico and native to the United States) at copper mines starting in the latter part of the nineteenth century. In addition to these two groups, the mines (at different times) attracted other ethnic groups, such as the English, Cornish, Scots, Germans, Irish, and Chinese. The percentages of individuals of these different backgrounds varied by camp. In regard to the presence of Mexicans, Huginnie noted that in some areas, they accounted for almost one-half

(48 percent) of all miners, whereas in other locales (such as in Globe-Miami) the number was much smaller, around 12 percent.[35]

What were relations like between the Spanish speakers and their majority American counterparts? Not surprisingly, the accepted standard was that better-paying, skilled posts were reserved for whites, and the lower-remunerated slots were the almost exclusive purview of the Mexicans. "Anglo men in Arizona distinguished themselves from Mexicans not only on the basis of race but also on the basis of labor ideology. The term 'Mexican labor' . . . embodied the notion that certain groups of people were suited to particular types of work. Anglos defined 'Mexican labor' as unskilled." These jobs included tasks such as development crews—cutting tunnels and opening mines for excavation. Of course, this translated into lower pay for the Spanish-surnamed.[36]

At another point in her research, Huginnie specified the differences in wages in 1900. "The most common daily wage for different groups of workers were as follows: machinists, carpenters, and mechanics, $4.00 to $4.24; miners, $3.50 to $3.74; timbermen and track layers, $3.25 to 3.49; other wage earners (including mill and smelter workers and common laborers), $2.25 to $2.49; miners' helpers (likely muckers), $1.75 to $1.99." Further, all of the foreman, engineer, and mechanic positions were held by whites.[37] In sum, Elijio, like many Mexicans, realized that conditions/pay were better north of the border, but he did not expect to be treated as an equal by colleagues in the mines.

The union of Elijio and María produced five children, the first of which, Marcelino, was born in Sanders in 1915 and died in 1985. Their other offspring were named Albert (1918–1971), Lillian (1920–1997), Ernest (1924–1983), and Mary (1932–2008). Respectively, the second and third were born in Winslow, Arizona, and Sterling, Colorado; both Ernest and Mary were born in Cheyenne. As with many of his countrymen, Elijio moved from job to job working to find the best possible return for his labor. The family later moved to El Paso, where Sanchez worked in a foundry during the early 1920s. Ultimately, Elijio became a laborer for the Union Pacific, arriving in Cheyenne. By the late 1930s, he had moved up to fire builder and then was an engine cleaner in the 1940s. María died of natural causes in 1941, and Elijio later remarried to a woman named Elsie who hailed from Los Angeles. Subsequently, he moved to California and died there in 1956.[38]

On the maternal side of the family, the Guadians arrived in Wyoming in 1915 and did not move around as much as did the Sanchez clan. Manuel began working for the Union Pacific shortly thereafter, initially as a section hand (he was employed at Horse Creek), and eventually moved to Cheyenne. There, he toiled as an engine cleaner at the city's roundhouse. He and Valina had five children: Susan (1916–2000), Michael (1919–2019), Rosemary (1922–1999), Mary (1926–1986), and Olga (1927–2015). With the exception of Susan, who was born in Horse Creek, all of the remaining offspring were born in Cheyenne. Just as in María Sanchez's case, Valina died at a quite young age. While the family records do not indicate the specific cause of Valina's death, she did ask Manuel to take her back to Romita so that she could die in her homeland. She did not wish to remain in Wyoming, a place she did not care for. The entire family, save son Michael (who decided to remain in the United States and went to live with an aunt in Garden City, Kansas) returned to Mexico for her passing in 1935 (at the age of thirty-six). After Valina's demise, the entire family returned to Wyoming, save Manuel, who reentered without permission and was later deported. He lived the rest of his life in Ciudad Juárez and died there in 1962.[39]

Given that both Elijio and Manuel wound up working for the Union Pacific, some of the stories from the La Cultura collection that deals with railroad workers (and their families) provide context for the experiences of the Latino story in this field. For example, Jose C. Fuentes, who was interviewed in January 1982, was born in Vial, Jalisco, in 1899. He arrived in Wyoming in 1923, moving there from Salt Lake City, Utah, and began working for the UP that same year. He had previously toiled for the Santa Fe Railroad starting in 1917. In Wyoming, he started working with an "extra gang," then moved to toil in the lumber house, finally serving as a section foreman for thirty years. Although he did not specify how much he earned at the end of his career in 1962, he did inform his interviewer that he started at a rate of 29 cents per hour.[40]

Paul Sanchez, interviewed in December 1981, was born in Mora County, New Mexico, in 1905 and moved to Wyoming in 1922 toiling in ranching and on the railroad, and also working construction in the building of the

Sinclair Refinery. His first job in Rawlins was in the roundhouse, but he also did engine repair. He did not specify how long he worked for the railroad but was laid off in 1924 after the completion of the refinery. Then, he moved to Portland, Oregon, and later San Diego, California. He returned to Wyoming in 1930 and worked for the railroad and also sheepherding until his retirement. He did note that his starting pay at the roundhouse was 38 cents per hour.[41]

Celso Palma Sandoval, interviewed in May 1983, hailed from the state of Chihuahua, where he was born in 1906, and arrived in Wyoming in 1931. His first work was in the beet fields near Laramie, but he eventually moved on to work laying and maintaining track starting at 37 cents per hour. He indicated that he started in 1931 but did not get seniority until 1934, due to the lack of a union. He informed his interviewer that once the organization gained recognition, there were "no issues after the union came in." In part because of the union's efforts, Celso managed to afford the purchase of a house in 1944 and finally retired in 1971.[42]

Interviewed in January 1983, Bernardo and Frances Archuleta (he was born in 1911, she in 1913) arrived in Wyoming in 1942, starting in Bryan and moving to Green River in 1957. Upon moving to the state, Bernardo began work with the Union Pacific, also toiling in the beet fields and on a ranch. While in the employ of the UP, he drove a truck, then moved on to serve the company as a flagger and finally operating switch lights. His recollection was that he was earning around $2 per hour at the time of his retirement in 1975. He noted that in his golden years, he relied on his pension as well as Social Security. Frances remained at home to raise their children but took a job as a housekeeper at Little America starting in 1958. Even under these conditions, the couple noted to their interviewer, all their children went to college.[43]

From these examples, it is evident that while there was certainly work available for Mexican Americans and Mexicans in Wyoming, when they worked for the railroads (and other endeavors) individuals tended to remain in lower-paying posts regardless of the length of service and any demonstrated ability.

That indeed was the experience of both Elijio and Manuel. Still, they managed to raise their families, and by the middle of the 1930s Marcelino from the Sanchezes, and Susan of the Guadians met in Cheyenne and from this union would spring the first generation of wrestling competitors. Their ties to sport would dramatically change the family's opportunities and made it possible to leave behind low-paying work such as toiling for railroads. Additionally, athletic successes functioned to provide clear counterscripts in the daily lives of competitors in this first generation, as well as presenting their capabilities in the state's newspapers for the majority population to see.

Marcelino Sanchez and Susan Guadian married in Fort Collins, Colorado, in 1936. He was age twenty-one, and she twenty. While he did not graduate from high school, this Sanchez was the first member of the family to compete on the state's athletic fields, playing football at the junior high school level. There is no clear indication from family lore as to why the couple decided to marry in Colorado. In an email to me from Art Sanchez, he stipulated that there were some issues with the local Catholic church not wanting to perform the ceremony. Thus, the couple went to Fort Collins and married in a civil ceremony conducted by the local justice of the peace.[44] Marcelino and Susan had a total of seven children: María Virginia (1936), Gilbert (1938), Beatrice (1939), David (1942–1976), Anita (1943–1943), Arthur (1944), and Raymond (1946).

Starting a family in the middle of the years of the Great Depression was not easy, and for a period of time Marcelino took advantage of the opportunities provided by the Work Progress Administration (WPA) and learned a trade as a hat blocker, working in that area between 1939 and 1941. Like many other young men of Mexican descent in Wyoming, he then worked for the UP during the war years. Subsequently, in 1946, he took a position with the Asher-Wyoming Company, a wholesale grocer located at 1506 Thomes Ave in the commercial sector of the city.[45] From interviews with family members, this job did not provide sufficient remuneration to support a family of six, and this patriarch eventually decided to join the US Army in 1947. As Arthur mentioned, his father's entry into the military "really helped stretch the family budget."[46]

Marcelino initially served his country while stationed in San Antonio, then New Jersey, before his assignment took him overseas to postwar Germany between December 1947 and June 1949. It was during this time that he trained as a medic, and this preparation would play a key part in saving his life. After the start of the Korean War in June 1950 he joined the

Eighth Cavalry Regiment. In November of that year, during the Battle of Unsan, North Korean and Chinese troops overran his unit and Marcelino became a prisoner of war (POW). Susan and the rest of the family received a notification that he was declared missing in action (MIA) shortly thereafter. It would be more than two more years (December 5, 1952) before they received notification of his status as a POW.[47]

The Battle of Unsan was the first large battle of the Korean War, and the first time that American troops faced off directly against both North Korean and Chinese Communist troops. It was also a rude awakening not only for infantry soldiers but also for American leaders, including President Truman, that with Chinese troops now in the war, this was not going to be a short conflict. These combined Communist troops ambushed the Eighth Cavalry Regiment and killed or wounded over one-third of those engaged. This battle was also the first in which American soldiers were taken prisoner by Communist troops, with Marcelino being among this unfortunate group.[48]

That he survived nearly three years as a POW is miraculous. Being a medic, Sanchez was able to monitor the physical needs of his American buddies, recognizing that his men had been living on a daily combat ration of 3,500 calories but were now issued only 1,200 calories consisting of mostly ground corn and millet, and no vegetables or protein.[49] The Communists announced after their success against the Americans at Unsan that they were adopting a program of "lenient treatment" of POWs, but Marcelino and the other 7,190 captured men never benefited from such a policy. Over half of these soldiers died in POW camps. Although helping with their medical needs, what Marcelino could not do was aid his fellow soldiers deal with what became known by psychologists of the era as "give-upitis," or the lack of a will to live. While similar conditions had existed in Japanese prison camps during World War II, and the brutality in the Korean camps may have been "somewhat" less, the conditions of cold and diet made the casualty rates just as high.

Marcelino's return to the states would have been much worse than that experienced by World War II POWs in that there was an assumption by the American Intelligence community that the mostly enlisted men had been "brainwashed." Even the "give-upitis" was blamed by some on the "soft life that American youth had led since the end of World War II;

and the emasculating effect of American 'Momism.'"[50] The Joint Intelligence Boards interviewed every returning POW on ships returning from Korea, with the interviews being conducted by military psychologists, psychiatrists, and intelligence officers. Said one returning POW: "We were interrogated every day for eight hours. Nobody was concerned about our health I can damn well guarantee you."[51] And while the Communists tried extremely hard to convince the POWs that their way of life was superior to the lives that Marcelino and others had left, they failed "big time." His return to society and the success he had in raising his Sanchez family are evidence of that.

Marcelino survived, in part, due to his training as a medic and his ability to provide at least rudimentary medical care to his fellow POWs. Ultimately, he regained his freedom with the release of the final American prisoners in September 1953, having spent almost three years in a Communist prison camp. For his service to his country and fellow troops, he earned a total of eight medals, including the Silver and Bronze Stars. He remained in the service until 1956, when he finally returned to his family. After these harrowing experiences, he worked in construction and as a shoe repairman before finally taking a post with the maintenance department of the Cheyenne Public Schools. He worked until the late 1970s, retired, and passed away in 1985.[52]

Given her husband's lengthy absence, Susan, who initially had been strictly a stay-at-home mom, had to seek remunerative work outside the family's domicile. First, she worked as a cook's helper for United Airlines and later moved on to a position in the housekeeping department at DePaul Hospital. Ultimately, she moved on to become a supervisor in that unit at this facility.[53]

The La Cultura project provides evidence demonstrating the limitations placed upon Spanish-surnamed women such as Mrs. Sanchez in terms of acquiring gainful employment in the state of Wyoming during the first decades of the twentieth century; indeed Susan's rise to a supervisory position at DePaul was unusual, as many interviewees found it nearly impossible to get work beyond housekeeping until past the 1950s.

Catherine Bustos, interviewed in July 1982, was born in Rawlins, but her family hailed from Mexico, coming to Wyoming around 1910. Her father, not surprisingly, worked as a sheepherder and later for UP.

Catherine attended her hometown's high school, graduating in 1933. At this institution, she was often referred to as a "dirty Mexican" and did not get advice from her counselors about pursuing any kind of a trade. Shortly after earning her diploma, Catherine worked full time as a maid at a local hotel before moving on to toil as a cook at a hospital for almost one decade. While there, Bustos indicated that her supervisor would often have departmental meetings and not invite her participation. She believes that she should have been promoted but was passed over. While employed and raising her children, she also took a correspondence course through the University of Omaha, earning a secretarial diploma. This post was her occupational goal, but she never managed to gain such employment, stating, "I never had the chance" to work in an office environment.[54]

Out of all of the La Cultura interviews reviewed, the one by Nellie Arias was among the most impactful, given that she was incredibly open about the discriminatory practices encountered both in her schooling and in her occupational experiences. Her parents arrived in Wyoming around the mid-1910s, and Nellie was born in Cheyenne in February 1919. She was one of the very few Mexican Americans who graduated in her class of 1936 (indicated that she was 3 of a total class of 203). In regard to pursuing gainful employment, she could not get a job due to there being "a lot of discrimination in Cheyenne." While going to school, Nellie emphasized the need to graduate because she did not want to end up cleaning hotel rooms or washing dishes. She excelled at taking shorthand and bookkeeping, but the instructor in that particular class did not encourage pursuit of this skill due to what was termed "your language problem." Potential employers in an office setting told her, "You have no business being here." Ultimately, Arias recalls, it was made clear to her that "this [housekeeping] was all I could ever do because of my origin." Further, she did not get much encouragement, "even by our own people." After facing so many obstacles (and eventually marrying) "I was discouraged many times, so I just finally quit" pursuing this particular goal.[55]

The experience of Alicia Sanchez is a bit different, in that she was born in 1936 and raised in New Mexico and did not arrive in Wyoming until 1951, when her father got a job with the street cleaning department of the city of Cheyenne. Alicia had graduated from Taos High School and initially managed to get a job with the local paper and then moved on to work at the Ft. Warren Air Force Base Credit Union. Even with these experiences, she was very adamant about the discrimination that she faced after arriving in the Equality State. She indicated to her interviewer that when applying for jobs, she was immediately asked about her "nationality." Once the interviewer posed that question, "right away, all of the positions were filled." Having moved on to work in lending, Alicia noted that she "fought to get where . . . [she was] now" and that she overcame most of the obstacles that were put in her path.[56]

All told, Mexican American women such as Susan Sanchez faced important hurdles when applying for work into the 1950s, but they continued to strive and achieved limited breakthroughs. It can be argued that part of the determination by the first generation of Sanchez wrestlers can be attributed to watching their mother support the family while Marcelino was a POW.

After moving to Cheyenne, the Sanchezes moved around quite a bit. At first, they were situated in the city's more ethnically diverse west side, near downtown. Later, they lived at the Frontier Villa until that building's demolition in 1955. Initially, this facility was erected to serve as housing for workers during World War II. After the cessation of hostilities, the units served as domiciles for low-income families. Given Marcelino's ties to the military, and the relatively low pay of Susan's job, these were the likely reasons for the family being able to live there. A 2018 article in a Wyoming newspaper quoted one resident who noted that the denizens of these residences were often reminded of their lower-class status by others but still looked back at their days there with a certain fondness. "Living like we did made me feel inferior, like I wasn't as good as the people who lived in the nice houses outside the Villa gates." Still, this same subject noted, "When I look back, I know that I had some truly wonderful times there, made some good friends, and came away with many memorable memories."[57] Afterward, the family moved to the Van Tassell Apartments. Ultimately, through the efforts of both Marcelino and Susan, the clan moved to their own home located at 512 West Fifth Street. It was here that Susan lived until her death at age eighty-four in 2000.[58]

In my discussions with both Gilbert and Arthur Sanchez, the two brothers recalled their childhood living in the various neighborhoods already noted. These were "comprised of multi-ethnic [African Americans, Asian

Americans, and poor whites] families that were mostly working-class people." These two Latino men's life experiences succinctly affirm much of what was argued in other works on Wyoming.

> We lived on the westside and the southside. . . . Most of the families came from Mexico, New Mexico, Colorado, and Texas. Almost all of our friends were Mexican. The men worked for the railroad, construction, or city. I recall the racial attitude of the city. We could not eat at certain restaurants or shops, but we were able to work in them. Other Wyoming towns were very discriminatory.[59]

In addition to facing prejudice, growing up without daily contact with their father made life exceedingly difficult for the Sanchez children. The separation was particularly problematic for the oldest boy, Gilbert. Not having a father to turn to on a constant basis left him vulnerable to the "mean streets" of Cheyenne, and, in turn, he came to view himself as a "street kid and not a good student at Corlett Elementary." In email correspondence with me, he classified himself as "a very hard kid to manage." While he did help his mother by delivering papers, shining shoes, and setting pins at a local bowling alley, he also got into "a lot of trouble."[60]

Soon, Susan determined that drastic action was necessary to keep her son from falling into more serious predicaments. Fortunately for her, three of the boys' aunts worked at the Saint Joseph Orphanage in Torrington. Through these contacts, she arranged for Gilbert to spend time at the facility, which operated under the strict auspices of the order of the Sisters of Saint Francis of Assisi. Here, the young Sanchez found his footing. The nuns made sure he did his homework, learned discipline, and, most important (it turned out), had access to books to inspire his goals and imagination. It was at the library at Saint Joseph that Gilbert encountered a book on Olympic heroes that had a great impact not only on his life but on subsequent generations of Sanchez youths. Gilbert noted that this work and his time at the orphanage "was the turning point in my life because the sisters helped me with my homework. My grades were much improved. I had chores and learned about the Catholic Church. I returned [just] before my dad was freed."[61]

With the encouragement and no doubt stern discipline of the nuns, plus the resumption of his father's guidance, Gil returned to the Cheyenne

Public Schools a more disciplined and focused young man. Still, in the late 1950s, not much was expected of a Mexican American youth in such institutions, and by most teachers. Another element was necessary in order to complete Gil's transformation from troubled young teen to dedicated student/competitor, however, and that occurred when he met Larry Brown, the wrestling coach at Cheyenne High School (CHS).[62] Before focusing on Gil's particular experiences in the classrooms of the Cheyenne schools, it is necessary to spend some time looking at what historians and other scholars have found to be the experiences of Mexican Americans in Wyoming classrooms over the early decades of the twentieth century.

There are a number of studies that document the experiences and circumstances of Spanish-surnamed peoples in various communities around the state. The earliest and most comprehensive of these is by T. Joe Sandoval, who completed a master's thesis at the University of Wyoming in 1946. His work examines various aspects of life of Spanish speakers in the following communities: Worland, Torrington, Wheatland, Rock Springs, Cheyenne, and Laramie. Here, he focuses on topics such as housing, schooling, and economic and social status in these towns. From what has been discussed so far, it should not be a surprise that conditions were not ideal. Importantly, Sandoval emphasizes that the majority of this group in the Equality State hailed not from Mexico but rather from New Mexico and Colorado. Thus, as he states, these persons, "although of different cultural backgrounds than the majority group, are not 'foreigners' as they are sometimes referred to by people of Anglo-Saxon extraction."[63] It is clear that shortly after the end of World War II, Sandoval made a case for treating members of this group as what they are, Americans born within the boundaries of the United States and citizens worthy of equality before the law. Such negative treatment of Spanish speakers, Sandoval noted, would haunt the United States: "Until our country succeeds in its own backyards it will have a hard time convincing the people [to the] South of the sincerity of the 'Good Neighbor Policy.' "[64]

The findings in the various chapters in his thesis and communities noted in the previous paragraph should not be a surprise, as Sandoval cited numerous examples of discrimination throughout the state. Some of the most egregious included keeping Latinos out of at least one restaurant and barber shop in Wheatland. The restauranteur interviewed argued that the reason for his decision was that his "white" customers would cease to do business with him if "Mexicans" were seen eating at the establishment. The barber simply claimed that he did not have to serve such persons, as there was a place in town that would accommodate the needs of this population.[65] In the chapter covering education, Sandoval mentioned the segregated schools Worland and Torrington and documented the dramatic decline in the number of children who remain in attendance as they moved into higher grades. By the time senior year rolled around, only eleven youths of this background were attending the two communities' high schools. Sandoval argues that the negative attitudes and low expectations of many teachers and administrators were partially to blame for the abysmal results. Yet another element that limited schooling was tied to the poor economic circumstances of most of these families. Particularly in the beet-field locales, the majority of the offspring would likely not start school until the end of the season, that time being late November.[66]

Another early research project found concerning the educational circumstances and experiences of Spanish speakers in state schools is the subject of a master's thesis by Keith Jewitt produced for the Department of Sociology at the University of Wyoming and completed in 1950.[67] For anyone familiar with the trajectory of the educational literature from this era concerning minority students, there are few if any surprises in the perspective presented in this work. Overall, these pupils were perceived as being not as successful, more likely to drop out, behind on reading and other academic scores, and far less likely to graduate.[68] A statement toward the end of one of Jewitt's chapters is very indicative of the way that teachers and administrators viewed students of this ethnicity during this era. After examining the "cultural" elements of this group, the author of this thesis notes that from "the historical material which was gathered it was possible to see that the cultural heritage of the group was one which was not conducive to the building of a desire for formal education."[69] While this statement is expected due to the bias just described, Jewitt's research does provide some valuable information as it discusses five factors he postulates as being influences of the grim statistics. These are economics, discrimination, bilingualism, mobility, and (once again) cultural issues. These topics are discussed in individual chapters.[70]

Again, there is not much unexpected in the examination of these topics. The economic and mobility sections discuss the disparity of wage scales, the low pay, and the constant movement that are the norm in the various industries where Latinos/as clustered. Jewitt particularly focuses on how these experiences impact students whose families moved as a result of their work in agriculture. The low pay (in all areas of employment) and the movement from place to place for those who toil in the fields generate low pay, generate a sense of inferiority, and are not conducive to "building up a desire for success in educational pursuits."[71]

In the chapters dealing with bilingualism and culture, we are presented with more of the same. While at least some of the persons interviewed for this project describe the ability to speak and write both Spanish and English as a positive,[72] Jewitt's final assessment takes a pessimistic perspective. Herein, he quotes one of his professors at the University of Wyoming (Dr. Emil Kauder—Department of Economics and Sociology) who discusses the many impediments to understanding English for those who start off with Spanish as their native language. In sum, Krauder argues that this obstacle might not be possible to overcome as "the rules governing the correct usage of the English language are diversified in nature and extensive in number." Thus, Jewitt contends, "we have here an indication that bilingualism may be an important handicap for the Spanish-speaking student."[73] In regard to culture, Jewitt provides a very stereotypical assessment in which he argues that the heritage of these student is one which

> does not allow the people to lose readily their identity in a new cultural system. In the past and still today the "mestizo" has been typified as having a lack of interest in matters concerning the whole community. He has been of necessity too concerned with the provisions of the necessities of life. Education has never been of importance to the Spanish-speaking individual of this category. It was and is a concept which cannot be suited to fit patterns of cultural and economic attainments of the group.
>
> With such a cultural heritage, one is able to . . . [provide] another partial explanation . . . [as to the reason why a large percentage] of the group in Laramie does not complete high school. After the members of the group have satisfied the requirements as established by civil law, they feel their responsibilities are at an end.[74]

While the majority of the reasons noted tend to blame Latinos/as for their failings, at least Jewitt does acknowledge that discrimination is a final factor in the equation that produces such bleak educational and societal results. In this chapter, he documents matters such as unfairness in the rental market, the treatment of customers doing business in particular establishments, and issues in intergroup dating,[75] in addition to the aforementioned limitations in employment. Still, Jewitt does present evidence that some "Mexicans" can be considered to be "good" and that at least the employers interviewed for this project would "hire a 'Mexican' as readily as they would a 'white.'" Another entrepreneur noted that he would not have any issues in loaning money to this group as they "might be comparatively slow in repaying . . . but he would not attempt to 'beat' the individual who had given credit."[76]

One final point from this chapter on discrimination impacts the story of the Sanchez clan that is the subject of this work. While many other "Mexicans" at Laramie High had difficulties, Jewitt notes that those who had success in athletic competition were more likely to be perceived as being "good." These are some particularly important observations supporting the main argument of this work. For example, Jewitt argues that "in the area of athletics there appeared to be little or no distinctions as to the majority or minority group membership. If the individual student possessed athletic ability, he was acknowledged as a teammate rather than an 'Anglo' or 'Mexican.'" Still, there were limits to this level of acceptance. "If a minority team member were to make an error under the strain of athletic competition, he would be likely to return to the status of 'Mexican' rather than remain a team member." Overall, "unless he possesses athletic ability or other abilities, the Spanish-speaking student is very likely to remain a 'Mexican' in the eyes of the 'Anglo' portion of the high school."[77] If a minority student could gain benefits by bringing local glory to his school's sporting teams, then how much more value would accrue to success at the state and even national level? How powerful of a counterscript could this be?

Another scholar who has documented the experiences of Latinos/as in Wyoming schools is Gonzalo Guzmán.[78] His research focuses on the "myth" that schools in the state were not segregated. Guzmán's research clearly demonstrates that they were segregated. Still, the situation did present some unique characteristics. Guzmán argues that the key difference in the state did not come down to strictly a "white" versus "Mexican" dichotomy in regard to segregating students. Rather, particularly in areas which the sugar beet industry predominated, no matter whether the children of laborers were Filipino, German Russian, Japanese, or Spanish-surnamed, prior to the years of the Great Depression, they all "attended school with the children of White Americans." Initially, the stated goal was to Americanize these pupils as "an 'immigrant' child worthy of Americanization at a time when similar movements almost exclusively were focused on European immigrants."[79]

This more idealistic scenario ended due to two critical circumstances: first, as parents of German Russian backgrounds began to object to having their children in the same rooms with Mexican pupils, and, second, as the state and community schools began to get support from New Deal programs and had to meet requirements initiated by the higher governmental level. By the end of that era, however, these students were now perceived as a "social problem," and that helped bring about the segregation of students in several communities by the start of World War II. One example can be seen in Torrington, which, by 1932 changed facilities holding both German Russian and Mexican students to having one exclusively for the Spanish-surnamed. Indeed where previously administrators had seen such children as worthy of integrating into American society, they were now classified as "maladjusted" and "backward because they are unable to speak the English language, and the White children do not accept them into the social life of the school."[80] Spanish speakers also endured discrimination outside of the sugar beet communities, with an example being the construction of a "Mexican" school in Worland by the mid-1930s, again using New Deal monies. By the time of the school's opening, local administrators openly "embraced the new inferior status of the Mexican student."[81] In sum, although there were some differences early in the twentieth century, by the end of World War II schooling of Mexican children in Wyoming was viewed "as a race problem" with most of the pupils this population perceived as not being suitable of integration into the broader society.

Not all of the interactions in a school setting were negative for Latinos/as during this era, however. In Gilbert's case, the fact that a white man stepped in and showed interest in the promise of a Spanish-surnamed youth was instrumental in his future success. Such relations have been noted as an important topic of research by one of the leading scholars of Mexican American history, Arnoldo De León. In a pathbreaking work from 1993 entitled "Our Gringo Amigos," De León argued that whites have always played a complex role in the experiences of Spanish speakers in the United States (though De León focuses specifically on Texas). Certainly, there is much documentation that Anglos have been racist and negative influences in the lives of Hispanics, but it is also important to note that a not insignificant number have stepped in (De León mentions social workers, military officials, religious—both Catholic and of other denominations, and labor organizers, to point out just a few; my research shows similar trends among athletic coaches) over the years to assist and partner with Latinos/as in a variety of causes. As De León argued at the end of his work:

> My intent has been to show simply that Anglos have played a greater role in the social advancement of Mexican Americans than generally credited. . . . What segments of the Anglo population responded to the needs of Mexican Americans? Did the Anglos take an interest in the entire community or just those belonging to the middle class? What mixture of circumstances motivated them to act?[82]

Coach Brown's influence on Gil would radically alter his life and that of his entire clan. The roadmap for the future suddenly came into focus: Wrestle for CHS; get an athletic scholarship at a college or university; and get a degree in something that would move him beyond the UP, the Asher-Wyoming Company, and even the custodial department of the Cheyenne Public Schools.

Initially, however, there was one other major, practical issue, and that was that Gil, who was fifteen at the time, was still attending McCormick Junior High, and his school did not have a wrestling program. No matter, as Coach Brown simply had his new charge take to the mat against athletes from his CHS Indians squad. Additionally, as Gilbert improved his skills, he passed along instructions to his younger brothers: Art, David, and Ray. Gil would only wrestle at CHS through the tenth grade, but he would be the first of the Sanchez clan to leave his mark, winning the

Wyoming title at 112 lbs. in 1956. Previously, he had demonstrated his potential on the mat by coming in fourth place at the state level as a freshman in 1955.[83]

In the state tournament, the Indians finished second overall, losing to the Laramie High Plainsmen. Gilbert defeated a competitor from Powell High School by a score of 8–2 for the crown. Interestingly, there were three other Spanish-surnamed competitors at this tournament who reached the ultimate or penultimate rounds: A youth with the last name of Martínez from the Rock Springs High School Tigers finished third at the 112 lb. bracket. Another member of that squad with the last name of Córdoba earned the state championship at 103 lbs., defeating a competitor with the surname of Madrid.[84]

While success on the mat opened some doors for Gilbert Sanchez, it did not mean that he was worthy of much attention from the state's press; neither was there much notice of the other Latino athletes noted. An examination of the *Casper Star-Tribune* article that summarized this tournament provided a fair bit of detail concerning the winners in the various groups, with the notable exception of the 103 and 112 lb. classifications. In those, the paragraphs describing the action tended to focus on some competitors who did not even reach the last rounds. Indeed, there is no specific mention or praise provided to the efforts of the likes of Sanchez, Martínez, Córdoba, or Madrid.[85] A publication of such counterscripts would have to wait for the time being. Gil would only wrestle for CHS that one season, but it would open up tremendous opportunities for him.

Though these Latino wrestlers were state title holders, the visibility they garnered paled in comparison to that given to other victors. Still, this was only the beginning of the Sanchez family's positive athletic recognition, and they would not be denied the respect due to champion athletes. More important, particularly for a family of modest means, the sport would open the door to collegiate scholarships and professional careers. In short, in the span of just a few decades, the hopes for a better life in the United States of Elijio and María and Manuel and Valina would begin to take shape in a most unexpected locale—the wrestling mats of CHS and, later, at various colleges and universities.

2

Athletics/Sports as a Part of the Latino/a Historical Literature

Starting in the Chicano Movement Era, roughly the late 1960s and into the 1970s, academics of the Mexican American (as well as other Latinos/as) experience in the United States have presented readers with myriad studies of numerous aspects of this populace's historical chronicle. Subject areas such as labor, political movements, religion, the role of women, the US/Mexican border, the maintenance of cultural traditions, community formation, and many, many other facets of life have been covered over the past fifty-plus years of scholarly output.[1] As noted in the introduction, a key overarching and ever-present theme of much of this production has been to present evidence of Molina's "counterscripts" in all aspects of community and individual life. How did Mexican Americans challenge discriminatory practices, assumptions about their inferiority (both physical and intellectual), and racism; build institutions of their own; and maintain a sense of their culture under trying circumstances? While there has been much discussion on these topics, it is only recently that scholars have begun to mine the historical vein of athletic competition/

https://doi.org/10.5876/9781646427529.c002

participation as an integral element of such efforts. An example of the lack of attention to sports as a key facet of Mexican American / Latino history can be seen in the fact that the interviewees of the La Cultura project from the early 1980s seldom mentioned this topic. The story of the Sanchez family can be seen as an introduction into what is a potentially rich source of study on the Latino/a population in the state of Wyoming.

Although focusing on a newer area of research, the past two decades have generated a rich and expanding literature that clearly demonstrates the role of sport as being a noteworthy element in the arsenal of counter-scripts. This chapter provides an overview of such studies and helps to place the story of the Sanchez family in historiographical context.

A recent, and very thought-provoking example of this trend appeared in a recent issue of *The Journal of Arizona History* written by a PhD student at the University of Arizona, Alex Nuñez (by the way, the grandson of long-time NBA referee, Tommy Nuñez), entitled "Switch-Hitting: Mexican Diaspora, Whiteness, and Tusconense Baseball, 1903–1954."[2] The significance of this essay is that it deftly summarizes some of the key questions that scholars of Latinos/as and sport have researched.

In examining this history, Nuñez commenced his essay with the story of a local (and all Mexican American) Little League team from the city of Tucson's south side and their participation in the finals of the West Regionals in 2019. This band of twelve-year-old athletes brought joy and great recognition to the city, and local fans were justifiably proud of their milestone. Nuñez, however, goes beyond the cheering that emanated from the local sports taverns and argued that "much more than just a game, baseball illuminated broader issues of race, class, and citizenship for Mexican Americans. . . . defining and negotiating the boundaries of membership in Tucson, a city that experienced tremendous anglicization in the first half of the twentieth century."[3] In examining this historical issue, Nuñez asserted three things: first, that participating in sports "helped forge a diasporic *mexicano* identity"; second, that this participation enabled the "*tusconenses* to foster identities as Americans in the face of growing socioeconomic disparities"; and finally, that such endeavors generated "moments in which Mexican Americans performed this convincing display of . . . fitness for citizenship [and] also reflected a successful transgression of deeper social and racial boundaries that permitted

Mexican Americans to claim elements of whiteness for themselves."[4] This last point, my study argues, is the most significant of the three. Just as Ray Sanchez was presented to the locals of Cheyenne as an "All-American" youth, successes on the mat helped other members of this family to commence a climb up the social and economic ladder and thereby claim a level of acceptance far above what was usual for Mexican Americans in the first decades of the twentieth century in Wyoming.

All three of these contentions are presented by the authors of the materials discussed in this chapter. There will be an examination of the Mexican American sporting experience in a variety of athletic undertakings including baseball and softball, boxing, football, soccer (both for men and women), and basketball. Additionally, there will be coverage of this populace's history in athletics in a fairly wide geographical area. The theoretical/historiographical arguments therein are also clearly visible in the story of the Sanchez family from Cheyenne through their connections to the high school sports and collegiate wrestling.

Baseball played a significant role in Mexican American barrios throughout the twentieth century. The game, which had been played in Mexico since the late nineteenth century, was one fairly enjoyable aspect of the otherwise brutal efforts during the years of the Porfiriato to transform the Mexican economy as well as to, theoretically, bring the nation into the "modern world" of both industrialization and international athletic competition. In addition, as Mexico industrialized, particularly in northern areas (and the Southwestern United States as well), the game was part of social life for these communities because "as agriculture and industry along the border regions. . . . developed . . . Mexican and Mexican American laborers north and south of the Rio Grande were exposed to the game."[5] As more such workers arrived in *el norte*, the game (particularly on Sundays) became an integral part of social life. There are several articles that tell this story (in addition to Nuñez's new effort in Arizona). Four significant essays are by José M. Alamillo, Samuel O. Regalado, Luis Alvarez, and Alberto Rodriguez. In addition, a book by Jorge Iber on the life and career of former Major Leaguer Mike Torrez (he of the infamous pitch to Bucky "Bleeping" Dent back in October 1978) provides insight into the significance of the game. All of these works shed light on developments that link directly with the arguments presented by Nuñez: the existence of communitywide efforts to create and sustain league play, the way that Mexican American communities managed to stage tournaments that brought together teams from various sections of the country, and last, the pride (both personal and communal) that these endeavors created.

In José Alamillo's essay "*Peloteros* in Paradise: Mexican American Baseball and Oppositional Politics in Southern California, 1930–1950," the author does an excellent job of demonstrating connections between sport, community organizations, and labor organizing. The diamonds of the region provided a place where families gathered to socialize (usually after church services), shared food and drink, and most important, allowed *jugadores* the chance to interact with each other and strategize efforts aimed at recruiting and improving the unionized presence in various places of employment. The games, while providing plenty of action between the foul poles, served a broader purpose.[6]

The works of Samuel O. Regalado and Luis Alvarez focus on the same geographical area but concentrate more on the issues of community groups that supported the teams/leagues, and the importance of the sport to the players. Succinctly stated, most of these men—who more often than not toiled in difficult, relatively low-paying occupations—utilized success on the diamond as a way to demonstrate their worth and masculinity before other members of their community. Additionally, in regard to the Alvarez essay, the emphasis of his project is on a team that represented a particularly successful Mexican American business institution: the Carmelita Provision Company. Last, his paper also covers the East L.A. Classic, a long-running football contest between what became two predominantly Mexican American high schools: Garfield High (the Bulldogs) and Roosevelt High (the Roughriders).[7]

The study by Alberto Rodriguez provides coverage of similar stories, but in the Rio Grande Valley of southern Texas. Rodriguez's study, however, also notes that pride in ethnic background on the diamonds of this area could also be found at the collegiate level, with attention paid to the many Mexican American players who toiled for the nearby University of Texas-Pan American, which is now known as University of Texas-Rio Grande Valley (UTRGV). His research documented athletes of this background taking the field for the Broncos (the teams for UTRGV are now known as the Vaqueros) as early as 1927. This essay also notes players of this ethnic background who played in local professional (minor and independent) leagues, some who signed with Major League baseball organizations, and the Mexican professional leagues.[8]

The work by Jorge Iber gives readers insight into the importance of youth baseball to the Oakland (mostly Mexican American) neighborhood of Topeka, Kansas. Here, Mike Torrez was an all-around athlete at Topeka High School but also played sports within his ethnic group's athletic sphere. One of his most consistent endeavors along these lines was playing basketball in Mexican American tournaments all over the Midwest. Further, his older brother, John Torrez, famously known as "Johnny Boy," was a legendary competitor in the Mexican American softball circuit, not only in Kansas but in Missouri and even into Texas as well. These endeavors (both in basketball and softball) helped join *comunidades* across numerous states and are a tribute both to these folks' athletic prowess and to quite sophisticated organizational efforts. The events helped, as Nuñez argued, to establish and sustain the sense of "Mexicanness" among the diasporic population across hundreds of miles of American territory.[9] For a complete study of Mexican American softball, a recent work by Ben Chappell is invaluable and expands upon all of these topics.[10] Last, a 2007 study by Katherine M. Jamieson documents the importance of the sport to opening doors of participation (and some negative consequences as well) at the collegiate level for young Mexican American women.[11]

As with the works on baseball, scholars who have written about Mexican Americans and boxing focus on issues such as masculinity and the value of the sport in regard to supporting cultural pride and retention. One popular trend of this sport has always been to pit fighters of different ethnic and racial backgrounds against each other, and this aspect, in part, contributed to the popularity of pugilism among Mexicans and Mexican Americans. Additionally, with the success (as early as the 1890s) of competitors such as Solomón García Smith (Irish father and Mexican mother, who won the featherweight title in 1897) of Los Angeles, the barrios of the United States have produced a substantial number of excellent pugilists (if not actual world champions).

Moving into the early twentieth century, we find such fighters as José Ybarra (who fought under the name of Joe Rivers), Joe Salas (the first Mexican American US Olympian), and Bert Colina (who won fifty-six of sixty-five bouts in the years between 1921 and 1929). A good way to understand Bert's popularity and his importance to fellow *mexicanos* can be seen in his fans' reactions to his fights, often cheering him on with shouts of "ándale, Co-lee-mah, ándale!" In later years, others such as Art Aragón (in the 1950s), Lefty Barrera (who competed in the 1960 Olympics in Rome), and (Chicano-Era icon) Rodolfo "Corky" Gonzales attracted fans. Of course, Corky's actions in the squared circle and fighting prowess helped in fashioning his image as a "militant" leader of the *movimiento*. Aragon's story demonstrates some of the complexity of Latino participation in sports. He was born in New Mexico and fought out of Los Angeles. During his career, he often triumphed over Mexican-born fighters, and this muddled the reception of *fanáticos* born south of the international border.

By the late 1960s and into the early 1970s, fighters such as Armando "Mando" Ramos and Carlos Palomino not only made names for themselves in the ring but also served as coaches who used their knowledge to help "provide a healthy environment and outlet for teenage frustration." The 1980s and beyond witnessed the continued "Latinization" of the ring and featured individuals such as Julio César Chávez (Mexican-born) and Oscar De La Hoya (who is Mexican American). Similar issues to those of Aragon occurred with De La Hoya concerning whether he was "Mexican" and "Macho" enough. Boxing experts have argued that De La Hoya's more tactical fighting style did not appeal to some Mexicans and Mexican Americans who preferred the more rugged "hard punching style typical of Mexican boxers."[12]

Among some of the most important works that provide further historiographical context for the sport are efforts by Gregory S. Rodríguez, Tom L. Romero, and Fernando Delgado; a book by Benita Heiskanen; and, most important, another tome by Troy Rondinone. Rodríguez's dissertation, entitled "Palaces of Pain—Arenas of Mexican American Dreams: Boxing and the Formation of Ethnic Mexican Identities in Twentieth Century Los Angeles," discusses how boxing helped shape *mexicano* identity. The sport served as a mechanism that bonded various disparate elements in the community and could be seen as a metaphor for struggles in other facets of barrio life.[13]

Romero's essay focused on the connections between Corky Gonzales's political activism and his time in the ring. While Corky boxed, he came to be accepted as a "good Mexican" who could be part of the Democratic political apparatus in Denver. In other words, he was acquiring some elements of "whiteness" and was someone who could be "counted on" to serve the party's political interests. It was only when he took the path of another "nationalism," that of a militant Chicano, that the "powers-that-be" came to view him in a different light.[14] Perhaps Corky's political transformation was too problematic of a counterscript for the Democratic leadership in Colorado?

Delgado and Heiskanen examine issues of gender identity (masculinity and femininity) in their works. Was, as noted, Oscar De La Hoya a "real" man who fought the way a "true Mexican" should fight, or was he "less so" due to not using straight-ahead tactics in the ring? How did De La Hoya's nativity in the United States influence fans' perception of him as a boxer, as a man? Heiskanen includes a chapter in her book that incorporates a discussion on the role of women (and particularly, Mexican American females) in this sport. Is this, some might argue, an undertaking that a Latina should participate in, or is it a vehicle for such *mujeres* to claim new athletic space for themselves?[15]

There is another essay by Heiskanen that ties in with the story of the Sanchez family. As noted in the introduction, and as will be clear in the chapters that follow, the competitors covered in this work are all relatively small in stature and in weight. Wrestling is one of the sports that provides opportunities for athletes of varied sizes. In her important essay "The *Latinization* of Boxing: A Texas Case Study," Heiskanen discusses how pugilists of Hispanic backgrounds have dominated the lower-size classifications in recent years. In regard to the United States, this has produced a substantial presence among this population in places such as the American West. Now, this does not mean that all such competitors are of relatively small sizes, as articles in boxing media clearly point out. However, in regard to the family under study in this work, grappling proved to be the key competitive endeavor (though not the only one).[16]

Troy Rondinone's work *Friday Night Fighter: Gaspar "Indio" Ortega and the Golden Age of Television Boxing* is more than just a biography of a pugilist born in Tijuana. "Indio" was a mainstay on early network televised fights during the 1950s, and his mere presence on the "tube" was impactful to not only persons of his ethnic/national background but also the broader American audience. For both sets of viewers, here was a *mexicano* who was tough and driven, and who regularly defeated individuals of other races/ ethnicities in one of the most masculine endeavors possible.

Watching this man on the screen displayed potency to whites (both in a positive and negative sense of the word, given the reaction of some to interracial fights), and possibilities to fellow ethnics. Rondinone quotes two individuals who thrived on Gaspar's appearances. A youth in Texas recalled that these bouts presented him with "a fearless and bold model of Latino musculature, tearing up opponents." Below the international border, an eight-year-old youth, Carlos Santana, his family itself recently arrived at Tijuana, was enthralled. The now-legendary guitarist reminisced about Ortega that he "looked so pretty when he fought." More important, it planted the notion of personal possibilities in Carlos's mind. "He did teach me certain things were available on a worldwide arena." Such success (locally or nationally) can impact the way that a minority youth can see him/herself. Additionally, this is yet another example of an athlete presenting a "counterscript" to a wider audience.[17]

One of the owners of the Olympic (boxing) venue in Los Angeles, Aileen Eaton, is quoted by Rondinone as giving her insight into why boxing was so popular with Mexican Americans / Mexicans. "There are no Mexican football players and no Mexican baseball players. . . . Boxing is their sport because there is no bullfighting or soccer."[18] As noted earlier, there were baseball players of this background in Southern California, and elsewhere. The following section demonstrates that Mexican Americans played football as well.

The game of football began in the elite Northeastern universities (places such as Yale, Harvard, and Princeton that now make up the Ivy League) in the years just after the Civil War. There has been much written about the start of the game, and the reasons for the sport's appeal at this moment in American history.[19] One of the first authors to write about the role of ethnicity in the game was Michael Oriard. In his 2004 work, *King Football: Sport and Spectacle in the Golden Age of Radio and Newsreels, Movies and Magazines, the Weekly and Daily Press*, this former Oregon State University scholar (who, by the way, played football at Notre Dame in the late 1960s and for the Kansas City Chiefs between 1970 and 1973) discussed a variety of issues, with ethnicity a focus in chap. 8 of this work. Here, we find some points that are particularly important to the story of the participation of

Latinos in the game. Just as with baseball, the gridiron was perceived as an agent of Americanization for recent immigrant populations. Indeed, Oriard noted that by the early decades of the twentieth century,

> sport meant one of two things within immigrant communities; the neighborhood and local sports clubs . . . that both preserved ethnic identities and fostered assimilation into mainstream American culture, and the school and professional sport that meant distinctly American success and more thorough absorption into the mainstream. To play football, whether at the high school or on a college or professional team, was to be thoroughly American.[20]

Of course, such opportunities were significant to the individual players who got to play at the various levels, but the importance went well beyond that of the specific athlete and his family. Again, as Oriard states:

> Polish and Italian youths were simply drawn to football in high school as a vehicle for achieving status. . . . [And] seeing them succeed, their communities celebrated such achievements highly prized in their new country, and more and more youngsters saw an opportunity to make it in America by following this example. Through this more "natural" process football contributed to the new immigrants' acculturation over time far more powerfully than such concerted efforts as the Americanization movement during the First World War.[21]

A recent work by Mario Longoria and Jorge Iber, in addition to recounting the 100+ year history of Latino participation in this sport, makes a similar argument for this population.[22] In addition to this book, there are two other articles and a second book that effectively connect the sport of football with Latino (and specifically, Mexican American) cultural maintenance and identity. The two essays are by Jorge Iber and the second book is by Frederick Luis Aldama and Christopher González.

Jorge Iber's essays are entitled "On-Field Foes and Racial Misperceptions: The 1961 Donna Redskins and Their Drive to the Texas State Football Championship," and "Mexican Americans of South Texas Football: The Athletic and Coaching Careers of E. C. Lerma and Bobby Cavazos, 1932–1965." The principal theme of both is similar: how success on the football field (and on the sidelines as a coach) helped counter stereotypes of the intellectual and physical limitations of Mexican Americans in football-mad Texas. In recounting the story of Donna High School, one of Iber's sources noted how whites perceived such *atletas*. Just before a play-off game against Sweeny High School, the Redskins' coach, Earl Scott, was approached by a colleague from the Bulldog sidelines who made his assessment of his mostly Spanish-surnamed foes abundantly clear. "Can these pepper bellies play? I mean, you never hear of any of them in the Southwest Conference." The final score of that contest was 32–14 in favor of Donna.[23]

The results of this victory still influenced the mostly Latino community almost forty years later, when a reporter from a Dallas newspaper interviewed locals about the team's storied season. In a community that endured many of the same racial and social issues as other heavily Mexican American towns in the Rio Grande Valley, this triumph was of major importance. When the team returned from Austin, many in the community showed their ethnic and religious affiliations by walking "down old Highway 83 to San Juan, eight miles away, to a religious shrine [Our Lady of San Juan Shrine in Pharr]. The basilica had long been regarded as the sight of a miracle."[24] Indeed, this was about as close as one could get to a miracle on the gridiron! Later in the newspaper article, then-principal of Donna High, Fernando Castillo, summarized the impact of the Redskins' triumph in 1961. "I was born in 1963 and heard about that team all of my life. That was the big talk. To be like that team was everyone's dream." Iber recapped this essay by arguing that "the success of these players permitted many of the Valley's Mexican American youth to envisage goals that previous generations could not."[25]

Iber's second essay focuses on two important but little remembered athletes (and one who also coached) who broke down barriers to the role of the Spanish-surnamed in Texas. Everardo Carlos "E. C." Lerma was one of the earliest Mexican American coaches in the state, taking over the reins of the Benavides High School Eagles in 1940, after a football career at Kingsville High School and (what was then) Texas A&I University (now Texas A&M–Kingsville). When Lerma took over this post, the reaction in town was of surprise, as many doubted whether a Latino could be an effective field general. Between that year and 1954, Lerma guided his charges to multiple titles, not only in football but also in track and basketball. As E. C. noted in an interview shortly before he passed away in 1998, "People just couldn't believe that a Mexican American could do as good of a job as an Anglo. Well, I think I proved them wrong."[26]

In the second half of the essay, Iber focuses on the playing career of Bobby Cavazos, who played halfback at Texas Tech in the early 1950s. In his senior year, Bobby, another native of Kingsville, led the Red Raiders in various offensive statistical categories, and helped guide the Red and Black to one of its finest seasons ever, finishing 11–1, including a victory over the Auburn Tigers in the 1954 Gator Bowl. By the way, Cavazos earned the MVP of that contest as the cap to his collegiate career. In part, this successful campaign helped to get Texas Tech admitted into the Southwest Conference starting in 1956. At a time when there were almost no Mexican Americans on the Lubbock campus, Cavazos's success on the gridiron helped to change some views of this population. In 1951, as Bobby was starting his Tech career, a local newspaper scribe, Don Oliver, noted that the players on the football team had to meet certain criteria. "We don't care where the boys come from as long as they are the 'right kind' of boys and can play winning football." Iber sums up this important change in the opinion of a local sports reporter by arguing that "clearly, Oliver and others at Texas Tech came to believe that Cavazos was one of the 'right kind' of boys. . . . Oliver's musings present an example of sports' power to 'destabilize' (serve as a counterscript to) the perceptions of some in the majority population."[27]

Another significant work to cover on football is Frederick Luis Aldama's and Christopher González's book *Latinos in the End Zone: Conversations on the Brown Color Line in the NFL*. This work not only covers Latino experiences in the NFL but also features in-depth interviews with three legendary athletes (all of them, Mexican Americans): Jim Plunkett, Tom Flores, and Joe Kapp. Plunkett and Flores are tied together as the first pair of Latinos to win (as player and coach) a Super Bowl (number XV with the Oakland Raiders after the 1980 season). The interviews discuss the difficulties each man encountered on their way to achieving football immortality. Similarly, the discussion with Kapp, who spent a significant amount of time north of the border playing for the Calgary Stampeders and the British Columbia Lions of the Canadian Football League (before moving on to play for the Minnesota Vikings and New England Patriots of the NFL), details the discrimination and doubts he faced given his Mexican American (and German) background.[28]

In addition to the first-person accounts, Aldama and González examine the question of why Latinos continue to be underrepresented on the collegiate football field. As recently as 2021, Spanish-surnamed athletes comprised only 3.4 percent of all gridiron players at the Division I level.[29] Given that Latinos amount to 18.8 percent of the US' total population that year, why are they so underrepresented?[30] These authors argue that education continues to be a substantial barrier to this population's entry into the football "pipeline." "Latinos were playing football in the streets as kids and even at school with organized sports. . . . This is where education and the family come to the fore. There is a cultural disconnect between the Latino family, the education system, and the capitalist football enterprise."[31] This is a crucial point in the Sanchez family's story, as the clan made excellent use of sport to move forward academically. Indeed, a number of the Sanchezes' *atletas* have, over the generations, made education their particular career path—giving back through sport and education what they gained in the classrooms and mats of Wyoming and elsewhere.

A final contribution to research on Latinos / Mexican Americans and football can be found in Billy McMillin's excellent (and award-winning) film from 2017, *The Classic*, which provides a history of the contest and uses extensive interviews with students and teachers as well as members of the broader barrio community to document the importance of the contest to East Los Angeles.[32]

Concerning *fútbol*/soccer, we find similar themes in the research. While there are many items that deal with this topic regarding the Latino community in the United States, this essay will focus on two specific items (one that deals with men, the other with women), and one book. First, there is an essay by Juan Javier Pescador of Michigan State University entitled "Los Heroes del Domingo: Soccer, Borders, and Social Spaces in Great Lakes Mexican Communities, 1940–1970," which provides readers with an overview of teams, leagues, and associated organizations in this region, but more important, argues that the sport and related events helped the men, their wives, and families present the wider community in places such as Chicago and Detroit that they were (just like white ethnics) part of "a working-class and leisure culture that emphasizes hard work, discipline, manhood, individuality, and competitiveness . . . and reflects both the shortcomings and aspirations of the Mexican and Latino experiences in the United States."[33] Thus, by playing this sport and challenging negative assumptions about them, the Mexicanos and Mexican Americans in these communities used soccer as a way to claim a sense of belonging in the Midwest.

Similarly, Paul Cuadros makes comparable statements about Latinas in the Siler City, North Carolina, area in his article "'Fútbol Femenino' Comes to the New South: Latina Integration Through Soccer." Here, the University of North Carolina journalism professor profiles various women who play the sport and details how their lives have changed as a result. In his summary, Cuadros makes an important assessment of the value of sport to these *mujeres* and to the broader community.

> Their status as athletes elevates these women beyond their traditional role in home. In addition, this new status . . . is a powerful indicator of sociocultural integration in the United States. . . . One of the things to consider . . . is how prominent they are among their people. . . . This cultural space . . . [is] where the community can come together and express itself freely in its own way.[34]

Last, a recent work by James Madison University sociologist David Trouille, entitled *Fútbol in the Park: Immigrants, Soccer, and the Creation of Social Ties*, demonstrates how immigrants playing in a park located in a fairly upscale section of Southern California have managed to challenge negative perceptions of them by locals, all the while building friendships, creating a safe space for themselves and their families, and "fostering individual and collective well-being."[35]

Moving on to basketball, there are two works—one an essay, the other an important book—which detail the significance of this sport to the lives of Latinos / Mexican Americans. The tome is by BYU professor Ignacio M. García and is entitled *When Mexicans Could Play Ball: Basketball, Race, and Identity in San Antonio, 1928–1945*. The author traces the story of the Sydney Lanier High School Voks and their impressive run on the courts of Bexar County and, later on, elsewhere in Texas under the leadership of Nemo Herrera, still the only coach in the history of the state to win state titles in two sports (baseball and basketball) in two different institutions (El Paso Bowie for baseball and Sydney Lanier in hoops). García summarized the importance of the game to Herrera's players and community by arguing that the coach "understood what obstacles they faced and would face after high school. If they focused on the limitations and the hardships, they might simply choose the path of others before them who remained in the barrio and stuck to what they knew. He wanted so much more for these young men."[36]

A similar story comes from yet another part of the country; this time the setting is Miami, Arizona (MHS), and the year is 1951. That season, the Vandals won the state championship with a squad that featured five (of a total of nine) players of Mexican American descent. Although there had been Spanish-surnamed players on this school's teams since the late 1920s, this team was the first in the school's history to claim a title with a majority Latino roster. To demonstrate the value of sport in changing perceptions of minorities among whites, the author of this essay, Christine Marin of Arizona State University, quoted one of the athletes discussing his trepidation upon first arriving at MHS. Although Tony Gutiérrez started playing in the late 1940s, and was not part of the title team, his thoughts reveal the importance of the game to Mexican Americans:

> *Mexicanos* had to be tough to be able to put up with what the gringos did to them. . . . They dressed better than I did, and they acted like the school was just for them. There wasn't outright discrimination there, but they made us Mexican kids feel like outsiders because they thought we weren't better than them. . . . [But ultimately] We were better than them as athletes, and that's when they started to like us. They wanted to win. And they needed us *Mexicanos* to win.[37]

While being teammates might not have overcome all obstacles, the act of playing together, and being successful on the court, helped to break down barriers to acceptance of Mexican American student athletes in this particular case.

As is evident from this chapter's discussion, there have been a significant number of scholars who have examined the impact of a wide variety of sports in the daily and communal lives of barrio dwellers in numerous areas of the United States over different time periods. The main theme in all of these works has been to present sporting activities and organizational efforts as a method of counterscripting widely accepted notions about the intellectual and physical inferiority of Mexican Americans (and other Latinos/as). The story of the Sanchez clan will extend coverage of such themes into the historical literature of the state of Wyoming. Although there are a number of studies that have focused on the history of the Spanish-surnamed in the Equality State, the account of this family's economic, social, and sporting trajectory will not only provide insight into the broader scope of Mexican American history there but will also argue that in some instances, sport proved to be a very effective mechanism for challenging racist beliefs and move a family into the mainstream of American society.

3

The Sanchez Name Begins to Stand Out in State Wrestling Circles

1956–1967

After two years of competition as a Cheyenne High School Indian and claiming the state title at the 112 lb. classification in 1956 Gilbert Sanchez decided to join the United States Marine Corps (USMC), and his pathway to further wrestling success took a unique turn. While only having completed through the tenth grade, his choice to join the military was not an unusual one in the overall trajectory of Mexican American history.[1] For if a young man of Mexican descent did not see much opportunity to finish school, or to move into a decent-paying job even after high school graduation (one that might lead to improved economic standing for himself and his future family), then service in the armed forces was a viable and common option. For many young men of this background, and certainly during the years post–World War II and Korea (as was the case with Marcelino), this seemed an avenue that afforded more-than-average prospects. In addition, the role of Mexican Americans in these two conflicts helped to stimulate the drive for full civil rights among this group.[2]

https://doi.org/10.5876/9781646427529.c003

Marcelino's service in the military eventually provided him access to a functional, though nonprestigious post in the Cheyenne Public Schools' maintenance department. While this job, along with Susan's paycheck, no doubt supported the family and even allowed them to purchase a modest dwelling, it was the societal/political changes that took place concerning the treatment and rights of Latinos from the 1950s on that made it possible for this couple's children to utilize the vehicle of sport to achieve successful careers in fields that required a college degree, and thereby transform the Sanchez family's social and economic standing for the better.

Before moving on to the particulars concerning the careers of Gilbert and Arthur, it is imperative that we briefly discuss how the aspirations of Mexican Americans, particularly those who were former military, transformed in the years after World War II and Korea. For this information, we turn to Raul Morin's pathbreaking 1963 work *Among the Valiant* and a recent master's thesis from the University of Wyoming by Emily A. López entitled "Mexican American Veterans, Class and Identity During and After World War II."[3]

Morin's work provides a summary of the service of individual *soldados*, their bravery and sacrifice during these conflicts. For our purposes, however, the key contribution of this manuscript can be found in chap. 17, the work's conclusion, wherein the author (himself a veteran of the European theater and the Battle of the Bulge with the Seventy-Ninth Infantry Division)[4] presented, likely for the first time in print to a broader American public, what this generation of *veteranos* expected after their return. While Morin was born in Texas and lived most of his adult life in Los Angeles, his argument fits in properly with the expectations of a man such as Marcelino Sanchez (and other Mexican American veterans in Wyoming) upon his return from captivity. Of course, the GI Bill provided opportunities to pursue further education, reduced cost for home loans, and offered medical and other benefits. Briefly, while there were still discriminatory events in many places (as noted in works on the life of Hector García, discussed in note 1 for this chapter), the World War II and Korean War Mexican American returnee had opportunities unimaginable to immigrants of the Sanchez and Guadian families. As Morin argued after his return from France:

> For too long we had been outsiders. . . . How long had we been missing out on benefits derived as an American citizen? Old timers had told us, and we had read in books how the early settlers had invaded our towns and had shoved us into the "other side of the tracks." . . . We never had any voice. Here now was the opportunity to do something about it.[5]

As a result, this generation, if not able to take advantage of such subsidies themselves, was able to instill in their children the sense that now there were greater chances for social and economic improvement. Interestingly, Morin even mentions that some Latinos were, in the postwar years, making their way beyond the "traditional" Mexican American sport in the boxing ring. Further, they were now moving into areas where they had not previously participated in large numbers, such as trades and professional employment. "Today, many of our people have entered the medical, legal and educational professions. . . . Many men and women have achieved high success in the entertainment and sport fields. . . . and sports—other than boxing—have been invaded by our veterans . . . all over the South-west where Spanish-speaking Americans abound."[6]

Again, historians have in the years since the publication of Morin's work complicated the analysis of how World War II and Korean War Latino veterans were treated by government agencies and the broader society (in other words, the reality was not as positive as Morin argued); however, there is certainly no debating the sense that these individuals embraced the notion that a page had turned in American social history and that they were not going to go back to being treated as "outsiders." Morin synopsized the hard-won sense of these individuals by stating:

> We developed intense pride in America. Our standard of living has improved 100 percent. As veterans, we have become serious-thinking Americans. We have enlarged our circle of friends to include not only Mexican Americans like ourselves, but Americans of many other nationalities. . . . World War II and the Korean Conflict were without a doubt the prime factors in having our economical, educational, and social status raised far above that which we had prior to World War II. It definitely made a great change in the lives of all Mexican Americans in the United States of America.[7]

Given this sense among veterans, it was logical that Gil looked upon the option of military service as a way to improve his future prospects. In addition, and this is truly a unique element in his story, he would also continue to wrestle under the auspices of the USMC and come into contact with not only excellent practitioners of the sport but also individuals who would open doors for him at institutions of higher education.

Emily López's work provides an effective and updated précis to Morin. In her thesis she agrees with the earlier study, stating that for these men, the "individual experiences serving in the War changed the way they saw themselves and in turn the way they expected others to see and treat them in the United States."[8] However, López provides a more nuanced analysis of the postwar movement to improve circumstances. While Mexican Americans from the middle class and more educated levels of the community pursued greater equality through civil rights groups (such as the League of United Latin American Citizens—LULAC—for example) and the legal process, those of the working class (such as the Sanchezes) "did not have a platform or needed skills and tools. . . . to combat inequality in a manner that Anglos would recognize before the War."[9] Additionally, she also researched the important element of how Anglos became more "receptive to changes" called for by postwar groups such as the American GI Forum (AGIF) in the areas of civil and other rights.[10]

López argues that there were two distinct types of racism confronted by veterans in the late 1940s and into the 1950s. The first category she calls "official racism"; this is the version of discrimination that was "enforced by laws and policies" (in other words, bureaucratic and institutional racism). The second classification she denotes as "social racism"; this featured discriminatory practices based on "personal opinion and social codes but not enforced or changeable through formal channels." Of the two varieties, the second is the more difficult to eliminate, as eradication is only "possible when the actors inflicting the racism begin to have internal changes within themselves and become willing to think and act differently." Right after these conflicts, particularly after World War II, was the time to utilize the "rhetoric of patriotism and democracy" and for Mexican Americans to push for changes in the way the broader society treated them.[11]

Toward the end of her study, López examines how veterans used this newly earned standing as a way to attack social racism. In discussing POWs, her research ties directly to a key aspect of Marcelino Sanchez's experiences. When discussing those who endured this fate, just like their white colleagues, this group of Latinos "realized that even after the immense sacrifices they made, they still were refused services as simple as being served in certain restaurants just as they had been before the war," but "they were emboldened to demand better." In turn, given the impressive military record of many of these men (and Marcelino certainly fits into this category), employers were often willing to allow such individuals to move into jobs that were previously closed to Mexican Americans.[12] While working in the maintenance department of Cheyenne Public Schools might not sound all that glamourous, it can certainly be argued that this was an improvement over the jobs that the patriarch of this clan held previously.

There is no indication from family members that Marcelino and Susan were politically active after Marcelino's return from military service; however, the Sanchezes did have plenty of examples in Wyoming (and in Cheyenne itself) of practices that treated Mexican Americans as second-class citizens. The latter part of the 1950s was the time to make abundantly clear to their children that there were ways to overcome such obstacles. It turned out that sport proved to be a particularly effective vehicle, at least for this family.

All of these trends took place in an evolving context, one in which many Anglos were willing to accept a greater degree of equality. "The fact that discrimination had been so condemned [by Americans] in Germany [and not to mention the fight against communism during the Cold War] allowed Mexican Americans to argue that racism was un-American."[13] While Marcelino was not able to take advantage of the educational benefits provided to him through the GI Bill, perhaps one or more of his sons might, and not only that, but in Gil's case, he would be able to continue to work on his wrestling skills while in the marines. Who knew what that might lead to? This was a time to claim opportunities for Mexican American veterans (or their offspring) because of the blood and tears rendered in the service of their country. Gil Sanchez would be the first to take advantage of this trend, and his success (in the classroom, on the mat, and in his professional career) would prove a powerful counterscript and set the tone for the family's future. He would make the most of it and set the pattern that his brothers, and subsequent generations of Sanchez men, would follow on the mat and in college classrooms.

Before moving on to the stories of Gil and Arthur, there are some technical notes that need introduction. First, as the story proceeds from here on, the Sanchez brothers will compete in one of the two styles of wrestling: Freestyle and Greco-Roman. A convenient definition of these two forms is found on a website called Grappling School. It defines the difference in the following way: "Freestyle permits holds both above and below the beltline using both arms and legs. In contrast, Greco-Roman forbids holding below the beltline." Freestyle is the newer form of competition. There are also differences in regard to pinning, as in the older form wrestlers cannot use their legs to flip opponents onto their backs, whereas in Freestyle the competitors have to guard those appendages. If a pin is not scored, then the way to determine the winner of a match is by points, and again, there are differences between the two styles (which I will detail). In Greco-Roman, the foes have to "rely on explosive upper body moves and quick positioning to throw opponents." In Freestyle, "there is more movement and fluidity" as wrestlers make one move after another to gain advantage. The sum total of such variances "require [athletes to] train in different ways," with Greco-Roman requiring more explosiveness and upper body strength.[14]

While pinning an opponent immediately ends a match, many such bouts are determined by points scored. Briefly, in Freestyle, points are scored by achieving takedowns, escapes, reversals, and near falls. The values are as follows: A fall (or pin) is worth three points, a near fall and reversal are valued at two points, and an escape earns one point. In order to score, a competitor must take their foe to the ground and gain control. Once that occurs, the athlete must maintain control for 3 seconds to score a takedown. Most matches run for 6 minutes. At the end of the match, the winner is the individual with the most points. If the score is tied, then the winner is determined by a best-of-three overtime period, which runs for 3 minutes. If the score is still equal, the referee determines the winner.[15]

A Greco-Roman match consists of two three-minute halves, and wrestlers can score points by executing holds, locks, throws, reversals, or takedowns. The level of difficulty in executing various moves and holds determines the points scored. Scoring is cumulative, with the points added up at the end of the two rounds. In the case of a tie, the winner is determined in the following order: highest-value move executed in the match and least number of cautions (infractions) issued against each competitor. If one athlete builds to an eight-point lead, they win by technical superiority.[16]

Gil's career on the mat for the marines benefited from his ties to the Corr brothers, Ed and Bert Jr. These siblings are legendary individuals in the state of Oklahoma and the state's long and distinguished wrestling circles. From 1952 through 1956 the twins wrestled on Sooner championship teams coached by Port Robertson. Each competed at 123 lbs., and both lost their starting spot on the team to another great Mexican American collegiate wrestler, Dick Delgado.[17] In addition to their place on the Oklahoma University (OU) team, the brothers each had navy Reserve Officers' Training Corps (ROTC) scholarships that were utilized to complete undergraduate degrees in social studies from the OU College of Education. They then moved on to the USMC, where each earned all-marine titles. They served until 1960. It was during this time that they came in contact with Gil Sanchez. It is not difficult to fathom that their time wrestling alongside Dick Delgado might have played a role in their decision to mentor/work with another young and talented Latino wrestler.[18]

In addition to his association with the Corr brothers, Gil gained international experience through his relationship with a fellow athlete named Hiroaka Aoki. If the name sounds familiar, that is because this wrestler, who is better known in the United States as "Rocky" Aoki, eventually founded the Benihana Restaurants chain. In 1958, however, Aoki competed for Keio University, and Gil managed to spend time training with him at this institution while stationed in Japan. The two became close friends, with Gil also spending time with the Aoki family while overseas.

In 1959 Rocky was part of a traveling squad that visited Norman and challenged a USMC team of which Gil was a part. By this time Sanchez had already claimed an all-marines title, following in the footsteps of his mentors, the Corrs. The Americans triumphed in this meet, by a score of 5–3, primarily because of their dominance in the higher weights. At this event, however, Aoki earned a decision against Gil at the 125.5 lb. classification. This meet was followed by another competition, this time including the military, the Japanese, and singlets from Oklahoma State University (OSU). Here, Gil triumphed over a high school wrestler named Ollney Mueller at 114.5 lbs., but then succumbed to Dick Wilson of the University of Toledo in the second round. These two meets were a tune-up for the main event: the Amateur Athletic Union (AAU) Championships that took place on OSU campus. Here, in the first round, Gil defeated an army wrestler named John Jordan before losing to a Japanese competitor named Mitsy Tamura, who fought for the Oregon State Beavers.

Given Gil's experiences in the marines (and the changes noted after World War II by Morin and López earlier), and the opportunities they provided, it is possible to briefly bring in voices (via the La Cultura interviews) of other Latinos from Wyoming to note how serving their country in the military opened up possibilities for educational and workplace advancement. While none of these individuals took the same (athletic) path Gilbert followed, donning the nation's uniforms made it possible for them to overcome some of the limits that had been unfairly placed in the path of betterment for many of the Spanish-surnamed in a state that supposedly valued "equality."

For example, José Montano, who was born in Mora, New Mexico, in 1912, arrived in Wyoming in 1925. He attended Rawlins High School but quit and worked low-paying jobs until joining the army in 1942 (through fall 1945). He noted that he served in China, Myanmar, and India during his enlistment. After returning from the conflict, he worked (not surprisingly) laying track for the railroad but eventually got a job at the Sinclair Refinery. Unlike the experiences noted in earlier interviews, while José started in what he termed a "work gang," he eventually moved up to a pipe fitter's helper, then a brick mason's helper, and served in the change house for a dozen years. He retired from Sinclair in 1973 after more than twenty-four years of employment. He noted that he never felt discriminated against after serving in the military.[19] While not achieving a high status in the company, the movement up the ranks by this interviewee is certainly a change from the earlier examples presented.

Henry Mascarenas was also a member of the marines, serving between 1953 and 1956. Like Mr. Montano, he too hailed from Mora. He came to Wyoming in 1947 and graduated from Natrona County High School. After serving in the military, he returned to Casper and became an apprentice to a radiator repairperson. His apprenticeship lasted for two years, and he started earning $1.75 per hour. After his training, he eventually opened his own shop and indicated to his interviewer that he had not encountered any type of discrimination in his work, business, or housing.[20]

Leo Richard Sánchez was one Spanish-surnamed individual who utilized his military benefits to attend college. He was born in Casper in 1935, and his father worked in the oil fields and was also a supervisor in a foundry. He indicated that his family was one of the first Hispanics to move from the northern part of Casper to the southern end of town. His father was able to purchase not only the family home but also additional real estate holdings. Leo attended Catholic school until high school, then went to Natrona County High School. He indicated that he served in the marines for four years but did not specify the years of service. Leo did state that upon leaving the USMC, he then went on to study at Casper College, Regis University, the University of Colorado for his BA, and then a master's degree from the University of Wyoming. At the time of his interview, he was a schoolteacher. In regard to his family's housing, Mr. Sánchez noted that the good reputation of his father, in particular, made it so that he could get a mortgage from a local bank. Finally, and in line with part of Gil's story, his military experiences and subsequent education made him insistent that his offspring continue their training after high school.[21]

An interview with Victoriano Trujillo provides more direct information concerning some of the not-unsubstantial changes that were taking place in group relations in Wyoming in the years after World War II. This interviewee was born in Douglas in 1937. His father followed the trajectory of the previous generation, working in sheepherding, construction, and lastly, for a quarter century, laying track for the railroads. Victoriano completed high school at Casper High, and then moved on to work as a telegrapher for the UP. In part, he picked up this skill because a high school counselor encouraged him to pursue vocational training. Trujillo also learned to be a taxidermist. Subsequently, he joined the navy and was a second-class radio operator between 1955 and 1959. Coming back to

Casper, he decided to pursue a career in education and earned an undergraduate degree at the University of Wyoming and, later, a master's from Clark College. Victoriano recalled that both Douglas and Casper segregated citizens during the 1940s and that he was often verbally abused by the local police while a teen. "We were told where our place was and that we were expected to, you know, toe the line." Even into the 1960s, some of these trends continued. Still, Victoriano managed to get multiple degrees, and at the time of his interview, he served as a reading teacher at Casper Elementary School and was active in local Republican politics. While not overcoming all roadblocks, and in line with the points raised in López's thesis noted earlier, the story of Mr. Trujillo does demonstrate that some shifts were occurring at the time that Gil began his collegiate career.[22]

After gaining a great deal of personal and on-mat experience while serving his country, Gil concluded his time with the marines over the summer of 1959. Given his extensive record of success, and the desire to continue his education, Sanchez then accepted an opportunity to compete for Lamar Junior College, which was located in Colorado, just a few hours away from Cheyenne.[23] Here, it is possible to see how the (Anglo) contacts created in the world of USMC wrestling paid off for Gil (and as noted in the De León article mentioned previously). As he indicated in an email to me, "A Marine friend knew the coach (Dan Sniff) at Lamar JC, [and] I was offered. I thought it best to go to a junior college to start college. I did OK in school and wrestling." As will become clear in the following paragraphs, he did better than "OK" in his time with the Antelopes.[24]

Gil started his time on the mat for Lamar in December 1959, and an early mention of his success came against Colorado State College, in a match where he pinned Ray Sandoval at the 123 lb. classification. However, even greater notoriety followed soon thereafter in April 1960 at the AAU Nationals in San Francisco, where Sanchez defeated his friend Aoki to claim the 114 lb. championship in Freestyle. He then earned a second national crown in Greco-Roman the next day, one of only two competitors to accomplish the difficult feat that year. In addition to these titles, Gil then moved on to the Olympic trials in Ames, Iowa, at the end of that month.

Here, athletes would compete in both styles, and the top competitors of the eight weight classifications would then go on to further training prior to heading to Rome to represent the United States. Gil started off well, with two victories before Mike Grandstaff of Norfolk, Virginia pinned him. Still in contention, he moved on to the third round, where he took on Dick Delgado of the University of Oklahoma. As a 1956 Olympian, Delgado was heavily favored over the less experienced Sanchez. Still, Gil held his own and lost a split decision to his fellow Mexican American, and this eliminated him from further consideration for the Olympic team in Freestyle.[25] Although jettisoned from the chance to represent his country in the newer format, Gil was still alive in the Greco-Roman portion of the competition just a couple of days later, where he won his first-round match by pinning Paul Wolf of Minneapolis at the 1:47 mark. He finished third in this meet, missing going to Rome.

As a final reward for his excellent year at Lamar, however, Gil then earned a scholarship to begin competing at the university level, accepting an invitation to suit up for the Colorado State University (CSU) Rams.[26] As had happened with his entry into Lamar, connections in the sport played an important part in providing this opportunity. Dan Sniff, the Lamar mentor, was a friend of CSU coach Ollie Woods, and he recommended that a transfer to this institution would be of benefit to the team and to Gil. While not achieving his Olympic dreams, Sanchez now had a full ride at Fort Collins, no doubt to the great relief of Marcelino and Susan. "Here was an opening for Gil to pursue a college degree without burdening his family's finances. Merely one generation removed from the clan's arrival from Mexico, [he] now had the chance to earn a degree and leave behind the low-paying jobs that his parents and grandparents had been locked into."[27]

The CSU squad was highly competitive in 1961, and they became a major force in the Skyline Conference for the first time in several seasons. Gil proved himself to be a key element of the Rams' resurgent mat fortunes. Included in this campaign were victories over the Colorado Buffaloes (in which Sanchez scored a pin against George Kent), Colorado School of Mines (featuring another victory by pin for Gil and breaking a nine-match losing streak against the Miners), and Colorado State College. In this last meet, Gil, subbing for an injured teammate at 130 lbs., lost his first match of the season, tying in points but losing the decision. The next couple of outings demonstrated that the team, though improved, still had a way to go before they could compete against a "blue blood" program in the sport, Iowa State University (ISU; which had finished second in the national finals in 1960). During their trip to the Hawkeye State, the Rams also fought against Iowa State Teachers College (now, the University of Northern Iowa). The match against the teachers was close, a 14–12 defeat, but the ISU Cyclones handled CSU, 22–4. At this event, Gil lost to Don Webster, 3–0. After this road trip, the CSU Rams returned to Fort Collins, where they awaited the Washington State University (WSU) Cougars. At this event, Gil was tied with WSU's David Wahl, 3–3, when he "wound up Wahl in a figure four leg-lock" and pinned his opponent. Then, Sanchez had the chance to compete against his home state's school, the University of Wyoming. His task that day was to go up against Dave Hanson, who had finished third in the national finals at 123 lbs. in 1960. The Cheyenne native surprised his Cowboy foe handing Hanson his first defeat of the season.[28]

Moving into the second half of the schedule, the local paper noted the team's improvement, and Coach Woods commended several of his charges, stating he expected them to make the NCAA tournament. Not surprisingly, Sanchez was one of the competitors mentioned by name. As the year progressed, Gil continued to prove his mettle, again stepping up to 130 lbs. in a dual meet against Western State University and the University of Utah. Facing individuals much heavier than him, he put up a brave fight but lost both matches, to Joe Oldfield of Western, 7–2 and the Redskins' (now Utes') best wrestler, Mike Bingham, 7–4. Fortunately, for the last match of the regular season, against the University of Denver, Gil was able to fight at his normal weight, and dominated Dave Stevenson, pinning his opponent at the 7:50 mark. The Rams headed into the Skyline Tournament after stomping the University of Denver Pioneers, 22–9, finishing with an overall record of 7–5.[29]

The struggle for the conference title took Gil and his teammates back to Wyoming, as University of Wyoming (UW) (a squad that had won nine of the previous ten championships) hosted the meet in Laramie. Given the improvement over the 1961 season, many considered CSU a contender to knock off the reigning Cowboys (along with the Utah Redskins). Sanchez took command of the 123 lb. classification right from the start, scoring the first pin of the event by pinning Terry Robinson of Utah State. He went on to decision Wyoming's Dave Hanson to claim the conference crown. Even more significantly, the Rams tied the Cowboys for the team title, with seventy-nine points each. This was the first time in the tournament's thirteen-year history that two sides tied for championship honors. Having earned these commendations, Gil then went on to also take the title at the AAU Rocky Mountain meet, polishing off John Neff of Colorado State College in the finals. His next stop would be at the NCAA Nationals, held that year at Oregon State University, in Corvallis.[30]

Gil had a bye in the first round of the national tournament but then faced a familiar foe, Don Webster of Iowa State. The result this time was just as in late January, with the Cyclone competitor defeating Sanchez 3–0, thus ending his efforts in the NCAA competition. Undeterred, Gil quickly moved on to the National AAU event, being held in Toledo, Ohio, seeking to defend his crowns in both styles. Unfortunately, he lost his Freestyle title, pinned by Dick Wilson of the hometown University of Toledo, who was the eventual overall champion at 114.5 lbs. Wilson duplicated Gil's feat from 1960, also taking the Greco-Roman title. While not able to reclaim his crowns, it had been an amazing first season of university-level competition for Gil Sanchez. He had won major titles, traveled the country, and continued to work toward a degree in secondary education (specifically, in social sciences); all of these trends were certainly counterscripts to the perception of Mexican Americans in these pre-Chicano-era years.[31]

Gil picked up right where he left off going into 1962, as he earned early season pins over opponents from Mesa Junior College and Western State and outpointed his foe from Colorado State College. Toward the end of January, the Rams stepped up their level of competition, travelling to Stillwater to face the OSU Cowboys. Here, Gil suffered his only defeat of the campaign, losing to Jyo Umezawa 3–0 at the 115 lb. category. He quickly rebounded, however, and earned two of the most significant victories of his time at Fort Collins, pinning Oklahoma Sooner wrestler Wally Curtis (who had finished third at the NCAAs in 1961), then toppling Lowell Stewart of Iowa State at 123 lbs. Although Gil shined on an individual level, both of these matches resulted in team defeats. Even more significant, however, the Rams, previously an "also-ran," tied the mighty Cyclones in their match, 13–13. The breakthrough season for both the squad and Gil individually continued with victories over Iowa Teachers', Wyoming, and Denver. Heading into the Skyline Tournament, Sanchez sported a 7–1 mark, with five of his wins via pins. He repeated as conference champion (although Wyoming won the team title and CSU finished second) at

115 lbs., pinning wrestlers from BYU and New Mexico before crushing his Utah Redskins foe, Steve Olsen, 16–4 in the finals. Now a two-time Skyline Conference title holder, he would, once again, move on to the NCAA Tournament, which would take place at Stillwater.[32]

By this point, reports described Gil as a wrestler who had "earned a fine national reputation" and was a third team All-American. In addition to Sanchez, other Rams heading to Oklahoma included Claude Gonzalez at 123 lbs., Kent Swendlund at 130 lbs., Roy Williams at 137 lbs., Tom Norton at 157 lbs., Ken Hines at 191 lbs., and Jerry Seely at the heavyweight classification. Of these competitors, three advanced to the second round (Gil had a bye). In his first match, he competed against John DeAno of the University of Illinois, defeating him by a score of 3–0. That moved him into the semifinals at the national level, to wrestle against Mark McCracken of the hometown Cowboys. Unfortunately, Gil did not have a chance to challenge another OSU foe to try to avenge his only defeat of the season, as he suffered a dislocated elbow and had to withdraw. He was also unable to compete against Okla Johnson of Michigan State in the consolation bracket.[33]

The CSU Rams' fortunes had certainly changed since the arrival of Coach Ollie Woods. From a poor program in the late 1950s, going into 1963 the team's national standing had improved drastically, and Gil was a key cog in the turnaround. "This year, CSU is already rated among the top 10 in the nation, and barring some unforeseen difficulties will raise some eyebrows around the country before the season's over."[34] While he had done well in his sophomore and junior years, Gil's senior campaign would be his best and take the Sanchez name to the highest levels of the sport.

Once again, he impressed from the first match of the season, this time competing at the 123 lb. weight for an injured Claude Gonzales and scoring an easy 13–1 victory over Done Romine of Colorado State College. Next, he scored a pin against Gary Pollard of Iowa Teachers' College. The Rams then took a drubbing at the hands of OSU in their next meet, and Gil's foe from 1962, Umezawa, once again got the better of him by a score of 5–3. The final three matches of the campaign resulted in two defeats for the team but continued success on Gil's part. First, he triumphed over Van Doughty of Western State, 9–3 (at 123 lbs.), then he topped Wally Curtis of Oklahoma, 8–1 at the same weight, and last, he shut out Bob Piper of BYU, 7–0. Overall, his season mark going into the conference tournament was a sparkling 6–2. Overall, the Rams finished with a less-than-sterling 5-4-2 team mark, however.[35]

Although the team title might not have been a realistic possibility, CSU had three athletes favored in their classifications: Gil (at his normal 115 lbs.), Gonzales (at 123 lbs.), and Ken Hines (at 191 lbs.). The squad featured a total of ten competitors, which, according to Assistant Coach Don "Tuffy" Mullison, made it possible for the Rams to field grapplers at their "proper divisions." For the third consecutive year, the other wrestlers in the conference (now called the Mountain Intercollegiate Wrestling Association) proved no match for Gil's prowess. He charged through the tournament, with his performance described as "outstanding." Sanchez pinned all of his opponents, finishing off Junior Sandoval of Colorado State College at the 4:05 mark to claim the crown. *Greeley Daily Tribune* sportswriter Bob Scales was effusive in his praise, complementing Gil not only for his athletic ability but also for his tactical excellence. "Sanchez exhibited clever wrestling with a knowledge and application of many pinning holds. In winning he used three different pins: starting with a half nelson, then a cradle and nailing Sandoval with a figure-four." As a team, the Rams finished second, losing out to Western State. The season and Skyline results made it possible for CSU to send seven entrants to the NCAA Championships. In addition to Gil, Gonzales, and Hines (who also won a conference title), Kent Swendlund, Larry Harrison, Tom Norton, and Fred Lett joined them in this competition.[36]

The 1963 NCAA Wrestling Tournament took place at a locale that would become infamous seven years hence, Kent State University in Ohio. Of the seven athletes competing for CSU, four won their initial matches: Sanchez, Gonzales, Hines, and Swendlund. After the second round, only Gil and Ken Hines remained in contention. In the 115 lb. class, Gil's first challenger was Bill Hughes of Bloomsburg State, whom he fell by a score of 11–5. Next, followed Ricky Graven of the hometown Golden Flashes, whom Sanchez pinned at the 2:31 mark. After this tilt came a familiar foe, Wally Curtis of the University of Oklahoma. The Sooner fell in this match by a score of 10–4. Next in line, now in the national semifinals, was another competitor from a historically dominant program: Lowell Stewart of Iowa State, ranked no. 1 going into the tournament at this weight. Gil dispatched this adversary with a pin at the 5:49 mark. Now, this young

Mexican American was going to compete for a national championship, going up against Arthur Maughan of Minnesota State-Moorhead. In addition to the distinction of trying to bring a national title to the campus of CSU, these final matches were also part of an episode of the *Wide World of Sports* on ABC. Now, not only would Gil get attention from the afficionados of the sport in Colorado and Wyoming, but he would compete (tape-delayed) in front of a national audience. Unfortunately, while this was certainly a monumental accomplishment, he succumbed to Maughan, getting pinned at the 8:11 mark of the match.[37]

The spring semester 1963 was an important one for Gil, and not only because of his success on the mat for the Rams. First, in January, his young wife, Dora Alice, became an American citizen. Next, he would be honored by his university at the end-of-the-year banquet for his outstanding performance in competition. Last, he achieved what Coach Brown had encouraged him to do back at Cheyenne High School: earn a collegiate degree. Gil majored in education (social studies) and would go on to have an illustrious career in that field. Still, his time on the mat was not yet finished.[38]

Shortly after finishing his academic career at CSU, Gil left Colorado on his way to the United States Military Academy (USMA) to participate in tryouts for the US World Championship Tournament team. Here, the goal was to make this squad and become part of a unit that would travel to Europe and compete at this prestigious event. Gil sought to qualify in both Freestyle and Greco-Roman divisions.[39] After participating in the tryouts at the USMA, Gil's next challenge came at the Rocky Mountain AAU Wrestling Tournament, which took place in Boulder, Colorado. Here, he competed in the 115 lb. classification, finishing ahead of another Wyomingite, Warren Grub.[40] Ultimately, the crown, in both Freestyle and Greco-Roman at 114.5 lbs. went to Gil's old friend, Rocky Aoki, representing the New York Athletic Club.[41]

Shortly thereafter, Gil, joined by his two brothers (Art and Ray) went to Pueblo to compete at the US Olympic (regional) Trials. The elites of the city of Cheyenne were so enthusiastic about their hometown heroes' prospects that the Junior Chamber of Commerce sponsored the three brothers' trip to Colorado. Here, for the first time, we saw in print all three of the siblings mentioned as wrestling prodigies.[42]

FIGURE 3.1. Gil winning his USMC title.

The Olympic regionals featured a highly unique situation, as Gil and Ray wrestled in the semifinals for the chance to compete against Glen McMinn of Arizona State for the championship at 114.5 lbs. Even more remarkably, Gil got to wrestle against Ray because Art, who had suffered an injured arm, forfeited a match to his brother. The two Sanchez competitors, both to Susan's joy and (probably) relief, managed a tie, with Gil moving on to the finals, in which he triumphed over McMinn. Ray finished in third place and did not get to continue on to participate at the national Olympic Trials. Gil, on the other hand, suffered an even more disappointing turn of events, costing him a chance to join the Olympic squad. As he was preparing to move on to the next level of competition, his doctor diagnosed him with a heart murmur, and "told me I had to quit wrestling."[43] At the national finals, a US Army soldier, Gray Simons, who had wrestled for Lock Haven University (but was then representing the New York Athletic Club), finished first at 114.5 lbs. and went on to compete for the United States in Japan.[44]

At the start of 1965, Gil's accomplishments, along with the up-and-coming stories of Art and Ray, merited a laudatory article in a Casper newspaper, which claimed that the "Sanchez Name Stands Out in State Wrestling Circles." Here the author argued that if one did not know about this budding family athletic dynasty, it was simply because "you are not a wrestling fan." The essay then goes on to list Gil's exploits and those, so far, of his younger brothers. Given the way that the Spanish-surnamed had been perceived in Wyoming, such a positive portrayal of a Latino family can be perceived as a challenge to many of the assumptions that existed at this time among the majority population of the Equality State, in other words, the very definition of a counterscript.

After the disappointment of his medical diagnosis in 1964, Gil hoped to get back to the mat in time to compete (hopefully alongside one or maybe both of his brothers) to see if he (or they) could represent the United States in the Olympics to be staged in their ancestral homeland in 1968. In order to prepare, Gil sought out two important clearances, first from his doctors, and then from (even more important), his wife. Both gave him their approval. "My wife says she is going to donate me to wrestling. . . . But I just can't stay away from it. All my brothers . . . are in wrestling or have been in it and it just runs in the family." He would make his comeback to the mat at the Great Plains AAU Tournament, held in 1966 at the University of Nebraska in Lincoln. If Gil and Ray were to compete at the same weight classification, they even had a plan so that both could make it to Mexico City. "'We could do it,' Gil explains, however, 'because he (Ray) could go in

Freestyle, and I would go in Greco-Roman.'" While proving himself more than capable of competing at this level (he was by now twenty-eight years old and the father of three), Gil dropped a 4–1 decision in the third round of matches to eventual champion in the 123 lb. classification, Floyd Johnson of Oklahoma State.[45]

Following in his brother's footsteps, David was the next member of the clan to wear a singlet, though he would not be on the mat for long, just his senior year at what was now known as Cheyenne Central High School. While this Sanchez brother was known to tussle with Gil, Art, and younger brother Ray in the family domicile, he preferred to play football and pole vault. According to a family publication, he was an all-state defensive lineman in his last season on the gridiron for the Indians. He did wrestle, even earning a regional title at the 127 lb. classification his senior year (1960) but suffered a neck injury prior to the start of the state tournament and did not participate in that event. He did not pursue athletics at the collegiate level but did earn a nursing degree at Laramie County Community College. He worked at DePaul Hospital, where Susan had toiled in the housekeeping department. Tragically, David died in an automobile accident in April 1976 at the youthful age of thirty-four.[46]

Art was the next member of this initial generation of Sanchez wrestlers. One of the first mentions of his achievements came in a competition against the Casper Mustangs in 1960 when he pinned Tom Rozel in the 103 lb. match. At this moment he was still in junior high but was on the mat for Central High. In his sophomore year in high school, he went out for the football team and got clipped on his left knee during two-a-day practices. He wound up in the hospital with an injured ligament. Given the limitations of technology at that time, his doctor believed the injury was a fractured patella, not a torn ligament. As a result, Art wound up in a cast for several weeks, followed by almost one month of rehabilitation. This injury caused him to miss the wrestling season for that academic year.[47]

The next documentation of Art's achievements focused on a dual event that consisted of Central versus Fort Collins High School (this school also wrestled against Cheyenne East High) toward the end of 1961. Here, Art and younger brother Ray were among the very few positives for the Indians in a lopsided 40–13 loss against the Coloradoans. Impressively, Ray pinned two opponents, Dave Barnes, at the 95 lb. classification at the 4:40

mark, and then Dan Abrams at 103 lbs. at the 1:26 mark. Subsequently, Art stopped Orville Reeves in the 112 lb. tilt at the 1:13 mark of the match. These victories by the Sanchez brothers accounted for the majority of the CCHS points in this confrontation.[48]

Throughout the 1962 campaign, Art shined with victories over opponents from Cheyenne East and Casper in January and then finished second at the state tournament to Rick Lucas from Laramie High School in the 112 lb. category. The following year yielded comparable results, as he once again made it to the state's highest level of competition but now at 120 lbs. Unfortunately, he did not advance as far as previously, losing to Anthony Olson of Worland in the first round by a score of 6–0. In addition to his time on the mat, Art also ran track and played football for the Indians. Overall, he was a three-year lettered athlete and captained the wrestling team his senior year.

After graduating high school in May 1963, he stayed in his home state and competed for the UW Cowboys. Here, he started off by claiming an AAU Rocky Mountain title in 1964 at 115 lbs. and competed against Gil at the US Olympic Trials. In the early months of 1966, the Cowboys pitted themselves against mat royalty, heading into Norman and sporting a sparkling 6–1 squad record, hoping to score their first team victory over the Sooners (along with two ties). Surely, the expectation was that this would be a competitive match. It was not to be, however, as not only did Art lose to Luke Sharpe by a score of 6–0, but the entire Wyoming side also failed to score a point against their opponents, losing, 27–0. Sanchez finished that season losing a decision to Ray Campos of the University of Utah 8–7 at the 130 lb. weight classification. At the end of this campaign, he finished third at 123 lbs. in the Skyline Conference tournament and made it to the NCAA Nationals held at Ames, Iowa, losing to Bob Fehrs of the University of Michigan in the second round. Overall, Art was a three-year lettered athlete on the mat at UW. As he approached completion of his undergraduate studies (in art education) in 1967, he announced his engagement to Mary Louise Gonzales of Rawlins. At the time, she was a junior majoring in elementary education. Simultaneously, Ray announced his intention to wed Mary Louise's sister, Jeanie. The nuptials took place in August. After finishing his degree, Art joined the navy and served on board the cruiser USS *Long Beach* for four years during the height of the Vietnam War.[49] Both brothers went on to successful careers in the field of education, to be detailed in chapters 4 and 5.

While Gil and Art Sanchez both had excellent high school and collegiate careers, and more important, used their athletic skills in order to earn undergraduate (and later, graduate) diplomas, it was youngest brother Ray Sanchez who achieved the greatest mat notoriety, particularly at the high school level. His feats at Cheyenne Central, and later at the University of Wyoming, received extensive coverage in local, state, and even national media. His efforts, along with those of his older siblings, were a constant reminder to Wyomingites that Spanish-surnamed youths were capable of being successful both in classrooms and in fields of athletic competition, thus, challenging the often-negative perception about this group on behalf of the state's majority population.

4

Ray Sanchez Has a Brilliant Future

1962–1981

While Gil and Art, and to a lesser extent, David, shined in their performances on the mat for the Cheyenne Central High School (CCHS) Indians, as well as for Lamar College, Colorado State, and the University of Wyoming, it was youngest brother, Ray, who garnered the most notoriety and acclaim as a grappler, retiring from high school competition as a multiple-time state title holder with an undefeated mark that eventually reached ninety-eight consecutive victories.

Given his success in bringing back the national AAU title in Freestyle wrestling to his hometown, plus a mention in "Faces in the Crowd" in the widely admired and read publication *Sports Illustrated*, it can be argued that Ray (along with his siblings) helped to markedly alter (among many, at least) the perception of Mexican Americans in the Equality State.

Once Gil started, he passed on the love of competition in this sport to his younger brothers. Ray, born in 1946, began the process of honing his mat skills through advice from siblings, and also benefited from the establishment (if only briefly, as it turned out) of a wrestling tournament

https://doi.org/10.5876/9781646427529.c004

at a local branch of the YMCA. As a seventh grader at Johnson Junior High School, Ray triumphed in his weight classification at this event (in part, because he was already scrimmaging with older CCHS competitors). This accomplishment set the stage for his move to Central, as a ninth-grade freshman in the 1961–1962 school year. Even prior to starting his regular career, Ray notched a 103 lb. crown at the Cheyenne Invitational in December 1961. Going into that season, Mike Christopulos of the *Wyoming Eagle* took note of Ray and quoted Central High Coach Len Kuczewski praising his new athlete. "I can't say enough good things about Ray Sanchez. He's a great little prospect. He's so smooth. He's probably a better prospect at this stage of this career than was his older brother, Gil."[1] Indeed, the 1962 Indians squad featured an all-star (and mainly Latino) group of champions from the Invitational, including Ray, Art (at 112 lbs.), Ray Hernández (at 95 lbs.), Dan Gutiérrez (127 lbs.), Manuel Sánchez (153 lbs.), Steve Reinhart (154 lbs.), and Bill Tolan (at 180 lbs.).[2]

Ray moved swiftly through competition in the 1962 campaign with triumphs (via both pins and decisions) against grapplers from Casper, Cheyenne East (at a regional meet), Torrington, Laramie, once again versus East (in an individual meet), Lingle, and at the (eastern) regional tourney. In this last match, Sanchez pinned his opponent, Ivan Eddy of Lusk, in a mere 26 seconds. All of these wins qualified Ray for the state finals, that year held in Laramie in late February. By this point in his freshman year, Coach Kuczewski realized that he was working with an utterly unique talent and boldly acclaimed, "I think that Ray will win the state championship. I don't feel that anybody can touch him."[3] The CCHS mentor's prediction proved prescient, as Ray did claim his first state title, pinning a Worland wrestler named Wright Fujikawa in the first round, decisioning a competitor from Powell named Steinbarger by a score of 8–2 in the semifinals, and once again beating Ivan Eddy for the crown in 103 lbs.[4]

His sophomore campaign was more of the same, and the local papers began to note this young athlete's lengthening streak. In an invitational tournament, *Wyoming Eagle* sports editor Eric Lundberg mentioned that Ray was now competing at the 112 lb. classification and had defeated all nineteen previous opponents. For the rest of 1963, area scribes continued to inform fans of the elongating number of triumphs. By the time that Sanchez pinned a Worland athlete named Garton in 34 seconds, the run had reached thirty. Heading into the February regional finals, Ray was once again at the 103 lb. level where he defeated all comers. Sanchez's first victim at the state tourney preliminaries was Sam Liams from Lander, followed by a Lingle wrestler named Ramos, and he then claimed his second title by beating Rudy Medina of Cheyenne East.[5]

A similar scenario played out the following year, though now the Indians had a new coach, Joe Dowler, who began an impressive run (including two state team titles in 1966 and 1967) beginning with the 1963–1964 school year at CCHS.[6] Now entering his junior year, Ray moved up to the 120 lb. weight, although he also wrestled at 112 lbs.[7] By the time that the regional tournaments began, he had earned the distinction of an individual story in the *Casper Star-Tribune*. Here, sports editor Stan Bowker heaped praise on the youngest member of the Sanchez clan, noting that his streak was now up to fifty-four consecutive victories while also briefly mentioning the exploits of brothers Gil, David, and Art. The primary focus of the article was on Ray's abilities on the mat, but Bowker also did, unknowingly, directly challenge key elements of how many Wyomingites perceived the abilities of the Mexican Americans in their midst.

First, he quoted Dowler praising his charge for his performance in the classroom. "Ray is not only a great wrestler, but he exemplifies high school athletics at its best. He trains hard, learns well and fast, and possesses the outstanding ability to compete." Here, we saw a direct counter to the perception of Spanish-surnamed persons in most parts of the United States during the middle decades of the twentieth century. Later, Bowker went further and turned his attention to Ray's other athletic talents, pole vaulting and weightlifting. Then, even more significant, the scribe detailed that Ray had a "high 'B' average . . . which will make it easier for him to carefully pick out the college he wants to attend." Lastly, Bowker closed by advising readers that newbies to the sport could learn from Ray and would be wise to imitate his techniques on the mat. "Newcomers to the wrestling game can really benefit from just watching Sanchez in action."[8] This article certainly presented a counterscript to what many Wyomingites read about Mexican Americans in their local papers.

Shortly after the publication of this article, Ray went on to challenge for the 112 lb. title, seeking to add it to his two previous 103 lb. crowns. In competition for Wyoming's eastern region, he once again moved on to the

FIGURE 4.1. Ray (front row, second from left) as part of the 1965 CCHS wrestling team.

state finals (held in Cody), defeating Lonnie Dickenson of Newcastle. In the semifinals, Ray overwhelmed Mike Willett of the hometown Broncs, 16–2. He then pinned Gene Bengston of Laramie High School to win his third consecutive championship.[9] Ray then topped off 1964 (now going into his senior year at CCHS) by winning in the 120 lb. classification at the Natrona County High School invitational event, held just before the holidays. Here, he pinned Bill Douglas of Worland and then Rick Hartman of Laramie to secure yet another title.[10]

The year 1965 brought Ray a final (at the high school level) amount of statewide glory, as well as national recognition. It also featured a stinging disappointment in not getting the opportunity to represent his country in international competition. Going into his senior year, this Sanchez brother had now earned seventy-four consecutive victories. He would now be (at least at the start of the season) slotted into the 127 lb. classification, though he subsequently moved down to 120 lbs.[11] By February it was once again time to prepare for the state tournament, which would take place in

Powell. This time, it introduced a new format, with no regional competitions scheduled, and instead featured three separate classifications based on the size of the various schools. Cheyenne Central High School competed at the AA level. Ray, of course, was there, and sought to defend his 120 lb. crown. His challengers for this final go-round were Wright Fujikawa of Worland, Steve Orester of Rock Springs, and Rod Lobof of Cody. The final featured Ray and Fujikawa and, as on previous occasions, the scoring was not close, with Sanchez winning, 12–5.[12]

As Ray walked off the mat for the final time as a high school competitor, the afficionados gathered saluted him with a standing ovation. Reporter Max Jennings noted that this was "something that has happened only rarely in tournament history." Jennings also stated that until this event in his senior year, "no high school wrestler in the state had scored an offensive point against this speedy mat man." He credited his amazing results to both physical and intellectual traits, with the latter element of Ray's abilities demonstrating a "canny application of knowledge . . . [that] is hard to believe." In sum, Coach Dowler simply argued that "Ray is without a doubt the best high school wrestler in the United States." Such a positive statement about a Mexican American teen rarely appeared in print in a Wyoming or other state's newspapers in the early 1960s.[13] Last, Ray earned notice in the trade publication *Amateur Wrestling News*, which named him the top performer in their 1965 High School Honor Roll (which consisted of the best fifty grapplers in the nation).[14]

Ray's outstanding results at the high school level helped him then move on to competition with athletes in the Amateur Athletic Union (AAU). He first moved on to the Rocky Mountain wrestling tournament, held at the University of Colorado in Boulder. Here, he won six consecutive matches at the 114.5 lb. class, and this feat entitled him to attend Nationals in San Francisco.[15] At the event in the City by the Bay, Sanchez faced Freestyle competitors from the high school, collegiate, and international levels. An excellent overview of the events at this tournament comes from a letter by Coach Dowler to individuals in the Cheyenne business community thanking them for assistance in financing the trip to California. Dowler summarized the 114.5 lb. field this way: "The Japanese National team had an entry, collegiate champions from all areas of the country were entered, wrestlers already graduated from college were there. . . . and a

FIGURE 4.2. Ray (far left) as an AAU National Champion in 1965.

few outstanding high school boys were there willing to risk their records against the nation's best." Thereafter, the coach presented a round-by-round synopsis of Ray's matches and the abilities of his opponents.[16]

In his first-round match, the foe was Bill Bush, a two-time state champion from New York state. Dowler stated that Bush was "extremely strong and presented Ray with a real challenge." Instead of trying to outmuscle his opponent, Sanchez "countered Bush's strength with balance and speed and eventually pinned him in 4 minutes and 21 seconds." The second match was not much of a contest, as Ray pinned Vic Sanchez of the Cerritos Wrestling Club from California in a mere 26 seconds. The third contest pitted the young Wyomingite against a collegiate athlete, Steve Johansen of Fresno State. This was no mere competitor, as Johansen had already claimed the small college championship in this category. "Ray completely dominated Johansen and won by the impressive score of 17 to 11."[17]

In the fourth round, Ray wrestled against a Greco-Roman specialist named Rich Henjyoji and faced something never previously confronted, being down (by a score of 5 to 0) after the first 5 minutes. It might have been easy for the youngster to throw in the towel after so much success, given his unfamiliarity with facing a deficit, but Sanchez proved up to the challenge as he and Dowler "made a few adjustments to the Japanese boy's style" and Ray heeded his coach's advice and promptly finished off the challenger by a mark of 11 to 5.

Interestingly, by this point in the tournament, all of the collegiate competitors had been eliminated.[18]

For the semifinals, Ray matched up against another state title holder, Dale Kestle of Michigan. This was the most even competition of the tournament, according to Dowler, who described Kestle as "the second-best wrestler in the weight." In this bout, Ray utilized not only his physical talents but also his tactical abilities. "I think this match was a real test as Ray was required to use a variety of moves and adjust to a number of difficult situations." Sanchez pinned his rival in the final minute. This triumph set up an improbable pairing for the national title, as the competition would be another high schooler, Dwayne Keller from Washington state. Whichever of the youths gained, the victory would be only the second high schooler to claim a national AAU championship. The title bout was never in doubt, as Ray triumphed, 21–9.[19]

Subsequently, his next step would be to decide where he would continue his mat career at the collegiate level. Given that Gil had wrestled at Colorado State, and Art was at the University of Wyoming, those were certainly possibilities. Still, there were many suitors, including wrestling "heavyweights" such as Oklahoma State University, Iowa State University, the University of Michigan, BYU, the University of Nebraska, and West Point.[20]

Even with his extensive winning streak, Ray had limited expectations considering the level of competition he would face in San Francisco. Many years later, he recounted various reminiscences of this national title run to his nephew, Jim Sanchez, by stating that "it was a little scary going into Nationals while still in high school. There were over twenty of the best college and high school wrestlers in the nation. . . . Really, I went to the meet just for the experience."[21]

This stunning achievement led to the hero's welcome when Dowler and Sanchez returned to Cheyenne as described in the introduction.[22] Even

FIGURE 4.3. Ray on the top of the podium as a national champion in San Francisco.

more accolades followed. For example, at the end of April, Ray received a letter of congratulation from Cecil M. Shaw, the superintendent of Wyoming State public schools. This educator informed Sanchez that he too used athletics to attend college and begin his professional career. Furthermore, this letter provided an overview of what wrestling was doing for the Sanchez family—helping them leave behind honest but modest and menial employment and take a step into middle-class status in the United States. "I firmly believe that it is the individual's spirit of competition and drive for success in all things that has made our nation truly great. . . . Your sportsmanship, deep desire to succeed, and great natural ability have made this state . . . very proud of you. You are indeed a credit to your home, school, and community." An earlier letter came from the state's governor, Clifford Hansen, in which he asserted that "you are an outstanding representative of Cheyenne and of Central High. . . . Your community, your state, and I know, your school, are awfully proud of you."[23]

Even as congratulations from officials rolled in, Ray did endure a great disappointment when, at the same time, he heard that he would not be part of an AAU-sponsored team scheduled to tour Europe that summer. Instead, squad mentor Bill Smith selected Rich Sanders of Portland, Oregon, who had won the AAU National crown at the 125 lb. weight, as the individual to compete at the 114 lb. weight while overseas. The reasoning Smith used to justify his decision was that he preferred to take individuals who were more "experienced" than Ray on the tour. Not surprisingly, Coach Dowler argued that Ray had earned a chance to represent his country. While he may not have had collegiate or international experience, it was hard to argue against Sanchez's history. Interestingly, a quick perusal of Sanders's webpage from the National Wrestling Hall of Fame leads one to question whether Coach Smith based his decision truly on "experience." There is no doubt that Sanders had an excellent career at the high school (three Oregon State titles and an 80–1 mark), collegiate (five national crowns coming at the NAIA, NCAA Division II, and NCAA Division I levels), and international (six medals) ranks before his untimely passing in 1972. However, he was just a bit older than Ray (Rich was born in January 1945). He was just a freshman at Portland State in 1965 and was wrestling at the higher weight (although he would later compete for the Vikings at 115 lbs.). Briefly, both individuals had tremendous success as high school athletes and were roughly the same age. It is worth asking whether the fact that Ray Sanchez was of Mexican descent played any role in being kept off of this squad.[24] Perhaps having a Mexican American represent the United States on such a team would have proven to be too much of a counterscript for Coach Smith.

Between the frustration of not going to Europe and late May 1965, Ray made the decision to join his brother Art at the University of Wyoming. New coach Joe C. McDaniel wrote to Ray in early June of that year and welcomed him to the Cowboys' family. He paid his incoming freshman a great compliment when he wrote that "I have seen you wrestle several times, and you reminded me of myself when I was wrestling. I believe that my style of wrestling will be to your liking." Further, the nationally recognized coach (and three-time national champion at Oklahoma A&M in the late 1930s) believed that the addition of this Sanchez brother would help to propel University of Wyoming wrestling to the highest levels of national prominence. "We plan to become a contender for National honors and know that you will play an important part in helping us attain that goal."[25]

The disappointment of not competing internationally was not the only setback Ray confronted in the months before moving on to the Laramie campus. In early August, he was involved in an automobile accident near Warren Air Force Base. He lost control of his automobile and hit a post, suffering "lacerations and bruises, but no broken bones." He was then taken to Memorial Hospital, where he was reported in good condition.[26]

Ray competed for the Cowboys' freshman squad and, not surprisingly, went undefeated during the 1966 season. Before that, however, he returned to AAU competition, winning the 115 lb. division at the Great Plains Wrestling Tournament, held in Nebraska in December 1965. In the fifth round of that event, Ray shut out Darl Weaver, 17–0 and then moved on to face a familiar foe in the finals, Rich Henjyoji of Oklahoma State. The two fought to a scoreless tie, but Sanchez finished first due to fewer black marks.[27] While on the UW junior varsity team, he also participated in a second AAU competition that took place in Boulder, Colorado (the Rocky Mountain Tournament), in March 1966, and there he won at the 123 lb. category. Later, he returned to the Cornhusker State in April for the AAU Nationals (competing unattached, not representing the University of Wyoming). Here, he faced another familiar foe, Dwayne Keller. By the semifinals, Ray had earned a bye and in the championship round he there faced Kenichi Kanno of Eugene, Oregon, pinning his foe at the 8:26 mark of the match. Once again, Ray reigned as national champion in 114.5 lbs.[28]

While Ray did much to establish himself as a prime competitor for his sophomore year at Wyoming (1967), he suffered a major injury in June 1966 while participating in tryouts for the United States' World Games squad at the University of Michigan. He had already proven his mettle by defeating both AAU and NCAA champions and already had qualified to be on the squad representing the US at the meet held in Toledo, Ohio. Unfortunately, injuries to his knee and ankle prevented him from competing.[29] Not to be deterred by missing out on this opportunity, Ray noted in December of that year that he still hoped to be ready to go when Olympic Trials began for the 1968 Games, which would be held in his ancestral home of Mexico (in Mexico City).[30]

The 1967 campaign introduced Ray to varsity competition at the collegiate level, and not surprisingly, he acquitted himself very well, although there were bumps along the way. For example, when the Cowboys competed in a match against wrestling royalty, the University of Oklahoma Sooners, the squad from Laramie fell at home by the lopsided score of

24–9. Going into this event, the team from UW had been undefeated but now dropped its first team match against ten victories. In this meet, Ray lost a decision to Bryce Rice, 8–4, for his second loss of the season. While tasting defeat was a new sensation, Sanchez continued to prove his value to the team as, even when he had to compete with an injured elbow in late February, he still managed to defeat an opponent from BYU, 9–2. This victory moved his season mark to 14–2.[31]

At the end of the season, he reinjured the elbow against Oregon State and was unable to participate in the Western Athletic Conference (WAC) Championships, as now teammate Wright Fujikawa competed at the 123 lb. classification in his place. Still, Ray was able to advance to the NCAA Nationals held that year at Kent State University between March 23 and 25. He entered the tournament with a record of 22–2.[32]

The NCAA field at 115 lbs. started out with a total of thirty-two competitors. Ray's first match was against Jerry Martínez of the University of Northern Colorado. There was little doubt about the outcome, as the Cowboy demolished his foe by a score of 26–5. Next up was Steve Cavanaugh of the University of Missouri. Here, Ray managed to pin his opponent at the 7:51 mark. The third round pitted Ray against Ken Melchoir of the University of Lock Haven and resulted in a 7–1 victory for the representative of UW. The semifinals in this classification were between Ray and Jim Anderson of the University of Minnesota in one bracket and Ron Iwasaki of Oregon State University and the aforementioned Rick Sanders of Portland State University (PSU). The PSU Viking defeated the OSU Beaver by a tally of 8–3. For Ray, this was the last hurrah in this competition, as he lost to Anderson by the same 8–3 score, thus ending his opportunity to become an NCAA national champion. This then moved him into the consolation bracket where competitors would fight for the chance to finish in the top four of their weight category and claim the coveted status of All-American. Because of his ranking, Ray had a bye into the third round of the consolation fights. His first bout here was against Dell Rhodes of the University of Colorado, a match he won, 5–0. Last, in the finals he faced Glenn McMinn of Arizona State University. The contest was a back-and-forth affair, but McMinn prevailed by a score of 7–6. Thus, he claimed third place in the tournament, and Ray came in fourth. Although falling short of his goal to win a national title at this level, Ray was only completing his sophomore year at Laramie, and there, he surely thought, would be other chances to win the grand prize of collegiate wrestling.[33]

Although he could not grasp the brass ring in the NCAAs, Ray still had a chance to defend his two crowns at the AAU level, and that opportunity presented itself in Lincoln, Nebraska, just a few weeks after the meet in Ohio. Prior to the event, the local paper did a story on Ray, and it provided insight into his eating habits and the first year competing at the collegiate level. Writer Chuck Woodling informed waitresses in the Nebraska capital to not be surprised if they were asked to bring Ray a steak for breakfast. Sanchez indicated to the scribe that the reason for this was so as not to gain weight. "After early morning weigh-ins, Ray eats steak for breakfast to get 'quick energy and protein' [then] skips lunch and gobbles a fruit salad for dinner. . . . 'I've had some real queer looks when I ask for steak, but I've always been able to get them.' " The article then goes on to point out that Ray is going for his third consecutive title, and how this might be the most difficult competition he has ever faced in AAU—particularly after the slog of a collegiate campaign. "This was my first year of wrestling a full college schedule, and I found out it can be quite a grind." Last, the article also provided an indication that Ray was still not over his elbow injury when he competed at the NCAAs and "he almost didn't come to the AAU meet because of the arm. After his first match Thursday, a quick win by a fall, he said he 'favored the arm a little bit.' "[34]

Sanchez moved through the early rounds, pinning Grant Henjyoji of the Multnomah Athletic Club, and then crushing Ron Rhodes of San Francisco, 34–2. By the fifth round of competition, Ray drew Greg Johnson of the Michigan Wrestling Club. The pair tied at 20–20. However, after this match, Sanchez had accumulated a total of six black marks, and that eliminated him from the event. Just as at the NCAAs, Ray fell short of his goal. Still, it seemed that there would certainly be more titles and opportunities in the future. Only it did not turn out that way.[35]

After completing his sophomore classes at UW, Ray had a decision to make: He could either go to Korea and Japan with a team from Fellowship of Christian Athletes, or he could he attend the tryouts for the US Pan American Games team in July (held in Minneapolis). A further consideration was simply to take summer 1967 off so that he could nurse his injured elbow. This is what Ray decided to do.[36]

The arrival of the fall term meant that Coach McDaniel's charges were to begin preparing for the upcoming season. The 1967 results were quite positive for the Cowboys, as the team finished with a 15–3 mark. Further, nine of the thirteen athletes returned for the 1968 campaign. Ray had had the most successful season, finishing as an All-American, but also on the roster were Don Miller, who finished sixth in the NCAAs at 167 lbs. and Leon Mickelson at 160 lbs., both of whom had won championships in their classification in the WAC; and, last Dale Kujah, who finished third in the WAC at 152 lbs. All seemed ready to go for the squad to achieve even greater heights than the previous year. While other articles noted that Ray's arm injury continued to be an issue, his goal was to be ready to go by January 1968.[37]

Unfortunately, the injury bug struck Sanchez again, and this time, much more severely. By the middle of January, Coach McDaniel informed fans that the worst had happened, and Ray, who had injured his back, would be out for the entire season. "We'll probably redshirt Ray this year because he would never be in top shape." Many years later, as he prepared for induction into the Wyoming Sports Hall of Fame (in 2009), Ray recounted what happened in that fateful month when a teammate came down awkwardly on his pelvis and damaged his back. "I hadn't had any injuries until that time. I was lucky that way, but when injuries hit, they hit me pretty hard. If I hadn't had that back injury, I think I could have won at least two national championships, gone to the world games again, and maybe gone to the Olympics." Instead, over the years since, he has endured four surgeries to try to correct the problem. He summarized his collegiate career in the following way: "There were a lot of goals I didn't achieve because of the back injury, and it was really disappointing."[38]

From there, the 1968 season spiraled into, at best, mediocrity for the team. By the end of February, as the WAC neared its tournament, the Cowboys sported a mark of 7-8-1 after losses to BYU, Arizona State, and Utah. Still, there was a glimmer of hope when after one month of convalescence, Ray announced that he would return in time for the ASU Invitational. Here, he defeated Hiram Scott 8–5. By the end of this season, he had achieved a personal record of 17–0. Even with his back injury, however, he still appeared on the Cowboy's roster for the start of the 1969 campaign, but he had to retire from competition. As he stated in his 2009 interview with *Wyoming News*, he had an illustrious career in high school, and in the limited time he competed for the Cowboys at the varsity level. Regrettably, he was unable to continue. While he could no longer participate as an athlete, the competitive juices still flowed, and when he graduated with a degree in English in May 1970, he began to share his knowledge and tactics with the next generation of Wyoming youths. His first task would be to revive the fortunes of a team that had won only two matches since 1968.[39]

Ray began his career at Lander Valley High School beginning in fall 1970. An article announcing his hire reviewed his success at Central, and at the start of his time at Wyoming, but then noted that "he never regained his sophomore heights" after suffering the injuries noted above. He also served as backfield coach for the football team in addition to teaching English. His tenure with the Tigers did not last long, as Ray decided to resign his post by April 1972. He stated that he wanted to return to school to pursue graduate work in educational administration. Instead, he took the same post at Rawlins, starting in May 1973. As at Lander, he also served as an assistant with the football team and taught English. During his time at Rawlins, Ray was able to coach some of the state's finest grapplers in a camp preparing them for matches against a touring Soviet exchange team in May and early June 1974. Ray continued coaching at Rawlins until the end of the school year in 1976.[40] He then went on to coach wrestling at a high school in Greeley, Colorado (Greeley West High School), finally hanging up his whistle in 1981.

A final, major honor came with Ray's induction into the University of Wyoming Sports Hall of Fame in 2012. To say the least, it was a long time coming. More than forty years after he donned a Cowboys' singlet for the final time, Sanchez now had his place among the legends of UW athletics. In an interview with the *Longmont Times-Caller*, one of Ray's sons, Scott Sanchez, reminded afficionados of the sport in Wyoming of the importance of this one Mexican American clan to wrestling. "When you talk about Wyoming wrestling, it's all about the Sanchez family—and it all starts with my dad." Indeed, Ray then summarized what the sport has meant to him, and the entire family, noting that "Wrestling has had a great impact on me as a person, on what I've done and what I've become. It's meant a lot to me and to my family."[41]

Ray spent the rest of his career teaching and as an administrator in the Denver Public Schools (at George Washington High—as the English AP and Honors teacher and department chair), then as diversity coordinator for Boulder Valley School District and Jefferson County Public Schools (as principal at Stein Elementary in Lakewood). It was at Stein that Ray helped turn the lowest performing Title I school in the district into the highest-ranked such institution. Unfortunately, he also slipped and fell while helping a student get up from a fall, and he, once again, reinjured his back. This led to a final surgery, and he retired in 2007. Since the early 2000s Ray and his second wife, Lynn (also a retired school principal), have lived in Longmont, Colorado. Together, they have a total of eight children (Ray's six are Raymond, Katrina, Britt, Scott, Megan, and Amy; Lynn's are Nikki and Leah).[42]

Prior to his induction into the Wyoming Sports Hall of Fame, he indicated to a reporter from the *Denver Post* part of the reason he finally decided to give up coaching, move into the classroom, and work in school leadership on a permanent basis. "I just didn't see the commitment when I was coaching. We had a couple of state-place winners in my four years. It was too easy for some of my wrestlers to quit. They didn't want to commit to the demanding workouts that are necessary to compete against the best."[43] While he may have seen a lack of drive in some of his charges, he (as well as Gil and Art) passed along a love for the sport (and of the educational profession) to the next generation of Sanchezes. Thanks to the efforts of their parents and grandparents, this generation had options and opportunities that would have been almost inconceivable to most Mexican families in the pre-revolutionary era. It is to that story we now turn.

5

The Next Generation of Sanchezes as Wrestlers and Coaches

1979–2023

As noted in the previous chapter, Ray's success on the mat and his efforts as an educator provide a powerful counterscript to the notion that Latinos in a place like Wyoming could only fill certain occupational spots. From the arrival of this first generation of grapplers' grandparents to the Equality State, their clan, and others of similar backgrounds, had been pigeonholed almost exclusively into menial, low-wage labor and categorized as having limited intellectual capabilities. While jobs in certain industries, such as the Sinclair Refinery, the railroads, mining, and a few other sectors provided a more or less sustainable living for many, there was little opportunity to move into professional employment that could grant access to a broader definition of the American Dream. Before proceeding to a discussion of the second generation, as well as a brief review of the educational and professional careers of Gilbert and Art Sanchez, it is important to note how Mexican American youths were perceived in Wyoming by many educators. As mentioned earlier when discussing the work of Gonzalo Guzmán in chapter 1, such pupils were considered a

https://doi.org/10.5876/9781646427529.c005

"problem" by the end of World War II. Had anything changed in the assessment of such students by the time that Ray, Gilbert, and Art commenced their careers in the field of education?

A 1970 master's thesis by Joyce A. Surdam from the University of Wyoming provides a disheartening answer to that question. This work, which focused on *estudiantes* at Laramie High School, argued that teachers at this institution perceived children of this background as being the offspring of a culture that was more concerned with mere survival at the present moment, rather than embracing the notion of future (economic and social) development. Further, they were presented as individuals being acted upon, and not as historical/social actors in their own right. Finally, they were described as being overly family centered rather than individualistic strivers, who were not politically engaged and not valuers of education and personal improvement.[1] Certainly, given the efforts of their parents and grandparents, such characterizations did not apply to the first generation of wrestlers in the Sanchez family. A final point by Surdam, however, does tie in with the generation that will be covered in this chapter, and that is greater political awareness (particularly with Frank Sanchez, as will be discussed). As noted by this Surdam, by the 1970s, "Mexican Americans . . . [had] become more politically aware and involved," and now in Wyoming and elsewhere, they were "more eager to pursue efforts to claim their civil and other rights."[2]

The La Cultura interviews also provide further documentation of some of the points made by Surdam. For example, an interview with Esther De Herrera, who was born in Rawlins in 1952, provides a sense of the negative attitudes toward Spanish-surnamed pupils. Her recollections at Rawlins High School were that many teachers were "critical of Mexican kids and probably had low expectations." She recalls that when she was in ninth grade the counselor suggested that she take general education offerings instead of classes that would prepare her to attend college. "Most of the Spanish kids were in general courses," in part because many of the instructors "did not think we had the capacity."[3]

Rafaela Rodríguez, who was born in Chihuahua in 1947 and whose family arrived in Wyoming in 1954, recalls similar situations in Casper. She indicated in her interview that she managed to complete through the eleventh grade but that the counselor at her high school never encouraged her to pursue any specific career. While she indicated that she wanted to be a stewardess, she never even applied for such a post. Instead, she worked in a plant assembling computer components. Her hope was that her children would be able to go to college "and become professionals."[4]

While the La Cultura interviews provide important context for some of the negative circumstances extant in Wyoming schools in the 1960s and into the 1970s, some interviews show that certain changes had occurred. For example, Oralia Gómez Mercado, who was born in 1941, attended and graduated from Washakie County High School. Although she classified her teachers and counselors as being "passive" toward her education, she recalled that she did well in math and history; while "counselled toward the commercial courses," she managed to complete her schooling, and also (over the years) took "lots of college courses," though she noted, "I don't have a degree, but lots of courses listed." Still, because of some of the government programs instituted during the Great Society years, she managed to get work first as a teacher's aide with Head Start, then, later, as a social worker with the same program, and eventually as an equal employment officer with the state Employment Security Services.[5]

A final interview that contextualizes circumstances in schools and a move toward better occupations comes from Abe DeHerrera, who had an interesting career in law enforcement and politics. Abe was born in Costilla, New Mexico, in 1942, and his family arrived in Wyoming in 1948. He attended Rawlins High School and noted to his interviewer that he was not encouraged to pursue a career. He did graduate, even though he faced a challenge from school administrators because he was already married. He subsequently worked on a pipeline, but eventually got a job as a police officer in Rawlins in 1965. By this time, he had four daughters, and a civil service job seemed like a good career move.

Abe also indicated that his hiring was not met with support by many of his fellow officers and that he often had to go to dangerous situations without backup. On the other side of the equation, "the Spanish people accused me of being a traitor." Still, his diligence and talent helped him move up the chain of command, and by the time of his interview, he was serving as a detective and also had served as chief for the department between 1977 and 1983. In addition, he took it upon himself to work with the Carbon County School District, serving as a board trustee for district

#1 starting in 1968. He summarized the changes he has seen in Rawlins, stating: "I think it's probably because of the openness that the younger generation has toward each other. . . . they seem to want to share thing better than it was done back in those days." Abe eventually served as a United States marshal for the District of Wyoming from 1996 through the end of the second Clinton administration.[6]

In summary, as the first generation of Sanchez competitors moved into school systems in Wyoming (and elsewhere), there were some positive trends alongside still lingering issues. Through their hard work, these three brothers would help build upon these developments for their students and athletes over the next few decades. In addition, they set an important standard for their children to follow, both on the wrestling mat and in the classroom. Before moving on to the exploits of the next generation of Sanchez athletes, it is necessary to provide a quick summary of the postathletic careers of Gil and Art Sanchez.

Starting with oldest brother Gil, upon completing his degree in social studies education in 1963, he taught and coached at Carey Junior High School in his hometown between 1964 and 1966. He then taught that same subject at Johnson Junior High, also in Cheyenne. It was during this time that he decided to pursue further studies and went on to get a graduate degree in history (as well as serving as a graduate assistant for the wrestling team) at Western State University in Gunnison, Colorado, graduating with an MA in 1968. After that, he worked as head coach at North High School in Phoenix, Arizona, until 1972. Next, he pursued a second master's degree, this time in guidance and counseling at the University of New Mexico. All the while, Gil kept teaching young grapplers the sport that had made it possible to begin the process of moving this family into the middle class.

In 1973, he served as an assistant coach for the Junior World Wrestling Championships held at Miami Beach Convention Center in late July. The competition would feature a total of twenty-two nations, and the event's promoter/director, local restaurateur Steve Evanoff, went all out to draw attention to the affair, even bringing in legendary wrestler Dan Gable, winner of a gold medal at the ill-fated 1972 Olympics in Munich (see next paragraph). While none of the twenty American competitors on this squad hailed from Wyoming, these young men (ages 16–20) got a world-class experience in competing against foes from international wrestling powers such as the Soviet Union, other eastern bloc nations, Turkey, Japan, and elsewhere.[7] Additionally, they benefited from the expert guidance of a marine and state champion with his own tales of international events.

While Gil never made it to the Olympics, he did get a taste of Olympian-style controversy at this event. Remember, this tournament took place just a few months beyond the legendary hullabaloo at the end of the US versus USSR gold medal game in basketball in West Germany, and a similar example of Communist-inspired cheating took place in Miami Beach. With Bulgaria having captured the overall Freestyle title, the two Cold War adversaries battled for the second-place trophy. It all came down to a match between Joe Carr and Aratsilov Magomedkhan at 163.5 lbs. Carr led 5–4 after two periods when, it appeared, a Soviet trainer applied a "foreign substance" to the towel used to wipe Magomedkhan's brow. When the referee noticed this activity, he tried to check on the situation. As he approached, the trainer took off running in the direction of the Soviet team's locker room. A check of that facility did not reveal the doctored cloth; thus, the match continued. Amazingly, Magomedkhan seemed to get a new burst of energy, and defeated Carr, 7–6, guaranteeing the second-place award to the USSR. Promoter Evanoff was not pleased, although he did apologize to the Soviet coaches for the bruhaha. Still, he recognized that "It's not beneath the Russians to partake of this kind of activity."[8]

After his exposure to Soviet sporting shenanigans, Gil returned to coaching, splitting the next six years between North High School in Phoenix (1973–1974) and his alma mater in Cheyenne as a counselor and coach (1974–1980) and serving as a role model for the students in his old neighborhood. Additionally, he also continued to serve his country as a staff member at the Olympic Training Center in Colorado Springs (1978–1981), as a coach for the Greco-Roman Schoolboy Team in Stockholm (1978), then at the Olympic Sports Festival in Syracuse, New York, in 1981. Meanwhile, he added one more educational accoutrement: getting certified as a school administrator by the University of Wyoming during the 1979–1980 school year. These credentials allowed him to serve as an assistant principal or principal for the remainder of his career. His final two stops were at Catholic schools (Holy Name in Sheridan, Wyoming, between 1997–1999, and St. Mary's in Cheyenne, between 1999 and 2000). Although he retired from his administrative duties, he continued to coach, this time as an assistant alongside his sons, Jim and Gil (whose careers will be detailed later in this chapter), in Nevada, Colorado, and South Carolina.[9]

Art's career followed a similar path. After his time as a three-year varsity athlete at the University of Wyoming, he hoped to begin his efforts as an educator, but the US Navy had other ideas. Shortly after receiving his diploma in art education, he received a draft notice. After passing his physical in Denver, he enlisted for a four-year hitch. During the Vietnam War, he served as a yeoman in the navigation department aboard the nuclear-powered missile cruiser the USS *Long Beach*. Later, he moved on to a Defense Department unit in Livermore, California. It was during these last two years in the service that two of his sons, Glenn and Greg, were born. He received an honorable discharge from the military in 1972 and began working on a master's degree at his alma mater. After completing this course of study, he secured a post in the Denver Public Schools, with his first stop being Manual High School for one academic year, and then spending the next fourteen years at Smiley Junior High / Middle School. After that stop, he spent another fourteen years as department head at Thomas Jefferson High. Meanwhile, two more children, Natalie and another son, Philip, were born to Art and Mary Louise (who also worked in education, as a library specialist for the Adams County School District). As had occurred in his life, with Gil introducing him to the sport of wrestling, Art did likewise with his sons. His coaching career featured stops at Manual in Denver (1975), George Washington High School in Denver (1982–1983), North High School in Phoenix (1984–1986), and finally, Thomas Jefferson High School in Denver (1995–1998). Even after retiring, Art continued to coach, serving as an assistant to his son Greg at Thornton High School (THS) in Thornton, Colorado, between 2003 and 2009.[10]

Now that Ray's, Gil's, and Art's accomplishments are summarized, it is time to move on to the second generation of Sanchezes on the mats of Wyoming and elsewhere. It is in this group of athletes that we see the dramatic transformation that sport had on the experiences and social standing of this Mexican American family. Whereas for the first generation of competitors, sport opened opportunities that their parents and grandparents could not have imagined, with this subsequent cohort competing on the mat and attending college were now expected. Again, as noted

FIGURE 5.1. Gil (far left) as a Junior World coach in the early 1980s.

in the discussion on Alex Nuñez's article "Switch-Hitting," mentioned in chapter 2, this group of Sanchezes had provided Wyomingites with "moments in which Mexican Americans performed this convincing display of . . . fitness for citizenship [and] also reflected a successful transgression of deeper social and racial boundaries that permitted Mexican Americans to claim elements of whiteness for themselves."[11] For Gil's offspring, Gil, Frank, and Jim; for Art's boys, Glenn, Greg, and Philip; and last, for Ray's sons, Scott, Britt, and Ray, wrestling opened further possibilities, so much so that one of these young men (Frank) would eventually serve as president of two collegiate institutions.

Since Gil started the family's ties to the sport, it is appropriate to begin an examination of the next crop of Sanchezes with his sons, particularly with the younger Gil, who had the most storied mat career of anyone in the family—competing in the NCAA finals on behalf of the University of Nebraska in his weight classification. One of earliest mentions of him (in 1979) noted that Gil was one of seven Wyoming wrestlers selected to participate at a two-week camp at the Olympic Training Center in Squaw Valley, California. He was listed as competing in the 98 lb. classification. Not surprisingly, the elder Sanchez was the coach accompanying this contingent. The instructors at the facility were to work with these youths in "wrestling techniques, weight training, psychological aspects of competition, nutrition, tactics, and strategy." Later, the group traveled to the National Sports Festival at Colorado Springs. The elder Gil argued that this process was designed to look toward the future of the nation's Olympic prospects. "The purpose of this program is to develop young wrestlers with potential for the 1984 and 1988 Olympics and future international competition."[12]

The start of the regular campaign brought even more notoriety to Gil, as he was considered a strong possibility for claiming a state title, although he was out for a while with an injury. Still, by the time that the state tournament rolled around, he ranked third in his classification and won the title at 98 lbs., defeating Jim Williams of Natrona County in overtime via "a bearhug and a trip to end the squabble in 0:37." Thus, yet another Wyoming state title now graced the Sanchez domicile.[13]

Gil's senior year at CCHS featured more of the same. Now competing at 105 lbs., he was considered a co-favorite to win another state title. Going into this season, he boasted a record of 55-8-1 with twenty-eight pins and two state crowns. Further, he was nominated as one of ten competitors from Wyoming for possible national honors from Wrestling USA and *Scholastic Coach* magazine. A committee comprised of both coaches and officials selected these athletes, and Gil was the top-ranked member of the group. He did not disappoint, claiming his third championship prior to graduation from CCHS in 1981. He also earned an All-American designation from *Scholastic Wrestling News* (now *Wrestling USA Magazine*) and then went on to participate on an all-star squad in July, putting up a valiant fight at 118 lbs. versus another three-time state title holder, Ed Risha of Douglas High School, but losing by a mark of 4–2.[14]

While his father and uncles had wrestled at Wyoming and Colorado State, Gil took the bold step to compete in the Big 8, the home of powerhouses such as the Oklahoma Sooners, Oklahoma State Cowboys, and Iowa State Cyclones. This particular member of the clan decided to cast his lot with a team that had recent success (finishing sixth in the NCAA

Tournament in 1981–1982) but that had endured a significant dry spell as a squad since the 1960s, without a national champion since 1963, no All-Americans since 1971, and last making the team tournament in 1961–1962.[15] Here, he would have the opportunity to compete against top-flight athletes and yet be able to be part of a program that seemed to be on the upswing.

Sitting out the 1982 season as a first-year student, he commenced competition for the Nebraska Cornhuskers in January 1983, at the Midlands Invitational, where he placed sixth at 118 lbs. Further, the team was optimistic for a successful season, as they ranked sixth in the nation by the *Amateur Wrestling News* preseason poll. Certainly, one of the key moments in the red-shirt freshman's campaign occurred when he returned to his home state to challenge the Cowboys in Laramie. Although Gil lost to Tim Nelson, Husker assistant coach Kelly Wright had high praise for his charge. "Sanchez just lost because he's a freshman. He's better than that kid. If he wrestles that guy again, he'll beat him. He was a senior and he is one of their best guys with a 15-5-1 record." At the conclusion of his first year of collegiate competition, Gil finished with a mark of 15-9-1, although injuries prevented him from participating in the Big 8 Conference tournament. Significantly, the UN squad made it to the national team championships and finished an impressive sixth in the nation. It looked as if the upswing would continue and Gil Sanchez would be a critical part of Big Red's drive toward even greater results.[16]

With a successful season under his belt, Coach Bob Fehrs was counting on Gil (now at 126 lbs.) and fellow sophomore Matt Campbell (at 118 lbs.) to become stalwarts for the 1983–1984 schedule. An early test came against the number-two-ranked OSU, and Nebraska received a rude awakening, losing 41–5. Gil suffered a lopsided defeat to the Cowboys' John Smith, 17–5. Additionally, he suffered an injured elbow that made him doubtful for upcoming matches against the University of Nebraska Omaha and highly ranked Oregon State University. Unfortunately, the damage proved too severe, and Sanchez was unable to compete against the Beavers. It seems as if the injury bug had struck most of UN's frontline starters at this point as grapplers at the 118, 126, 142, and 150 lb. weights were unable to spar. "'That's almost half of our team out,' Fehrs said. 'Consequently, with half a team, it's tough to do much.'" Although he returned to action in mid-December,

Gil was not up to his usual level of performance, failing to place at the Midlands Invitational. Things did not get any easier for the Huskers as they confronted the Cyclones early in the new year of 1984. Gil had a particularly difficult chore, scheduled to line up against Kevin Darkus, a two-time All-American who came in with a 27–0 mark. Instead of facing this foe, however, Coach Fehrs forfeited the 126 lb. match and instead moved Sanchez up to 134 lbs. The hope was that Gil could manage against George Patterson, because he was only "a junior college guy." Unfortunately, the strategy backfired, and the ISU competitor triumphed, 17–8.[17]

Certainly, Gil's sophomore campaign featured disappointments and injuries, but he did contain memorable triumphs, including one that must have resonated powerfully with his father. In January 1984, the Cornhuskers traveled to Fargo to compete against the North Dakota State University (NDSU) Bison. While NU came out a winner by the score of 31–15, and Gil won his match 5–3, it was his opponent at 126 lbs. that made this match so special, for the foe in this tilt was Jack Maughan, the son of Bucky Maughan, who had defeated the older Gil at the 1963 NCAA championship. This high point of the season did not last long, however, as once again Sanchez missed a match against Oklahoma due to an infection. Still, he had a 11-4-2 mark heading toward the end of the season. As the Big 8 Tournament approached, unfortunately, he was still not up to par and lost in a preliminary round 10–7 to Alfred Morgan of the University of Missouri. Although a frustrating year personally, Gil managed to be part of one of the best teams in the history of Nebraska wrestling, as it finished fourth in the team standings and brothers Bill and Jim Scherr each won national titles at 190 and 177 lbs. respectively.[18]

Obviously, replacing two national champions means that a program is going to have to "rebuild" to maintain a level of competitiveness. With Gil entering his junior year, he would be one of the principal cogs for the Huskers. He quickly began to demonstrate his value to the squad by finishing second at 134 lbs. in the University of Nebraska Omaha Open, which featured more than 400 participants from twenty different institutions. Still, the injury gremlin struck the team's side again, and, as Coach Fehrs noted, some of his new recruits "have reached a plateau." Thus, even more rested on the performance from seniors such as Chris Marisette and junior Gil Sanchez. The year did not get off to a bright start, as the

FIGURE 5.2. Gil Jr. (right) competing on behalf of the Nebraska Cornhuskers' wrestling team.

Huskers lost to Iowa State 34–4 in mid-November. While the team score was indeed lopsided, Gil lost a close match to Jeff Gibbons, 6–5 at 134 lbs. Things improved later in the season, as the team swept the United States Air Force Academy and Central Oklahoma State (University of Central

Oklahoma) by scores of 45–0 and 33–11. Gil finished that dual meet with three consecutive victories. Next, he once again triumphed over Jack Maughan, with Nebraska once again trouncing the Bison, 29–9. His winning ways continued versus Chris Anderson of the University of Tennessee at Chattanooga, Scott Lane of University of Nebraska Omaha, and Kurt Lage of the University of Missouri. By this point in the season, late January, he now ranked as the thirteenth best grappler at 134 lbs. In late February, after once again recovering from injury, Coach Fehrs inserted him into the 142 lb. category, and he defeated Alex Magafas of Drake University, Des Moines, 13–2.[19]

As the season reached its apex, the Huskers were a force to contend with at the national level, sporting a mark of 16–5 heading into the conference tournament. Gil was also on a tremendous streak, as noted by interim coach Tim Neumann. Indeed, the Huskers' goal was to have all ten competitors at the Big 8 event qualify for Nationals. To accomplish this monumental task, all the individuals would have to finish in the top three of their respective weight classifications. Neumann singled out various members of the squad, with Gil getting a tremendous amount of praise. "He's wrestling fantastically. He has technical falls over his last six opponents."[20] As the event reached the final pairings, Gil challenged Nick Neville of the Sooners, who triumphed, 5–2. Nevertheless, by coming in second in this competition, Gil punched his ticket to Nationals held on the campus of the University of Iowa. Here, Sanchez once again faced a Big 8 foe, Leo Bailey of Oklahoma State, who defeated him by a score of 9–6. Overall, however, the Wyoming native now figured prominently at the national level, finishing the year with a mark of 24–7 and making it clear that yet another member of the Sanchez clan was poised to challenge for a national title in the 1986–1987 season.[21]

Gil Sanchez's senior year featured a continuation of the excellent wrestling displayed toward the end of his junior campaign. He started out by winning his classification at the Wyoming Open in mid-November and followed that up with one of the most significant triumphs of his mat career. At the first meet of the season, against the OSU Cowboys, Nebraska lost, 27–11. However, the meet featured Gil wrestling against a familiar foe, John Smith. By this time, the heavily favored Smith was now a gold medal winner at the Goodwill Games and looked to defeat Sanchez as he had done previously. With the score tied at six in the third period, Gil escaped his foe to take a one-point lead and then put him down on his back to secure a 13–6 triumph. The crowd at the Bob Devaney Sports Center cheered wildly as the Huskers took a brief 6–4 lead in the team score. Unfortunately, the Cowboys then took four of the remaining five matches to seal their victory. Still, the focus was on the impressive victory at 134 lbs. "I've wrestled him tough the last two years, but I've never gotten any respect. Now, maybe I will get that respect." Coach Neumann, just like Coach Dowler had so many years earlier, then stated that Sanchez had bigger aspirations than a single triumph. "He's shooting for a national title, and he showed that tonight." As if that weren't enough, Gil then followed up with a dominating performance at the Northern Open Wrestling Tournament, recording four pins in five matches and shutting out Wisconsin's Tim Fitzpatrick 11–0 in the title match. "He just dominated everyone. He's looking unstoppable now. Anytime you're named the outstanding wrestler at a tournament where the whole Iowa team is there, you're doing a good job." At this point, his season mark stood at 15–1.[22]

The impressive run continued at the Northern Iowa Open, as Sanchez decisioned Barry Davis, who had earned a silver medal in the 1984 Olympics and was a three-time NCAA champion. This then brought his season record to 21–1, and his career mark now stood at 82-26-3. At that point, he held the fourth-highest winning percentage in the history of Nebraska wrestling. Coach Neumann credited the improvement in his charge to the work Gil did with Mark Perry, who was a two-time All American at Oklahoma State. "Mark had one semester with him last year, all summer and then the preseason this year. He's really helped Sanchez with his technique." Eventually, the local paper in Lincoln did a story on Gil and expounded on the role that the sport has played in his life and that of his family:

> I won a state championship as both a junior and a senior. . . . My dad, who is still at Cheyenne Central—he's now a counselor—and my four uncles all went to Central. . . . My dad, who was my high school coach, placed third as a junior and second as a senior in the NCAA tournament when he was in college at Colorado State . . . I've had good regular season records every year, but then something would go wrong. My freshman year I got

> hurt the week before the Big 8 meet. Then, my sophomore year, I had another good season but got a staph infection in my knee and got really sick. That ended my chances that year. . . . This time, I hope to stay away from injury and keep things rolling.

By the middle of January, Gil sported a 34–1 mark and was now considered the second-best grappler at 134 lbs. in the nation. As the season reached its final weeks, Sanchez even notched a victory against Jack Cherry of Oklahoma. To add to the fairytale aspect of the season, the Huskers beat the Sooners in a match, 25–16, a true rarity. As Coach Neumann noted, "Nebraska has had a real good wrestling history during the past eight years. But as far as I'm concerned, this ranks as one of our biggest wins ever." Last, going into the Big 8 Tournament, Gil notched another milestone in a dual meet against Wyoming and North Dakota (NDU). In the competition against his home state's university, he defeated Chad Taylor, 17–2 for his ninety-ninth career triumph. Then, and anticlimactically, NDU forfeited his weight classification for him to reach the century mark in wins.[23]

Going into the Big 8 Tournament, as usual, OSU and ISU were favorites to win the team title. However, individual championships and a trip to the Nationals were at stake as well. Nebraska, which had recently defeated Oklahoma in a meet, hoped to come out with a third-place finish in the competition and, ideally, send several athletes to the NCAAs. Of course, the anticipation was that Gil would meet his OSU foe, John Smith, again in the finals of the 134 lb. category. Given that he stood with a mark of 35–1, with the lone defeat to Smith, Sanchez was confident he would win the title. "It will be tough, but I think I can get him again. I've been working all year . . . because last year I didn't wrestle very well in the finals. Now, I'm wrestling good, and I don't have any big injuries, so I'm ready." The predicted final matchup took place, but unfortunately, Gil lost to Smith, 14–3. His record dropped to 42–2, with both defeats at the hands of his Cowboy nemesis. Still, he now qualified for Nationals and could have a final chance to get even.[24]

The inevitable matchup between the two titans of this category proceeded apace, with Gil defeating Buddy Blaha of Virginia, 16–2, then scoring a technical fall against Joe Gribben of Northern Iowa, 16–1. In the third round, Andre Miller of Wilkes put up a bit more resistance but succumbed, 11–4. This was followed by Paul Clark of Clarion, who lost to Gil by a score of 7–4. On the other side of the bracket, Smith pinned Tim Rokha of Drexel, then scored a technical fall against Dan Mantauch of Michigan State, 23–8. Jim Frick of Lehigh also lost to Smith in the same manner, via a technical fall, 22–7. Finally, in the semifinals, the OSU grappler trounced Rob Johnson of Ohio University, 20–9. The match that fans at the University of Maryland had so anticipated would happen, as the two Big 8 foes would fight for a fourth and final time with the national championship at stake.[25]

The individual won-loss records of the two were indeed impressive. Gil came in with a mark of 46–2, and Smith was 42–1. No matter the outcome, Coach Neumann expected an epic tilt. "Gil is the only wrestler in the country who can compete with Smith. Smith destroys everybody else he faces, but with our new strategy for Gil, it's going to be one heck of a match." The strategy did not pan out, and Smith triumphed by the lopsided score of 18–4; thus, Gil endured the same fate his father had back in 1963. Still, his accomplishments were extraordinary. He finished the year with a mark of 46–3 and was the fourth all-time winningest competitor in Husker history, with a record of 107-28-3. More important, he was also an All-American on the mat and part of the All-Academic Big 8 team with a 3.2 GPA in the other family business: education. He would then continue to participate in the US Wrestling Federation Senior Open, where he won four of six matches, finishing second in his category after suffering a knee injury. Last, he began to participate in a series of coaching clinics that prefigured an important part of his future endeavors.[26]

Gil's next steps in life combined his sport and work as an educator, as he became an assistant coach for the Huskers starting in 1987. Among the successes he participated in were when Coach Neumann earned the title of Coach of the Year in the Big 8 after the 1988–1989 campaign. In addition to mentoring, Sanchez continued to compete on the mat. In June 1989, he participated in a US Olympic Festival mini tournament in Oklahoma City and finished second in the 136.5 lb. category. Impressively, he lost in the finals to Randy Lewis, a 1984 Olympic gold medalist, by a score of 10–9. Two years later, he was a member of the No. 2 team in a dual match versus the Soviet Union and faced Miazbeh Antrev at 62 kilograms (136.5 lbs.). Next, he also won the 1991 Canada Cup Championship in Toronto as well as participating in dual meets versus Cuban, Soviet, and Korean teams. Further, he was third at World Team Trials Freestyle that year. Last, he also served as one of the coaches for the All-American All-Star Team that competed in Germany in 1991. All these competitions, plus his work as a Husker assistant, finally led to a head coaching job—at Clemson University starting in July 1992. "I'm very excited about becoming the head coach of the Clemson wrestling program. It has been my dream to be a head coach at a Division I school at this early stage of my career. Everything has fallen into place for me here at Clemson."[27]

The Clemson University wrestling program began in 1975 and had produced one national champion, Noel Logan, in 1980, prior to Sanchez's arrival on campus. Gil replaced Eddie Griffin, who had served as the Tigers' leader since 1984. During Griffin's tenure, the team enjoyed much success, with 1988–1989 and 1989–1990 being particularly good years, as six members of the squad reached Nationals those seasons. Thus, when Gil arrived on campus, the cupboard was well stocked with talent. The personnel present on campus, plus Sanchez's leadership, saw the crowning of a second national champion, Sam Henson, at 118 lbs., and the squad finished thirteenth at the NCAA Tournament in 1992–1993. Additionally, three Tigers claimed Atlantic Coast Conference (ACC) individual championships for the first time in program history. Of particular interest is how Henson credited his head coach for helping him get to the national title. "Henson credits Sanchez for refining the combativeness which defines him. . . . Sanchez insisted on disciplined practices. 'Sam was very good as a freshman, but the maturity level didn't come until later. He hated to drill. He just liked going "live" all the time. He wants to dominate, not just win.'" As a team, the 1993–1994 season was Clemson's best, as they finished seventh as a squad at Nationals, Henson won a second consecutive championship, three grapplers won ACC titles, and the Tigers finished second in the ACC Tournament.[28]

Going into the 1994–1995 season, there was reason for both optimism and concern. First, an article appeared in February 1994 that indicated the possibility of Clemson having to cut some athletic programs. While the men's and women's swim teams were the focus of the piece, athletic administrators also advised Gil to restrict his recruiting costs. This edict came at a time when Sanchez was in the middle of that process (including getting commitments from five high school All-Americans), had just hired Sam Henson as an assistant, and was facing a "retooling" after graduating various seniors. In addition to these concerns, Gil had just signed up to have his Tigers visit his alma mater and compete against Coach Neumann's squad—certainly, with an eye to measuring himself against his mentor's lofty standards. Unfortunately, this match turned out to be a disappointment, as the Huskers triumphed, 38–0. By this point in time, February 1995, Clemson stood at 4–11 in team meets. Just one week later, Gil Sanchez resigned his position as the Tigers' head coach.[29]

The announcement surprised many on campus and off. When asked about his decision, Gil indicated that he had other opportunities he wanted to pursue. "I've enjoyed my time at Clemson University," he asserted, but it was the right time to move on. He would leave the school with a winning record, 31-28-1, but a 4–13 mark his final season. Shortly after the notification, Clemson reported that an ineligible athlete might have competed in place of an injured teammate. The violation appeared to have taken place at the Virginia Duals in mid-January when Dan McCollum participated in a match as Paul Seim. Seim was nursing a knee injury and did not even make travel for this event. Even with the mounting evidence, Gil stood his ground, noting, "I don't have all the facts yet and I want to make sure I'm talking to the right people. But of course, that would concern anybody."[30]

The in-house investigation was not the only unwelcome news for the Clemson program, as roughly one month later, the school made the decision to eliminate wrestling from its athletic offerings. The need to hire a new coach, as well as the necessity of upgrading facilities led to this outcome. In total, the move saved $350,000 for Tiger athletics (out of a $20 million budget). With twenty-eight athletes on the squad, the school guaranteed funding for each competitor for one more year but would review such efforts on a case-by-case basis from then on. Meanwhile, the internal report on the alleged violation neared completion by late March 1995. In total, administrators found three regulatory breaches. By this point, Gil had confirmed that indeed he did use an ineligible competitor and owned up to his mistake. "I think being a young coach, I am going to make mistakes and I made a big one here . . . but I admit my mistake." While it was certainly a serious blunder, the review documented no other violations. Thus, it can be fairly argued that the pressure of a losing season, as well as the possibility of an end to the program, created the circumstances for this poor decision. Even with this blot on his otherwise excellent record, he quickly found employment at the University of Missouri as an assistant.[31]

Gil continued to use his connections to present the best of the sport to young people in his new domicile. To wit, he worked with his former protégé Sam Henson to hold clinics in the Columbia area in both 1995 and 1996. While at Mizzou, he also followed another family tradition and completed a graduate degree in educational administration. Still, he had found a place to call home in South Carolina, and an opportunity arose to return to the Palmetto State in 1999, when a former Tiger grappler, Carey Schoener, recommended him to his boss at Battery Creek High School, Principal Greg Oliver, for the head coaching position at the institution. The hire, even with the Clemson baggage, was considered "the biggest news ever to hit South Carolina prep wrestling." In addition to his coaching skills, Oliver was impressed by Sanchez's honesty and willingness to accept responsibility. "When I was 24 years old, I certainly wouldn't want every mistake I made to be publicized. He's been man enough to admit what he did. We're not trying to hide anything, and Gil's not trying to hide anything."[32]

Initially, things did not go well for the Dolphins, as they started the season 0–5, but finished with a 9–13 record. Going into the 1999–2000 season, Sanchez expressed optimism that the team was moving in the right direction. Indeed, he argued that this squad had the potential to field up to three future state champions. By the middle of the first decade of the 2000s, Gil had moved into administration, serving as an assistant principal at Hilton Head Island Middle School. Nevertheless, he continued to recruit youths to value this sport. Late in 2004, he pulled off a major coup by bringing in Rulon Gardner, who won a gold medal in the 2000 Sydney Olympics to the area, so the "kids will have a chance to hold a gold medal and . . . [have] a once in a lifetime thing." In addition to his regular duties, Sanchez continued to coach, and soon worked as an assistant at Hilton Head Island High School.[33]

One of his major reclamation projects at this institution was in collaborating with a young man named Calvin Murray, a wrestler who started his career with an 0–19 mark but with Gil's help finished fourth in the state at 112 lbs. in his junior year. By 2014, Gil now served as an assistant principal at the institution that made it possible for him to return to South Carolina: Battery Creek High. Finally, he moved on to serve as a coordinator for the Beaufort County School District in 2022. In sum, many of the lessons learned on the mat made it possible for Gil to earn the post he currently holds. He did not let John Smith or a youthful mistake keep him from moving forward, just as his father had taught him in the CCHS gym and in the Sanchez home back in Wyoming.[34] At this point of his career, ensconced as a respected professional in a state with a relatively small Latino population, Gil was a shining example of a counterscript of the athletic, coaching, and intellectual limitations that some might still attach to the Spanish-surnamed.

Jim Sanchez followed in his older brother's footsteps and joined the Huskers' program starting in 1986. He had a great deal of success while at CCHS. In 1982 has was part of an All-Wyoming Cultural Exchange team selected to tour Holland over a three-week period in the summer. He won all eight of his matches during this tour. When he returned home, he won the Grand Nationals in Greco-Roman wrestling held in Lincoln, Nebraska, at the 88 lb. classification. The title earned him a spot to represent the United States at the Schoolboy World Cadet Festival, held in Fullerton, California, in August. This tournament was described as a "steppingstone to future international and Olympic competition." In order to attend, the Cheyenne Wrestling Club asked citizens to contribute to a fund (with a goal of $700) to cover expenses. Jim did his family's wrestling tradition proud, as he managed to claim this title at the 98 lb. classification. After his return to Wyoming, Jim indicated that the trip was a wonderful opportunity, and not just because he brought home a gold medal. "It was a great experience getting to see and meet young wrestlers from around the world. . . . I also want to thank all of the businesses, relatives, friends, and people who have contributed to the Cheyenne Wrestling Club. Without them, I wouldn't have been able to compete."[35]

By the start of his junior year at CCHS, he was considered one of the favorites to win a state title and was ranked as the number one competitor in his category in a statewide coaches' poll. Like others in his clan, he did not disappoint and defeated Joe Facinelli of Lander in the finals to claim his first state crown. After this title, he then had another memorable summer and was part of a second Wyoming Cultural Exchange Team that traveled to Taiwan; on this tour, he won all four of his matches. Following this achievement, he went on to compete in the largest and most prestigious competition—the Junior National Wrestling Championships, which took place in Cedar Rapids, Iowa. The five-day competition fielded athletes from all fifty states. Here, Jim won the Greco-Roman tournament with seven consecutive victories and then placed third, with a 7–2 mark, in Freestyle.[36]

During his senior year, Jim continued to accumulate accomplishments. In early January 1984, he was the lone bright spot for a state team that competed against a Japanese squad in Laramie. Of the eight matches, Jim claimed the only victory for the locals as he tied with Mayutama Hitoshi 13–13 but won based on criteria.[37] He then continued to claim another state title in February (but at 105 lbs.). He also was selected as a Gatorade All American, a team that consisted of sixty wrestlers from thirty states. Last, he also was part of an All-Star team that competed against the best wrestlers from Pennsylvania in the *Pittsburgh Press*–Dapper Dan Classic. In that city's paper, he received a writeup that noted he had finished his high school career with a mark of 79–8 and "no opponent got closer than six points" in his senior campaign. The Keystone State competition was tough, however, and Jim wound up losing his one match to Jim Martin of Danville via a pin. By the way, Martin's high school record was 158–2, and he would go on to win a national title while competing for Penn State University.[38]

Following his final year as a high schooler, Jim continued to participate in international competitions. In 1984 and 1985, he represented the US in the Espior (20 Under) World Championships. In 1984 the US team wrestled in the Stockholm Open, where Sanchez won four matches and defeated a Bulgarian competitor named Georgien Nedialho in the finals at 105.5 lbs. In 1985, he again wrestled in the Espior World Championships in Colorado Springs, a meet in which forty countries participated. In the trials to represent the US, he triumphed against Junior National champions Dan Knight of Iowa and Kurt Howell of Delaware. Both of these foes were four-time state title winners as well as Junior National Champions. In the first round of the World Championships, Jim lost to a Russian, and in the

FIGURE 5.3. Jim (front row, second from right) as part of the 1984 World Greco Roman Team.

second round, he succumbed by one point to a Chinese foe. In email correspondence with me, he noted,

> Representing the United States in the world championships was the highlight of my career. Following this, I competed in the US Nationals in the Open Division and placed fourth which qualified me for the World Team Trials. There, I placed second behind three-time Olympian Mark Fuller. The top four wrestlers . . . then wrestled in the Olympic Sports Festival. I lost to two competitors I had previously beaten and placed fourth. In 1986, I suffered a separated rib at the Espoir and didn't compete. That was my last year in the 20 and under division.[39]

After graduation from CCHS, Jim moved to Lincoln with his brother Gil to hone his mat skills and prepare for the 1985 Junior World Championships (just mentioned). He then walked on at Nebraska in fall 1986 and started getting noticed. His first action came against Athletes in Action, in which he won by a technical fall over a 1986 All-American named Jay Olinger. Later that season, as the Huskers suffered a series of injuries,

Sanchez moved up to the 118 lb. category and helped NU defeat Drake University, 23–15. By this stage of the season, the team's mark stood at 12–6 and they were ranked fourteenth in the nation.

In 1987, the Huskers' coaches asked Jim to focus on Freestyle wrestling instead of Greco-Roman, as they thought it would help him at this level. The lowest weight for this style in college was 118 lbs. As had happened previously, Jim was small for the classification. After the end of the NU season, he entered the 114.5 lb. weight, which Freestyle offered, and wrestled at the US Open, at that time sponsored by Sunkist Kids. Gil had been assisted by this group, and Jim's father approached representatives at the meet and asked if they would underwrite this son as well. The corporate types indicated that if Jim placed at the US Open, they would indeed provide such assistance. Jim placed fifth in that competition, defeating Oklahoma State All-American Eddie Woodburn. Since the champion in his classification was a man named Sato from Japan, Sanchez ranked fourth and qualified for the Olympic Festival in Freestyle, which would determine the US representative for the World Championships. In his bracket, he faced two-time NCAA All-American Jack Cuvo from East Stroudsburg University, losing the first match 18–15, winning the second match 11–9, then succumbing in the tiebreaker after suffering a shoulder injury during his victory. Cuvo would go on to place second in the trials. In 1988 and '89 Jim won the Division I (D-I) NCAAs at 118 lbs. for his school. In summary, while his record was not as impressive as that of his brother, Jim lettered three times at Nebraska and graduated with a degree in education.[40]

Jim made his mark as a teacher and coach over a long and distinguished career. First, he served as an assistant, from 1990 to 1997, then as a head coach between 1998 and 2011. He worked at Eldorado High School in Las Vegas between 1998 and 2000, then moved on to Valley High School in the same municipality between 2001 and 2004. The majority of his coaching career came at Loveland (Colorado) High School, between 2005 and 2011. As he finished his time as a coach, Jim also completed yet another Sanchez family tradition, earning his master's degree from Northern Colorado in 2011. He has also served as dean of students at this institution since 2005 and continues to work there currently. Here, his mentoring has helped produce 11 state champions, 17 state finalists, and 32 state placers.

The success of his charges continued on to the collegiate level, with multiple competitors earning national recognition. The most impressive individuals he coached for the Indians, now renamed Red Wolves (and in his private coaching practice, Gold Mine Wrestling), include Andrew Alirez (whom he tutored for four years at Gold Mine), who was a four-time state champion and won a national title at the University of Northen Colorado; Tyler Graff was another four-time state winner and four-time All-American at the University of Wisconsin (he also made the World Team and represented the US at the World Championships, placing fifth); Connor Medbery was a three-time Colorado champion and an All-American at Wisconsin as well; finally, Josh Kreimier was a three-time state finalist and three-time NCAA qualifier for the Air Force Academy.[41]

The third member of this group of Cornhuskers was youngest brother, Frank, who was born in Gunnison, Colorado, in 1968 while Gil worked on his first master's degree. The family did not return to Wyoming until 1974, after his father's second advanced degree from the University of New Mexico. It was at about this time that Frank recalled traveling with Gil to an exhibition somewhere in Montana and realizing the significance of what his dad could accomplish on the mat. "I remember being in awe of how my father moved and how powerful he was. This was one of the earliest memories connecting me to wrestling." It was not long afterward that Frank began his own efforts in the sport, starting at age six, competing at the 45 lb. level and winning at the Grand National Tournament in 1974 or 1975. Frank then continued honing his skills at the Cheyenne Wrestling Club. In his earlier years, the primary training locale for this group was the CCHS gym, as Gil (then working as a counselor and coach) would open the facility for practices.[42]

By the time that he entered high school, Frank contributed further to the family's wrestling lore. In 1985, as a junior at CCHS, Frank was already rated as a "highly regarded 98 pounder" and a potential challenger for statewide honors. By the time the Wyoming tournament rolled around, he was, not surprisingly, competing for the state crown against George Sánchez (no relation) from Rawlins. In this match, George defeated Frank, 9–7. When I interviewed Dr. Frank Sanchez, at that time president of Rhode Island College (RIC), the sting of defeat still stuck with him all these many years later. "I really should have won that title; I still replay that in my mind." While he may not have won that title, shortly thereafter Frank had an opportunity to participate in what had become another Sanchez tradition, that is, representing his country and state in international competition. In June of that year, he was part of a cultural exchange squad that would participate in various tournaments in West Germany starting at the end of the month. It is important to understand what these opportunities meant to individuals such as Gil and Frank Sanchez. Here were young Mexican American athletes, from a family of modest means, who now had an occasion to travel to various parts of the world, experience other cultures, and gain inspiration not only to continue competing in this sport but also get a sense of broader possibilities. As one of the directors of the program (through the Wyoming Amateur Wrestling Association) that both brought foreign teams to the state and also sent locals overseas, Don Candelaria noted, "The best (virtue) is the cultural aspect. Before we leave, we study the countries we're going to. We stay with families, and we're able to learn a great deal more about the countries that way. . . . It gives us a great opportunity to have fun and experience other people." For his senior year, Frank moved up to 112 lbs. and appeared headed for another chance at the state title, but unfortunately he broke his arm two weeks before the state tournament, thus ending his high school career.[43]

Frank earned a partial wrestling scholarship to become a Cornhusker, and he competed as a redshirt freshman. His arrival in Lincoln, however, had an interesting impact on his career trajectory. In our interview, he noted that he was not particularly cognizant of his "cultural affinity" while living in Cheyenne. This could have been, in part, because his father and uncles had been successful on the mat for CCHS, had earned degrees, and had, to an extent, moved into a more middle-class standing. Thus, his experiences were different from those of many of the Mexican Americans in Wyoming who labored still in lower-paying, less-skilled occupations. Upon arriving in Nebraska, however, Frank began to interact with some of the other individuals of this ethnic background (he estimated that there were around 200 or so on campus), many of whom hailed from communities of long standing such as Omaha, North Platte, and Scottsbluff, and whose experiences were different from those of this Sanchez family. In this milieu, Frank began to think about becoming more active in campus causes instead of continuing to pursue wrestling. Given the efforts of prior generations of his clan, he had such a choice available. He also indicated that his coaches had recruited another competitor at his weight classification, Iowan Jason Kelber (who would go on to become a three-time All-American at NU). These two points led to his decision to give up the sport.[44]

A final point found in Nuñez's work is worth mentioning here in regard to Frank's academic and professional trajectory. In addition to the ability to perform "fitness for citizenship" as noted earlier, participating in sports, Núñez claims, also helped Mexican Americans "forge a diasporic *mexicano* identity." Indeed, Frank became much more aware of his people's circumstances once he left the more middle-class life his family had managed to create and began interacting with Mexican Americans from the various Nebraska-based communities. As will be described, it was participating in sports that helped push Frank Sanchez in the direction of social and educational activism that would lead him to the presidency of two academic institutions.

Upon taking this weighty decision, Frank soon joined up with fellow Mexican Americans in a group called MASA (Mexican American Student Association), and it was here that he came to realize a talent for organization and a fervent desire to work with underrepresented populations on college campuses. He eventually became the group's president. Among the many activities he participated in during his time at NU, one major highlight was when MASA invited the legendary labor leader and activist Cesar Chavez to campus in 1990. Indeed, Chavez actually stayed in Frank's modest domicile while in Lincoln. Frank and his colleagues also worked to bring attention to circumstances for Mexican Americans at the institution. Among the five points MASA presented was a request for increased attention to multicultural affairs and the needs of first-generation students.

Frank graduated with a bachelor's degree in psychology with minors in Chicano studies and speech communications. He then proceeded to attend his father's alma mater, Colorado State, in order to complete a master's degree in higher education. His thesis focused on the creation of a program designed to improve the college retention of first-generation, low-income, and Hispanic students; this effort then allowed him to move on to a minority fellowship at Indiana University working under the direction of a noted scholar in the field of student engagement and institutional responsiveness, George D. Kuh. He completed his doctoral studies in 1997 and then began work on his dissertation. It was during this time that he commenced his professional work at various universities. His first job was at DePauw University in multicultural affairs. Next, he returned to Wyoming and worked as assistant director for housing in the division of Academic Affairs and Housing. He was there for two years. Next, he moved on to a heavily Latino institution, Adams State University in Alamosa, Colorado, where he was vice-president for student affairs for six years. The following step up the institutional ladder was in a similar capacity but at a much larger institution, the University of Colorado Denver for five years. After that, he moved to the City University of New York as vice-chancellor for CUNY, where he remained for another five years. Finally reaching the pinnacle, he took on the presidency of RIC starting in 2016.[45]

It was during his tenure at RIC that Frank sat down for an interview with the editor of the professional publication *Dean and Provost*. The title of this article was "Learn What It Takes to Become a College President." Here, Frank laid out his advice to those interested in higher education administration concerning how to achieve such a significant position. The traits he suggested included being flexible (ready to adjust), having decisiveness, and being prepared for challenges. When asked about how wrestling might have helped him to develop such traits, he argued that "sport and academic success are tied to the work ethic. Competition, knowing you can overcome challenges [remember his defeat at the hands of George Sánchez?] plays out in the niches [academic and professional] you pursue. . . . all of the years of wrestling helped open doors to what followed." One thing for certain is that in the early twentieth century Elijio and María Sanchez and Manuel and Valina Guadian could never have fathomed the possibility that one of their grandchildren would, in the matter of one generation–plus, have risen from working at honest, but low-skilled, low-paying labor in Wyoming, to become president of an institution of higher learning. After a successful stint at RIC, as of June 2023, Frank returned to New York state to become president of Manhattanville University in Harrison.[46] Certainly Frank's experiences are the

FIGURE 5.4. Frank Sanchez, President of Manhattanville University, Harrison, New York.

most compelling example of a counterscript produced by the athletic experiences of the Sanchez family, though there are many more examples of this trend by others in the clan.

As with their cousins, Art's three sons continued to participate in wrestling, and utilized their ties to the sport to, again, earn college degrees and begin professional careers. The first sibling to take to the mat was his oldest son, Glenn (born in 1971), who competed at THS in the years between 1986 and 1989. He then walked on at his father's alma mater, as part of the squad for the UW Cowboys over the 1989–1990 season. Like his cousin Frank, however, he eventually decided not to continue wrestling and focused on his academic pursuits. Unlike the other Sanchezes detailed so far, Glenn decided to pursue a career in engineering, graduating with a bachelor's of science in architectural engineering from Wyoming in 1995. While completing this degree, he was already working in the field, serving as an assistant construction engineer for a firm in his hometown of Thornton. Later, he decided to pursue further education, completing a master's in architecture at the University of Pennsylvania (completed in 1997) and a second master's in civil engineering at nearby Villanova (finished in 2002).

Since 2008, Glenn has owned and operated his own firm, Glenn Sanchez Property Development LLC, with offices in both Philadelphia and Denver. In an email to me, this Sanchez wrestler was very modest concerning his accomplishments on the mat. "I wrestled from approximately age 6 to college, however, my wrestling career was the least impressive of the family with no major awards." Still, in an interview he did note that the sport, and the family's tradition therein, certainly had a "psychological/mental . . . values/drive [influence] that continue to be an enormous impact on my life, work ethic and way of thinking." Specifically, in a discussion with me, Glenn noted that the legacy has impacted the way that he deals with his own daily work as an architect/engineer. "I do a lot of 'hands on' construction. . . . I'm responsible for this. I guess that a lot of that comes from the fact that wrestling is a one-on-one sport, and that mentality was instilled in me by my father and other members of the family."[47]

Greg, Art's second offspring, began his career at Thornton High School, where he competed between 1987 and 1990. In his sophomore year wearing a Trojan singlet, he was a varsity regional qualifier and followed that with a trip to the state tournament the following year, though he did not place. His best performance came as a senior, where he started the state tournament defeating Aaron Lenz of Loveland. He next faced Jeremy Geidel of Thompson Valley, besting his foe by a score of 14–6. Ultimately, he came in third place in the 160 lb. category, garnered All State Honors, and earned a spot on the All-Front Range League Conference team. One noteworthy accomplishment in this season came when he defeated David Fife, a 1989 state champion in the third-place match. The final mention of Greg as a high schooler occurred in June 1990 at the Colorado High School All-State Games, when he lost to Clint Pipher of Hotchkiss, a two-time state champion, by a score of 10–5 at the 168 lb. classification.

From there, he moved on to wrestle for the University of Northern Colorado, competing for the Bears between 1990 and 1992. In a conversation with me, Greg indicated that his time on the mats of UNC were "not very noteworthy." He redshirted his first year and only wrestled and lost one varsity duel as a sophomore. Further, Greg noted in his correspondence, "My own wrestling accomplishments are not as storied as many others in the Sanchez family, but our family's wrestling culture has played a big part in my personal life development." He graduated in 1995 with a degree in secondary education, specializing in social studies. He did his student teaching at his high school alma mater, spending fall 1995 at Thornton High School, where he also was a volunteer assistant wrestling coach. He has been in the Social Studies Department at Horizon High School in Thornton since 1996, additionally serving as assistant head coach for the Hawks between that season and 2002. Then, he took over as head coach, serving in that capacity until 2009. Not surprisingly, Art was at his son's side throughout these campaigns, filling the role of co–head coach. In Greg's years as a head coach, he and Art had the challenge of starting the Horizon wrestling program from scratch. While they had some state qualifiers, there have not been any state placers (in other words, competitors who have finished in fourth place or higher at the state level). In recent years, Greg returned to an assistant coaching position until 2021 and can always be found at Horizon matches working the scoreboard and operating the clock at home events.[48]

The youngest of Art's three boys is Phillip, who was born in 1977 and competed at Thornton High School between the years 1993 and 1995. Interestingly, in his correspondence with me, he not only discussed the positives of sport, and the opportunities provided, but also shared the frustrations caused by injuries truncating what he believed could have been an excellent career. "In my opinion, my wrestling career fell flat on what I had set my goals to be. . . . I had some of the best role models growing up with my family, I had some of the best coaches and access to a wealth of the knowledge of the sport, but unfortunately, the glory was not for me." Still, as his cousin Frank noted in the article referenced earlier, the family traditions developed via athletic endeavors (a fierce work ethic, competitiveness, and a drive to overcome challenges) helped Phil surmount his vexations and eventually led him to a successful time on the mat and multiple years as a coach in the highly spirited area of California wrestling (in addition to his teaching duties).[49]

Phil's varsity career at Thornton included a fourth-place finish in his weight class all three years. While he did not think that this was sufficient, he did note in his correspondence that the top three finishers in his district each year all went on to place first, second, and third at the state level. Losing out to the top three grapplers in the state at your weight classification is certainly deserving of praise. Further, Phil also indicated that he competed in his last two years at THS with an ACL injury. He then moved on to the University of Northern Colorado in 1995, redshirting because of surgery on his knee. In 1996 and 1998, he was a member of the Bears' squad. An interesting tidbit from his time at UNC was that there was yet another intersection between the Sanchez and Maughan families, as Jack Maughan, whom Gil wrestled, was one of Phil's coaches with the Bears. There was yet another connection between this clan and another family mentioned previously. Jim's protégé—Andrew Alirez's father, Andrew Alirez Sr—fought against Phil in the finals of the Colorado Junior National team, and beat Phil in that match. The senior Alirez went on to place fifth in Nationals that year.[50]

Instead of participating for the UNC team in 1998–1999, Phil wrestled at the Olympic Training Center in Colorado Springs and took part in international competitions against foreign teams from Slovakia and Bulgaria. He also worked out with members of the USA wrestling team. Subsequently, he returned to UNC for his senior year (1999–2000), but once again the injury bug hit his ankle at a team scrimmage and left him unable to complete a season in which he felt he could potentially make it to Nationals. He did, however, continue to participate in athletic competitions, though now in judo. Although finding an outlet during this time for his competitive nature in judo, the injuries and perceived lack of success did have an impact on Phil's relationship with wrestling. "It took me eight years, removing myself from the sport to even try to coach."

He did participate in this aspect of the "family business" while working as a PE instructor at Palm Springs High School between 2008 and 2015. He then moved on to Cathedral City High School and served in that capacity between 2015 and 2017. One of his main goals as an educator is to develop in his students a lifelong commitment to physical activity. To this end, he has worked with local charities to bring in an afterschool climbing/bouldering club using a wall at the institution. Another element of Phil's work as an educator has been to introduce his students to sports not traditionally associated with your "typical" high school or middle school gym class. For example, collaborating with a colleague named Bridgette Kennedy, he instituted an archery program at James Workman Middle in 2016. Here, students learn the fundamentals of the sport, are taught appropriate safety techniques, and are given the opportunity to enjoy an area of athletic competition that is not dependent on a particular body size (such as wrestling) and are introduced to an endeavor that they can continue throughout their lives. As Phil's associate noted, "Archery has increased our students' focus and patience; improved character traits, concentration, and skills; and had a positive effect in their schoolwork and daily life." This sounds a lot like the impact that wrestling has had on so many of the competitors in the Sanchez clan. In sum, Phil is passing on many of the traits that he learned from his family and from his experiences in sport to the next generation.[51]

The first of Ray's sons to take to the mat was his namesake, born in 1969, who competed for Greeley West High School in Colorado between 1985 and 1987. During his time on the mat for the Spartans, he was a district and conference champion and also won a state title in Freestyle at 112 lbs. In his senior year, he went into the state tournament with a mark of 22–4 and missed making it to the final four competitors at this weight, losing in overtime to Bryan Borquez of Brighton, 4–2.[52] He then followed his dad's footsteps and competed for the Wyoming Cowboys between 1987 and 1988. He redshirted his freshman year and was on the varsity as a sophomore. Raymond recalled that he finished with "around a .500 record." Going into 1989–1990, this member of the Sanchez clan took a different route and gave up wrestling to pursue his talents on the stage, primarily as a member of the Centennial Singers, a group that performed to help celebrate Wyoming's 100th anniversary of statehood. All the while, Ray continued to pursue his studies in biology with hopes of eventually attending medical school. Ultimately, he decided that this was not his preferred field of study and instead decided to focus on chemical engineering. Given this, the senior Ray recommended that his son transfer to the Colorado School of Mines.

Upon his arrival in Golden, Ray felt that he had not yet put wrestling behind him, and then took to the mat for the Mules between 1991 and 1992. Once again, he had around a .500 record. In 1993, Ray earned his desired degree and has worked in that field for various companies, including King, Buck Technologies, Haliburton, Stim-Tech, and American Woodmark. He also owned his own company, Sanchez Engineering Consulting, between 2011 and 2017. This firm started as a result of his work at Stim-Tech, for which he did consulting. Eventually, this endeavor grew to provide similar services to other companies in the oil and gas industry. He is now a senior process engineer at WL Gore and Associates in Flagstaff, Arizona, where he leads a team that is charged with applying the coating to medical devices. When asked to comment on the significance of wrestling to his family and his life, he sounded a note similar to that of his siblings and cousins: "Wrestling really has molded me into the person that I am. I often felt that I was behind the eight-ball in regard to academics and athletic talent. What I learned from the sport is to keep working, fighting, and going. That background of pushing yourself has been invaluable. Indeed, I have been able to pass along this family belief/tradition on to my own children." In his spare time, Raymond also continues another family custom, by serving as a volunteer coach for his son's former high school: the Lee Williams Volunteers in Flagstaff.[53]

Ray's second son, Britt, born in 1974, competed for Rawlins High, then at Greeley West High School and finally at George Washington High in Denver between the years 1989 and 1993. His best season on the mat was as a sophomore, when he finished the year with a mark of 12–3. As happened with other members of his family, a substantial injury (in his case, a concussion) stymied his progress as a grappler. Additionally, Britt's real athletic passion was for the gridiron, and he was more successful at this endeavor, although he did wrestle again as a senior. He even had a chance to walk on to the University of Northern Colorado football team. As he indicated in an interview, "It was too hard to be a student, an athlete and a father,"[54] so he decided to train as a computer technician. All the while, he continued to play football for various semipro teams in Arizona. Indeed, he played at this level between the ages of twenty-four and forty-five. His skills eventually generated notice by the Iowa Barnstormers of the Arena Football League, and the organization offered him a contract at the age of twenty-eight (for a whopping $28,000) in 2002. Not surprisingly, he turned down the offer.

At the age of thirty, Britt joined the US Air Force and still serves as of 2023. He first worked as a firefighter and then switched to an even more dangerous undertaking working in efforts involving chemical, biological, radiological, and nuclear combat rescue (CBRN). These are the individuals who, wearing hazmat suits, respond to such incidents all over the world. In addition to his work in the military, Britt also works as a wide receiver and running backs coach (since 2019) at Desert Ridge High School in Mesa, Arizona. When asked to summarize what his family's sporting history has meant to him, Britt noted that this background helped prepare him mentally and physically for the dangerous work he has done over the past decade. "Sport has created many opportunities for my family. It has also instilled in us the value of athletic competition that has made it possible for us to learn from defeat and not give up under difficult circumstances. We have been able to learn much from both victories and defeats."[55]

Among Ray's offspring, the most successful on the mat is his youngest son Scott, born in 1975, who added to the Sanchez trophy case and won two Wyoming state titles while competing for Rawlins High School in 1992 and 1993. For his first crown, he went into the state tournament ranked first at 125 lbs. In the first round of the meet, he defeated Greg Meyer of Wheatland, 12–1. Next, in the quarterfinals, he decisioned Javier Muro of Worland by a 7–1 mark. Finally, in the title faceoff, he triumphed over Scott Burgener of Lyman, 8–5. Not surprisingly, Scott also earned the designation of All-Conference as well. The following year, as a senior, now wrestling at 130 lbs., he continued to dominate the competition. At that state tournament, he defeated Troy Pitman of Powell, 9–4; significantly, Pitman had been the state champion at this classification the previous year. Scott then demolished Chad Johnson of Worland, 16–0 in the quarterfinals. Last, he bested Lee Aullman of Star Valley, 7–0 in the title match.[56] After graduation, Scott attended the University of Wyoming, and earned a bachelor's degree in math education, with his first job being at Boulder High School in 2000–2001. He then went on to work as an assistant coach for Colorado icon Gary Daum at Niwot High School, starting in 2001. Under the tutelage of this legend, Scott added even more knowledge than what he had gained from his father and uncles. "He [Daum] was probably the only person I would call a mentor. He was just an awesome guy. . . . I already knew a lot about wrestling, but he taught me how to run a practice, talk to parents, and work a budget."[57]

After Coach Daum's retirement in 2005, Scott took over the mentorship of the squad and guided the Wizards through 2014. In keeping with yet another element of the Sanchez family tradition, Scott earned two master's degrees while at Niwot. His first was in instruction and curriculum (from the University of Colorado) in 2007, followed by another in administration in 2010 from Grand Canyon University. Subsequently, he returned to his home state, taking a post as a math teacher at Johnson Junior High in Cheyenne, followed by stints as a behaviorist at two local elementary schools. Next, he moved on to his father's alma mater at Cheyenne Central High School between the years of 2016 and 2019. Here, he felt that his assignment teaching lower-level math courses (whereas he had taught calculus at Niwot) was not a proper utilization of his knowledge and skills, and given that he had earned a third master's (this time in analytics from CSU in 2017), Scott felt that a move to the private sector was in order. Thus, he took a job as a data analyst with Blue Cross Blue Shield of Wyoming between 2020 and 2022. Still, the sport was not far from his mind. Not surprisingly, as happens with many educators, he could not stay out of the classroom and returned for one more year as a teacher, this time at Carey Junior High School. Here, he also served as an assistant coach for the wrestling team and got to collaborate with his own son, Sammy, then an eighth grader. Finally, another opportunity opened with his former company, and now Scott is back in the insurance field as a supervisor.[58]

As is apparent from the discussions above, the second generation of Sanchezes who competed in wrestling (and other athletic endeavors) did much to contribute to the plethora of this family's sporting achievements. While not all were as successful as the first generation on the mat, the fact that all of the members of this cohort achieved academic and professional accomplishments clearly demonstrates the importance that sport and the educational opportunities it provided have had on this Mexican American clan. By the third decade of the twenty-first century, the Sanchezes had moved into the ranks of the middle class and above and produced multiple examples of the impact of participation in sport as a key element of Latino community life. The final chapter in this work will take a brief look at the third group in this line to participate in wrestling and also provide a cursory look at other Spanish-surnamed individuals and families who have achieved success in wrestling in the state of Wyoming.

CONCLUSION

The Most Recent Generation of Sanchezes on the Mat and the Significance of Sport in Latino/Hispanic History and Life

The third generation of Sanchezes to take to the mat is much smaller than the previous cohorts. In part, this can be tied to the fact that, given the higher social and economic status of the various members of the family, offspring now have greater choices in regard to competitive and educational opportunities. Given this trend, there are just two members of this group who have participated in the sport to a degree resembling that of their fathers, uncles, great-uncles, and grandparents: Sammy Sanchez, Scott's son, and Zachary Sanchez, Raymond's son.

In my interview with Scott, he mentioned that Sammy began his wrestling career during the first grade and trained, as had so many others in his family, at the Cheyenne Wrestling Club, through the fifth grade. He then moved over to Carey Junior High School. Here, Scott was able to work with his offspring during the years he taught at Cheyenne Central. Sammy then enrolled at Cheyenne East High School, where he took to the mat on behalf of the Thunderbirds. In his freshman year, this youngest grappler in the Sanchez line did well. Indeed, during his last year at

https://doi.org/10.5876/9781646427529.c006

Carey, he defeated many of the opponents who were competing against him as high school sophomores in 2023. It is clear that Sammy not only learned the physical "tricks of the trade" but also imbibed the family lore and philosophy. "It's always been wrestling for me. I never really tried other sports. I love going out to wrestle in big matches, I always have. I had a lot of confidence coming into the season, and I have only gotten more confident."[1]

A perusal of newspaper articles shows that he made significant progress during his first year of high school competition. Early on in the season, Sammy lost via pin to Dylan Sorenson of Kelly Walsh at 106 lbs. but then turned right around and pinned another athlete from that same school, Jackson Focke, in a mere 24 seconds just a few days later. Toward the end of this campaign, his mark stood at an impressive 31–13, and in mid-February Sammy triumphed over Cache Wood of Sheridan, 7–3, to claim the Class 4A-Regional championship. Going into state, he ranked as the fourth-best competitor in his weight classification. The assessment of this young grappler by his coach, Thad Trujillo, mirrored that which had been stated about previous athletes from this clan: "He's made a lot of growth in the past 12 months and is really bought in. He's found a new gear and had gotten a lot of confidence. It's nice to have a freshman who's not afraid to take chances and loves to compete." Unfortunately, in the state semifinals, Sammy lost to Tristen Tromble of Natrona County, 14–5. While he wound up two matches short of adding another title to the family mantle case, it seems to be only a matter of time, and more hard work, before the Sanchezes make room for yet another trophy.[2]

Raymond's son Zachary also did well in his time on the mat. He started by competing in USA Wrestling's kids' division, where he collected multiple titles in the mid-2000s. He then moved on to the high school ranks in Wyoming and placed sixth in the state as a freshman, and fifth as a sophomore. When the family moved to Arizona, he began competing for the Lee Williams High School Volunteers in Flagstaff. He stepped away from the sport during his junior year but then returned to grappling and finished his high school career with a 30–3 mark as a senior, placing fifth in the state in 2015. Zachary decided to not pursue the sport at the collegiate level but followed in his father's footsteps by earning a degree in engineering from Arizona State University in 2019.[3]

While the Sanchezes of Cheyenne have a storied history in the annals of Wyoming wrestling, they are certainly not the only Spanish-surnamed family to have left an indelible mark upon the sport in the Equality State and thereby to have provided multiple examples of counterscripts. In 2010 the *Casper Star-Tribune* presented its readers with a list of truly elite grapplers, listing all of the four-time and three-time state champions. Ray Sanchez is the only Hispanic who is a member of the four-timers, but there are quite a few such names among the three-time titlists. Among these are David Zúñiga of Worland (1984–1986); Jesse Abeyta of Rawlins (1989–1991); Oscar Frías of Lovell (1994–1996); Justin Gonzales of Mountain View (1994–1996); John Cisneros of Lusk (1999–2001); Rafael Chávez of Rock Springs (2002–2004); and Julius Ríos of Torrington (2003–2005).[4]

Another important element in the story of Latino participation in Wyoming wrestling is the number of families that have utilized this competition as a mechanism to gain a degree of acceptance in schools throughout the state going back as far as the early 1950s. A researcher of the sport, Spencer Condie, shared an interesting list of the most renowned clans in this endeavor with this author. In total, he counted thirty-seven Spanish-surnamed families that had produced at least five place winners and one state title. The Sanchezes have generated the most individual crowns, with 11 titles and 19 placers over their storied, multigenerational history. Other prominent lines include the Ramos of Lingle (5 titles and 8 placers); the Cisneros of Lusk and Laramie (5 titles and 9 placers); the Trujillos of Worland (5 titles and 12 placers); and finally, the Hernándezes, also of Worland (4 titles and 19 placers). In an email to me, Condie argued, in addition to Cheyenne, that Torrington, Worland, Green River, and Rock Springs are the most important towns for studying the history of Latino participation in wrestling in the state.[5]

In addition to Condie's research, another locale to look for Latino competitors who have made their mark is in the individual champions list for the state. Here, the first Spanish-surnamed champion listed (the first tournament took place in 1949) was Gus Rodriguez of the Rock Springs Tigers, who triumphed at 103 lbs. in 1952 and then repeated the feat at the same classification the following year. In 1954 another Tiger, Nolan Martínez, claimed the crown at the same weight. In 1955, Bob Fernández of Worland was the champion at 112 lbs., and in the following season,

Jake Córdova of Rock Springs followed in the footsteps of Rodriquez and Martínez at 103 lbs. Thus, by the time the Sanchezes of Cheyenne began their run, with Gil Sr.'s crown in 1956 at 112 lbs., many of Wyoming's wrestling aficionados were accustomed to seeing Hispanic competitors achieve statewide success. Indeed, that same year, Jake Cordova of Rock Springs also won at 103 lbs. Thus, individuals of this minority group were bringing notoriety and positive attention not only to themselves, and their group, but also to the individual towns they represented. Many others have followed in the footsteps of these pathbreakers over the subsequent decades, not only in Wyoming but in other parts of the country (and at the high school and collegiate levels).[6]

There is one mention of wrestling in the La Cultura oral histories that merits brief mention here: Joe Ramirez Jr., who was born in Hawk Springs in 1940 and attended THS in the 1950s. In his interview, he mentioned that he had won the state title at the 154 lb. classification in his junior year. Unfortunately, a check of the "champs list" for wrestling in the state of Wyoming does not list him as the winner at that weight anytime during the 1950s. Additionally, no record of his participation in this event was found in state newspapers during those years. Last, a perusal of his obituary (he died in 2016) does not mention any such accomplishment. While that information in the interview might not be accurate, it should be part of the historical record that Joe did mention that he did wrestle and played football at Torrington. He also made one observation that does bear upon some of the points made in this work about the Sanchez family and the impact of athletic participation on how minorities are viewed by the majority population. "My oldest brother, Harold, was pretty athletic. He set some records that haven't been broken yet (as of the early 1980s) and my sister, Sally, she was, to the best of my knowledge, the only Mexican cheerleader and also crowned homecoming queen. So, therefore, our family was looked at fairly good."[7]

Given the effect participation in this sport has had on this one family, what broader understandings/themes can be drawn from this study? As noted, the examination of the impact of sport on the lives/history of Latinos/Hispanics (and Mexican Americans in particular) is a relatively new area of study for historians, but this does not mean that the historiographical cupboard was bare. The current work will hopefully add another element (and area of sport) to that developing enterprise. Additionally, as articulated in the work by Grenardo mentioned in the introduction, success by minority athletes, sharing their stories via various mediums, and, most critically, having interactions between different racial/ethnic groups via sport can be a constructive element in overcoming racial misperceptions and breaking down barriers.

While a body of work exists regarding Latinos/as' endeavors in baseball, football, soccer, and to a lesser extent, basketball, this is the first academic treatment by a historian examining the role of wrestling in the lives of Mexican Americans.[8] More broadly, there are researchers in other fields (primarily in education) who have provided a further sense of how sport influences the educational opportunities and results of Spanish-surnamed individuals, something that Grenardo did not touch upon, with his work focusing almost exclusively on African Americans. The story of these Sanchezes provides a historical example that upholds much of what scholars in these fields have articulated in their research.

Part of the argument made in this work was that success in sport has been a mechanism Spanish-surnamed individuals have utilized to challenge assumptions about their capabilities (both physical and intellectual). While improved treatment by classmates, aficionados, and newspaper reporters were certainly of value, as is clear in the case of this family, what have academics found is the impact for former competitors of participating in athletics on future financial and educational decisions? There are two important studies that deal with this question from an economic perspective. In 2000, John M. Barron et al. published an essay entitled "The Effects of High School Athletic Participation on Education and Labor Market Outcomes" for the *Review of Economics and Statistics*. Here, they argued, "There is a clear link for men between athletic competition and both formal education and wages. . . . the reason we find that former high school athletes fare better in the labor market than their non-athlete counterparts is that athletic involvement enhances productivity." Seven years later, Ewing followed up on the topic with an article entitled "The Labor Market Effects of High School Athletic Participation: Evidence from Wage and Fringe Benefit Differentials," which yielded similar results. "Confirming the findings of Barron et al. . . . I find that former high school athletes earn more than their nonathlete counterparts, all else equal." Thus, once Gilbert Sr. took up wrestling at the suggestion of Coach Brown at Cheyenne Central High School, back in the mid-1950s, he began the process of moving not only his own future but that of his siblings and subsequent generations, onto a path whereby the cohorts of competitors produced more college degrees than state titles in wrestling, thus dramatically transforming the family's economic and social standing.[9] This is not to denigrate the efforts of Gil Sr.'s parents and grandparents but merely to point out that he, when given the opportunity to display his talents in an area of athletics, created an aperture for the pursuit of further education and that, in turn, helped him achieve a middle-class lifestyle and salary, as well as setting a standard followed by many others in his family.

In regard to how wrestling came to be a tradition for this family (and the significance thereof), scholars in the field of sports administration have done work in this regard. In 2017 Lindsey Darvin et al. published an article in the *Journal of Amateur Sport* entitled "¿Por Qué Jugar? Sport Socialization among Hispanic/Latina Female NCAA Division I Student Athletes."[10] Here, various scholars researched key factors that played a role in the "socialization, motivational and persistent participation processes" of these competitors. Why were these critical elements in the lives of athletes? Because, as the authors argued, "youth participation in extracurricular activities, including sport, have been shown to enhance self-esteem, social behavior, emotional regulation, and ethnic identity, which are all important aspects used by Latino youth to cope with negative experiences such as discrimination."[11] While the Darvin project focused on Latinas, the components mentioned are evident in the Sanchez family case study.

Darvin et al. asked interviewees three key questions: (1) how did the student-athletes develop an interest in their particular sport?; (2) what role did family/siblings play in that selection/interest?; and (3) what influenced the competitors to persist so as to make it possible for them to reach the collegiate level?[12] The participants' responses focused on ties to sport being ever present in the various families; the fact that either parents or siblings participated in competition; and finally, the role that parents, siblings, and (significantly) coaches (many of whom were not Hispanic) played in fostering the internal motivation to become sufficiently proficient, thus making it possible to participate at the university level (whether at D-I or a lower division).[13] Not unexpectedly, all of these elements are visible in the history of the Sanchez family. The persistence displayed made it possible for the first cohort to attend college (at a time when this was a rarity for Mexican Americans). The fact that Gil, Arthur, and Ray competed at this level, and earned degrees, made it possible (and expected) that the second generation (and now some in the third) would continue on similar paths.

In recent years, there has been a generous amount of research done on the relationship between Hispanic/Latino students, their academic achievement, and sports. Again, the results presented in these works mirrored the experiences that took place over the various decades of the Sanchez family's ties to wrestling. For example, Juan M. Hinojosa's 2018 dissertation from Texas A&M University–Kingsville, entitled "The Effects of Athletic Sport Teams Participation on Hispanic High School Student Academic Achievement" documented the value of such involvement by youths attending an urban institution populated predominantly by students from a low socioeconomic background.[14] Hinojosa focused on three specific areas of academic success (or lack thereof): grade point average, class attendance, and discipline referrals for individuals in grades 9 through 12.[15] Significantly, he found that the GPAs and the attendance of those who played sports (vs. nonparticipants) were higher for all grade levels. The only negative result occurred in regard to disciplinary matters, where athletes had a lower number of referrals for the ninth and tenth graders but then a slightly increased number for juniors and seniors.[16] We need only refer back to Gil Sr.'s experiences at the orphanage and then his connection to wrestling at CCHS to get a sense of the difference athletics (and the nun's "gentle persuasion") made in his life.

Another study focusing on Spanish-surnamed high schoolers and athletics is by Luis A. Inoa from 2018 and entitled "Latino Males in the U.S. and the Effect of High School Sports Participation on a Multi-Dimensional Construct of Academic Engagement"; it presents a more nuanced understanding of the relationship between Hispanic athletes, academics, and their schools. Here, the goal was not only to examine the impact of sport on GPA but to scrutinize "the ways in which socialization into sport paves the way for . . . school engagement, which facilitates academic engagement, which advances educational achievement/attainment."[17] Inoa's results do show that Spanish-surnamed young men who played sports for their high schools in tenth grade graduated at a higher rate (in 2006) than did nonparticipants (94% versus 84%). Further, by 2012 26 percent of all Latinos surveyed had earned an associate degree; for those who were a part of a high school team, the percentage was slightly higher, 28. The amount for noncompetitors was only 20 percent. Significantly, of those who were on teams in both the tenth and twelfth grades (by 2012), 35 percent had earned at least a two-year college degree.[18] Those who played for a secondary institution as a sophomore and senior also had higher GPAs, graduation rates, college enrollment, and degree attainment than those who did not.[19] Two major differences, however, occurred when Inoa divided the Latinos into ethnic groups; in this case, for those of Mexican descent the difference in earning of a two-year degree was not statistically significant and neither was a sense of engagement with the school.[20] Clearly, this was not the case in the story of the Sanchezes, as not only did they earn degrees (and advanced ones in several cases), but the ties to their schools, in particular Cheyenne Central, were of great importance and of long-lasting duration.

In 2013 Sylvia Martínez and Evan Mickey published an article in the *Journal for the Study of Sports and Athletes in Education* entitled "The Effects of Participation in Interscholastic Sports on Latino Students' Academic Achievement," scrutinizing the influence that participation in athletics had on math scores for such pupils.[21] The results were generally positive as they argued that "participation in high school interscholastic sports has consistent benefits on students' math scores."[22] Further, the authors noted that students with aspirations to continue their education beyond high school were more likely to participate in sports than those who did not harbor similar goals. One caveat these researchers did mention, however, was that those students who worked in order to help their families were, not surprisingly, less likely to participate in competition.[23] In the Sanchezes' case, except for the first cohort, participating in sports was more likely not only because of the family history in wrestling but also because Gil, Art, and Ray earned degrees and provided their offspring a better financial situation than they experienced. While they certainly were not wealthy, their professional careers in education made it easier for the second generation of Sanchez wrestlers to hit the mat and move on from there. This detail ties in with what Martínez and Mickey argue, that it is imperative for schools and communities to make greater efforts to help provide entrée into athletics for Hispanic youths because "increasing access and encouraging Latino students to participate in interscholastic sports could be a way to bolster academic achievement among this population."[24]

So far, all works noted in this chapter have focused on Spanish-surnamed athletes at the high school level. There are some works, however, that take us beyond that period and examine how such athletes navigate life in a collegiate setting. Two recent dissertations, one by Manuel Silva at the Claremont Graduate School and the other by Guillermo Ortega at the University of Houston, provide insight into how these student athletes manage to get to college, how they deal with classroom and competitive activities, and how they manage to persevere in order to complete undergraduate degrees.[25]

Silva's effort focuses on topics such as whether athletes felt welcomed at their institutions, the difficulty in leaving their families, and the importance that kin placed upon their collegiate education. In his research, Silva found that the overwhelming majority (almost 97%) of both male and female competitors "felt welcomed" at their institutions of higher learning.[26] In the Sanchezes' case, not one member of the first generation, which we could have expected to have faced the greatest amount of resistance, mentioned not being treated well. There may be some important reasons for this. First, in Gil Sr.'s case, he had spent time in the Marines and traveled widely, thus making him more "mature" than many of his colleagues. Second, he attended Colorado State University, which had a significant number of Latinos on campus, even in the early 1960s. Third, given that he was the first person in his family to go to college, he understood the great opportunity (and responsibility) that wrestling for the Rams provided for him and the rest of the clan. Finally, once Gil Sr. started the trend, and with the great success that Art and Ray had in Wyoming (and the fact that they wrestled for the Cowboys), the impact of the trends noted in Olmsted's dissertation would have been of benefit.[27]

Silva also questioned his interviewees regarding the significance of family values on the athletes' move into collegiate sports. Again, nine out of ten of the respondents (both male and female) indicated that this was a positive element in their participation.[28] As noted throughout this work, once the values instilled through wrestling became part of family custom, it was expected that the Sanchez youths would wrestle (or, in the case of later generations, participate in other sports). Finally, Silva also mentions the significance of high school coaches in encouraging athletes to pursue their collegiate athletic dreams.[29] The opportunity/inspiration planted in Gil Sr. by Coach Brown back in the 1950s concerning how wrestling could provide an education and a way out of lower-paying labor set this family on the path to a new way of life. Certainly, the ability to grapple, the intense training and the physical skill of all concerned over the decades played a key role, but it was that initial spark that helped open the family's route to the future.

One of the key elements covered in Ortega's dissertation intersects with the Sanchez story in two ways. First, and not surprisingly, he discusses that his research showed that Latino athletes tend to interact less with the broader campus community (students and faculty) than they do with their fellow athletes, thus creating a lack of engagement with the university. This component of their experience makes it more difficult for such individuals to be successful on college campuses and to graduate.[30] In the case of the Sanchez family, we see a different outcome, particularly with Frank Sanchez. As noted in chapter 5, when Frank arrived at Nebraska, his connections with fellow Chicano students served as the impetus for his decision to leave wrestling and become involved in efforts to improve the educational circumstances for fellow Latinos—ultimately leading to his doctorate and career in university administration.

So, what does it all mean? First, this work will hopefully stimulate further historical research on the role of athletic competition (both in revenue-generating sports—such as football and basketball—and non-revenue-generating sports—such as wrestling) in the lives of the Spanish-surnamed throughout the United States. There is, at this stage of the game, a decent number of investigations into this history concerning baseball, football, soccer, and basketball. We have a sense of how these sports have impacted individuals and communities, but more needs to be done regarding endeavors such as wrestling, softball, track and field, and volleyball, among others. Second, by looking at the historical stories of athletes in such areas, historians can connect their work to scholars in other fields, such as education, to provide academicians and the general public a sense of the importance (both historical and current) of scholastic athletic competition to efforts to improve educational outcomes for the largest minority group in the United States. It makes sense that sharing inspiring stories such as that of this Sanchez clan can benefit our communities. Finally, given the Sanchez family's long tenure in Wyoming—and their interactions with employers, educational facilities, and other institutions—this story will add a new element to the historical literature of the Spanish-surnamed populace of the state.

In 2015 a group of sociologists and public policy specialists examined the impact of the current trend in which fewer and fewer low-income and minority students are participating in high school sports due to a variety of economic and other reasons. It is worth quoting part of their summary here:

> Playing soccer or marching band [or wrestling] is not simply a fun activity; these activities teach valuable lessons in teamwork, communication, and perseverance—all of which pay off later in the workplace. For children from less-advantaged backgrounds, the social connections and character traits gleaned from extracurricular activities may offer the key to upward mobility and a secure middle-class life. Furthermore, participation in such activities may plant the seeds of future political participation, setting children on the path toward social connectedness and civic involvement rather than isolation and disengagement. . . . [Currently] These low-income students are losing a chance to develop grit and perseverance, work alongside others, build valuable connections with mentors, and learn how to lead. As a result, their ability to climb the economic ladder may be jeopardized. Living up to our national creed of equal opportunity requires closing the extracurricular gap as swiftly as possible.[31]

While the this quote from academicians does an effective job of encapsulating the value of sport to youths, the elder Gil Sanchez, provided an even more succinct summary of the importance of athletics (and other extracurricular activities) to his family and the broader population of Spanish-surnamed youths in an email to me when he noted, "In our family we have educators, engineers, and other professions. Not to mention a college president. All because a 15-year-old boy named Gilbert Sanchez from Cheyenne, Wyoming decided to become a wrestler."[32] Hopefully, this story will inspire others to pursue athletic competition not only (given its immediate and long-lasting benefits) for its own sake but also for the possibility that it may change the social and economic standing of many other families.

Notes

Introduction

1 Lew Freedman, *Jump Shot: Kenny Sailors, Basketball Innovator and Alaskan Outfitter* (Portland, OR: Westwind Press, 2014); Irv Moss, "Sailors Still Big Shot in Wyoming History," *Denver Post*, April 6, 2009, accessed March 15, 2022, https://www.denverpost.com/2009/04/06/sailors-still-big-shot-in-wyoming-history/; "Kenny Sailors: Basketball Pioneer—Our Wyoming," Wyoming PBS, accessed March 15, 2022, https://www.youtube.com/watch?v=C7hKqooYdQU.

2 See Robert W. Cohen, *The 50 Greatest Players in Green Bay Packers History* (Guilford, CT: Lyons Press, 2018); and Rick Roddam, "The Five Greatest Athletes in Cheyenne's History," June 5, 2015, accessed March 15, 2022, https://kingfm.com/the-5-greatest-athletes-in-cheyennes-history/.

3 SI Staff, "The 50 Greatest Sports Figures from Wyoming," *Sports Illustrated*, December 27, 1999, accessed March 15, 2022, https://vault.si.com/vault/1999/12/27/the-50-greatest-sports-figures-from-wyoming. See also Associated Press, "Richard 'Rink' Babka, discus Medalist at 1960 Olympics, Dies at 85," January 17, 2022, accessed March 15, 2022, https://www.espn.com/olympics/trackandfield/story/_/id/33087030/richard-rink-babka-discus-medalist-1960-olympics-dies-85.

4 Mark Kidston, "Ontiveros Family: Born to Illegal Immigrants, Mexican American Couple Builds Family, Future in Wyoming," *Billings Gazette*, April 9, 2011, accessed March 16, 2022, https://billingsgazette.com/news/state-and-regional/wyoming/born-to-illegal-immigrants-mexican-american-couple-builds-family-future-in-wyoming/article_6752c685-d77d-5940-a117-608782335060.html.

5 SI Staff, "Faces in the Crowd," *Sports Illustrated*, March 15, 1965, accessed March 16, 2022, https://vault.si.com/vault/1965/03/15/faces-in-the-crowd.

6 A good place to look for an examination of the differences between the two types of wrestling, Freestyle and Greco-Roman, can be found here in William Tackett, "Freestyle vs. Greco-Roman Wrestling: What Are the Differences?," Tackett Jiu Jitsu (March 6, 2024), https://grapplingschool.com/freestyle-vs-greco-roman-wrestling/. Tackett's description is as follows: "The difference between Freestyle and Greco-Roman wrestling is that Freestyle permits holds both above and below the beltline using both arms and legs. In contrast, Greco-Roman forbids holding below the beltline. Only males compete in Greco-Roman, while Freestyle is open for both males and females."

7 Jorge Iber, "The Sanchezes of Cheyenne, Wyoming: The First Generation of a Family of Wrestlers at the Local, State, and National Stage," *Annals of Wyoming* 92, no. 4 (Autumn 2020–Winter 2021): 2–17; quote from 14.

8 Iber, "The Sanchezes of Cheyenne, Wyoming."

9 Wyoming earned the nickname "Equality State" due to it being the first territory in the United States (in 1869) to permit women the right to vote and hold office. The seal in the center of the state's flag suggests that it is a place for "equal rights." Unfortunately, this has not always been the case for various groups in Wyoming.

10 Jorge Iber et al., *Latinos in U.S. Sports: A History of Isolation, Cultural Identity, and Acceptance* (Champaign, IL: Human Kinetics, 2011) is just one of the many works on this topic. An extensive discussion of these items will be presented in chapter 1.

11 Natalia Molina, *Fit to Be Citizens? Public Health and Race in Los Angeles, 1879–1939* (Berkeley: University of California Press, 2006) and *How Race Is Made in America: Immigration, Citizenship, and the Historical Power of Racial Scripts* (Berkeley: University of California Press, 2014). Of particular interest from this second work are Molina's introduction and chaps. 1 and 2.

12 It is common when making such a statement to refer to Jacques Barzun's memorable quotation from his 1954 book, *God's Country, and Mine: A Declaration of Love Spiced with a Few Harsh Words*: "Whoever wants to know the heart and mind of America had better learn baseball." Given the passage of time, and the dramatic changes that have taken place in the landscape of American sport (e.g., baseball is no longer the most watched/followed sport, with football, both professional and collegiate, now at this spot), Barzun's analysis has come under scrutiny in recent decades. For an example of this type of analysis, see Gerald Early, "Birdland: Two Observations on the Cultural Significance of Baseball," *American Poetry Review* (July/August 1996): 9–10, accessed March 16, 2022, https://www.writing.upenn.edu/~afilreis/50s/baseball.html.

13 Iber et al., *Latinos in U.S. Sports*. Of particular interest for this introduction are chapters 3 and 4.

14 Molina, *Fit to Be Citizens?*, 9–10.
15 Molina, *Fit to Be Citizens?*, 61.
16 Molina, *Fit to Be Citizens?*, 53.
17 Molina, *Fit to Be Citizens?*, 69.
18 Molina, *Fit to Be Citizens?*, 77.
19 Molina, *Fit to Be Citizens?*, 111.
20 Molina, *Fit to Be Citizens?*, 117.
21 Molina, *Fit to Be Citizens?*, 121.
22 Molina, *Fit to Be Citizens?*, 147.
23 Molina, *How Race Is Made in America*, 6.
24 Molina, *How Race Is Made in America*, 7, 10, and 11.
25 George J. Sanchez, *Boyle Heights: How a Los Angeles Neighborhood Became the Future of American Democracy* (Oakland, CA: University of California Press, 2021), 68.
26 For information on this group of settlers, see Christopher Long, "Old Three Hundred," *Handbook of Texas Online*, accessed March 24, 2022, https://www.tshaonline.org/handbook/entries/old-three-hundred.
27 The quotes are noted in Iber et al., *Latinos in U.S. Sports*, 72. See also Arnoldo De León, *They Called Them Greasers: Anglo Attitudes Toward Mexicans in Texas, 1836–1900* (Austin: University of Texas Press, 1983); quotes from 6–7, 34, and 67. Another important work in this vein is Marc C. Anderson, "What's to Be Done with 'Em'? Images of Cultural Backwardness, Racial Limitations, and Moral Decrepitude in the United States Press, 1913–1915," *Mexican Studies/Estudios Mexicanos*, 14, no. 1 (Winter 1998): 23–70.
28 Material quoted in Iber et al., *Latinos in U.S. Sports*, 67–68. See also David Julian Chavez, "Civic Education of the Spanish-American" (MA thesis, University of Texas, Austin, 1923), 58–59 and 108–117.
29 Material quoted in Iber et al., 73. See also Florie S. Dupre, "Play as a Factor in the Education of Children" (PhD diss., University of Texas, Austin, 1925).
30 For his obituary, see, accessed March 24, 2022, https://news.google.com/newspapers?id=O5AxAAAAIBAJ&pg=5400,6981528&dq=elmer-mitchell&hl=en.
31 Elmer D. Mitchell, "Racial Traits in Athletics," *American Physical Education Review* 27, no. 3 (March 1922): 93–99.
32 Mitchell, "Racial Traits in Athletics," *American Physical Education Review* 27, no. 4 (April 1922): 147–152; quotes from 148, 148, and 150.
33 Mitchell, "Racial Traits in Athletics," *American Physical Education Review* 27, no. 5 (April 1922): 197–206; quotes from 201 and 202.
34 Genevieve King, "The Psychology of a Mexican American Community in San Antonio, Texas" (MA thesis, University of Texas, Austin, 1936), 60; Albert Folsom Cobb, "Comparative Study of Athletic Ability of Latin American and Anglo-American Boys on a Junior High School Level" (MA thesis, University of Texas, 1952), 2.
35 Merrell E. Thompson and Claude D. Dove, "A Comparison of Physical Achievement of Anglo and Spanish American Boys in Junior High School," *Research Quarterly* 13 (October 1942): 341–346; Bruce Walsh-Shaw, "Sociometric Status and Athletic Ability in Anglo American and Latin American Boys in a San Antonio Junior High School"

(MA thesis, University of Texas, 1951), 18–19; final two quotes in this paragraph from Iber et al., 116 and 75.

36 Brett Thomas Olmsted, "Los Mexicanos de Michigan: Claiming Space and Creating Community Through Leisure and Labor, 1920–1970" (PhD diss., University of Houston, 2017).

37 Olmsted, "Los Mexicanos de Michigan," 139.

38 Olmsted, "Los Mexicanos de Michigan," 140.

39 Olmsted, "Los Mexicanos de Michigan," 155 and 156.

40 David A. Grenardo, "It's Worth a Shot: Can Sports Combat Racism in the United States?," *Journal of Sport and Entertainment Law* 12 (2021): 237–318.

41 Grenardo, "It's Worth a Shot," 245, 246, 275, and 310.

42 Grenardo, "It's Worth a Shot," 275.

43 Grenardo, "It's Worth a Shot," 246 and 316.

Chapter 1: The Sanchez Family Arrives and Settles in Cheyenne: 1915–1956

Portions of this chapter first appeared as Jorge Iber, "The Sanchezes of Cheyenne, Wyoming," *Annals of Wyoming* 92, no. 4 (Autumn 2020–Winter 2021): 2–17.

1 Peter Standish, *The States of Mexico: A Reference Guide to History and Culture* (Westport, CN: Greenwood Press, 2009), 139–153.

2 Standish, *The States of Mexico*, 140 and 145.

3 Alan Knight, *The Mexican Revolution*, vol. 1: *Porfirians, Liberals, and Peasants* (Lincoln: University of Nebraska Press, 1986), 91.

4 Knight, *The Mexican Revolution*, 92 and 132. See also Margaret E. Rankine, "The Mexican Mining Industry in the Nineteenth Century with Special Reference to Guanajuato," *Bulletin of Latin American Research* 11, no. 1 (January 1992): 29–48; and Standish, *The States of Mexico*, 144–145.

5 For information on this trend, see the following: Ruth Gomberg-Muñoz, "Not Just Mexico's Problem: Migration from Mexico to the United States, 1900–2000," *Journal of Latino-Latin American Studies* 3, no. 3 (Spring 2009): 2–18; Fernando Saúl Alanís Enciso, *They Should Stay There: The Story of Mexican Migration and Repatriation During the Great Depression* (Chapel Hill: University of North Carolina Press, 2017), chap. 1, "Migratory Movements Between Mexico and the United States, 1880–1934," 11–19; and Manuel G. Gonzales, *Mexicanos: A History of Mexicans in the United States*, 3rd ed. (Bloomington: Indiana University Press, 2019), chap. 5, "The Great Migration," 129–162.

6 Jeffrey Bortz and Marcos Aguila, "Earning a Living: A History of Real Wage Studies in Twentieth Century Mexico," *Latin American Research Review* 41, no. 2 (2006): 112–138; quotes from 117, 116, and 119.

7 Moramay López-Alonso, "Growth with Inequality: Living Standards in Mexico, 1850–1950," *Journal of Latin American Studies* 39, no. 1 (February 2007): 81–105.

8 López-Alonso, "Growth with Inequality," 102–103.

9 Knight, *The Mexican Revolution*, 1:133.
10 Knight, *The Mexican Revolution*, 1:100, 199, 237, 259, 358–359, and 461.
11 Trisha Venisa-Alicia Martínez, "Living the Manito Trail: Maintaining Self, Culture, and Community" (PhD diss., University of New Mexico), 68.
12 Martínez, "Living the Manito Trail," 72 and 74.
13 Martínez, "Living the Manito Trail," 91.
14 Vanessa Fonseca, "'Donde mi amor se ha quedado': Narratives of Sheepherding and *Querencia* Along the Wyoming Manito Trail," *Annals of Wyoming* 89, nos. 2 and 3 (Spring–Summer 2017): 6–12; quote from 10–11.
15 Virginia Sánchez, "Pal Norte: The Sanchez and Espinoza 1940s Family Migration from Mora County, New Mexico to Cheyenne, Wyoming," *Annals of Wyoming* 89, nos. 2 and 3 (Spring–Summer 2017): 16–24; quote from 16.
16 Peg Arnold, "Wyoming's Hispanic Sheepherders," *Annals of Wyoming* 69 (Winter 1997): 29–42.
17 Arnold, "Wyoming's Hispanic Sheepherders," 30–31.
18 Arnold, "Wyoming's Hispanic Sheepherders," 33–34.
19 Camila Montoya, "Not a Sweet Deal: Mexican Migrant Workers in the Sugar Beet Farms of the Midwest and Mountain States, 1900–1930" (MA thesis, Michigan State University, East Lansing, 2000), 18 and 19.
20 Montoya, "Not a Sweet Deal," 23, 25, 31, and 32.
21 Montoya, "Not a Sweet Deal," 35.
22 Alephonso García, "Beet Seasons in Wyoming: Mexican American Family Life on a Sugar Beet Farm near Wheatland During World War II," *Annals of Wyoming* 73, no. 2 (Spring 2001): 14–17.
23 Ellen Schoening-Aiken, "The United Mine Workers of America Move West: Race, Working Class Formation, and the Discourse on Cultural Diversity in the Union Pacific Coal Towns of Southern Wyoming, 1870–1930" (PhD diss., University of Colorado, 2002); Miguel A. Rosales, "A Mexican Railroad Family in Wyoming," *Annals of Wyoming* 73, no. 2 (2001): 28–32; William L. Hewitt, "Mexican Workers in Wyoming During World War II: Necessity, Discrimination, and Protest," *Annals of Wyoming* 54, no. 2 (1982): 20–34; and Jennifer Macias, "The Years After World War II: Latinx Families in Wyoming," *Annals of Wyoming* 89, nos. 2–3 (Spring–Summer 2017): 25–31.
24 Schoening-Aiken, "The United Mine Workers of America Move West," 2 and 5. In addition to Rock Springs, Schoening-Aiken mentions locales such as Reliance, Winton, Cumberland, and Hanna. Not all of these locales had substantial numbers of Spanish-surnamed individuals. Indeed, she indicates that, in Cumberland, after 1911 "the company employed no African Americans and no Japanese or Mexican immigrants (20)."
25 Schoening-Aiken, "The United Mine Workers of America Move West," 63–64 and 95.
26 Schoening-Aiken, "The United Mine Workers of America Move West," 337–343.
27 Rosales, "A Mexican Railroad Family in Wyoming," 28–32.
28 Rosales, "A Mexican Railroad Family in Wyoming," 30 and 32.
29 Hewitt, "Mexican Workers in Wyoming During World War II," 20–34.

30 Hewitt, "Mexican Workers in Wyoming During World War II," 28.

31 Hewitt, "Mexican Workers in Wyoming During World War II," 29–30; quote from 30.

32 Macias, "The Years After World War II," 25–31.

33 Some of the older projects dealing with this topic include the following: Daphne Overstreet, "ON STRIKE! The 1917 Walkout at Globe, Arizona," *Journal of Arizona History* 18, no. 2 (Summer 1977): 197–218; and Joseph F. Park, "The 1903 'Mexican Affair' at Clifton," *Journal of Arizona History* 18, no. 2 (Summer 1977): 119–148.

34 Andrea Yvette Huginnie, "'Strikitos': Race, Class, and Work in the Arizona Copper Industry, 1870–1930" (PhD diss., Yale University, 1991).

35 Huginnie, "Strikitos," 28, 40–41, and 44–45.

36 Huginnie, "Strikitos," 53–54 and 58.

37 Huginnie, "Strikitos," 95–96 and 98. Note that Huginnie researched mine censuses between the years 1890 and 1930, but the wage figures only appeared in the documents from 1890 and 1900. In this quote, she used the figures from 1900.

38 Email from Arthur Sanchez to author, February 15, 2023. See also email from Jim Sanchez to author, April 26, 2020; and Iber, "The Sanchezes of Cheyenne, Wyoming," 6.

39 Email from Arthur Sanchez to author, February 15, 2023.

40 Jose C. Fuentes, oral history interview, January 1982, for the La Cultura Hispanic Heritage Oral History Project, OH 868.

41 Paul Sanchez, oral history interview, December 1981, for the La Cultura Hispanic Heritage Oral History Project, OH 858.

42 Celso Palma-Sandoval, oral History interview, May 1983, for the La Cultura Hispanic Heritage Oral History Project, OH 903.

43 Frances and Bernardo Archuleta, oral history interview, January 1983, for the La Cultura Hispanic Heritage Oral History Project, OH 844.

44 Email from Art Sanchez to author, March 14, 2023.

45 For information on Asher-Wyoming, particularly the history of its building, which is on the National Register of Historic Places, see the Waymarking web page, accessed February 22, 2023, https://www.waymarking.com/waymarks/WMHW3G_Asher_Wyoming_Co_Wholesale_Grocers_Cheyenne_WY.

46 Email from Arthur and Mary Louise Sanchez to author, April 26, 2020.

47 Iber, "The Sanchezes of Cheyenne, Wyoming," 6.

48 David Halberstam, *The Coldest Winter: America and the Korean War* (New York: Hyperion, 2007), 41–44.

49 Max Hastings, *The Korean War* (New York: Touchstone Books, published by Simon and Schuster, 1987), 291–292.

50 Philip Wylie, *Generation of Vipers*, 2nd ed. (London: Dalkey Archive Press, 1996), cited in Judith Keene, "Lost to Public Commemoration: American Veterans of the 'Forgotten' Korean War" in *Journal of Social History* (Summer 2011); 44, no. 4, *Social Memory and Historical Justice* (Summer 2011): 1095–1113.

51 Lewis H. Carlson, *Remembered Prisoners of a Forgotten War: An Oral History of Korean War POWs* (New York: St. Martin's Press, 2002), 220–221, cited in Judith Keene, "Lost to Public Commemoration: American Veterans of the 'Forgotten' Korean War."

52 Iber, "The Sanchezes of Cheyenne, Wyoming," 6.

53 Iber, "The Sanchezes of Cheyenne, Wyoming," 7.

54 Catherine Bustos, oral history interview, July 1982, for the La Cultura Hispanic Heritage Oral History Project, OH 824.

55 Nellie Arias, oral history interview, no date listed, for the La Cultura Hispanic Heritage Oral History Project, OH 904D.

56 Alicia Sanchez, oral history interview, August 1982, for the La Cultura Hispanic Heritage Oral History Project, OH 842.

57 Kristine Galloway, "Frontier Park Housed Hundreds in Federal Housing Project Frontier Villa," *Wyoming Tribune Eagle*, July 22, 2018, accessed February 23, 2023, https://www.wyomingnews.com/news/local_news/frontier-park-housed-hundreds-in-federal-housing-project-frontier-villa/article_0bc39e02-8d73-11e8-a423-3b3d60b2f8cd.html.

58 Iber, "The Sanchezes of Cheyenne, Wyoming," 7. See also *Cheyenne, Wyoming, 1940–1955: WWII National Defense Work Shortage of Living Quarters Justifying the Construction of Federal Housing Projects*, (Thousand Oaks, CA: UBuildABook, 2016).

59 Iber, "The Sanchezes of Cheyenne, Wyoming"; quote from 8. Also, email from Gilbert Sanchez to author, April 7, 2020.

60 Iber, "The Sanchezes of Cheyenne, Wyoming."

61 Email from Gilbert Sanchez to author, April 7, 2020.

62 Email from Gilbert Sanchez to author, April 7, 2020.

63 T. Joe Sandoval, "A Study of Some Aspects of the Spanish-Speaking Population in Selected Communities in Wyoming" (MA thesis, University of Wyoming, Laramie, 1946), 3.

64 Sandoval, "A Study of Some Aspects of the Spanish-Speaking Population," 4.

65 Sandoval, "A Study of Some Aspects of the Spanish-Speaking Population," 35.

66 Sandoval, "A Study of Some Aspects of the Spanish-Speaking Population," 39, 40, and 49.

67 Keith Jewitt, "The Spanish-Speaking Students in Laramie High School, 1940–1950" (MA thesis, University of Wyoming, Laramie, 1950).

68 Jewitt, "The Spanish-Speaking Students." For an examination of the specific statistics, see chaps. 2 and 3, 7–39.

69 Jewitt, "The Spanish-Speaking Students," 42–43.

70 Jewitt, "The Spanish-Speaking Students," 43.

71 Jewitt, "The Spanish-Speaking Students," 44–51 and 69–77; quote from 76.

72 Jewitt, "The Spanish-Speaking Students," 62.

73 Jewitt, "The Spanish-Speaking Students," 63.

74 Jewitt, "The Spanish-Speaking Students," 88.

75 Jewitt, "The Spanish-Speaking Students," 53, 56, and 58.

76 Jewitt, "The Spanish-Speaking Students," 55 and 56.

77 Jewitt, "The Spanish-Speaking Students," 57–59.

78 Gonzalo Guzmán, "Education for a New Race: White Schools, Child Labor, and Creating the Mexican in the Equality State, 1917–1941" (PhD diss., University of Washington, Seattle, 2018); " 'This Change You Know': Schools as the Architects of the

Mexican Race in Depression-Era Wyoming," *History of Education Quarterly* 61 (2021): 392–422.

79 Guzmán, "Things Change you Know," 396–399; quotes from 398 and 399.

80 Guzmán, "Things Change you Know," 406 and 410.

81 Guzmán, "Things Change you Know," 411 and 415.

82 Arnoldo De León, "Our Gringo Amigos: Anglo Americans and the Tejano Experience," *East Texas Historical Journal* 31, no. 2 (1993): 72–79; quote from 77.

83 Email from Arthur Sanchez to author, March 14, 2023.

84 Iber, "The Sanchezes of Cheyenne, Wyoming," 8–9.

85 "Plainsmen Win State Mat Title; Mustangs Place 7th," *Casper Star-Tribune*, March 18, 1956. In the final chapter of this work, I will cover the careers and successes of other Latino families and individuals on the mats of the state of Wyoming.

Chapter 2: Athletics/Sports as a Part of the Latino/a Historical Literature

1 Obviously, there is a limited literature extant from prior to the Chicano Era, but the volume of this literature increased dramatically after the 1960s. While the list that follows is extensive, it is by no means exhaustive. See Zaragoza Vargas, *Labor Rights Are Civil Rights: Mexican American Workers in Twentieth-Century America* (Princeton, NJ: Princeton University Press, 2005); Lori A. Flores, *Grounds for Dreaming: Mexican Americans, Mexican Immigrants, and the California Farmworker Movement* (New Haven, CT: Yale University Press, 2016); José M. Alamillo, *Making Lemonade out of Lemons: Mexican American Labor and Leisure in a California Town, 1880–1960* (Urbana: University of Illinois Press, 2006); Brian D. Behnken, *Fighting Their Own Battles: Mexican Americans, African Americans, and the Struggle for Civil Rights in Texas* (Chapel Hill: University of North Carolina Press, 2011); José Angel Gutiérrez, *The Making of a Civil Rights Leader* (Houston, TX: Piñata Books, 2005); Yolanda Alaniz and Megan Cornish, *Viva La Raza: A History of Chicano Identity and Resistance* (Seattle, WA: Red Letter Press, 2008); Reies López Tijerina, *They Call Me "King Tiger": My Struggle for the Land and Our Rights* (Houston, TX: Arte Publico Press, 2000); Jorge Iber, *Hispanics in the Mormon Zion, 1912–1999* (College Station: Texas A&M University Press, 2000); Jay P. Dolan and Gilberto M. Hinojosa, eds., *Mexican Americans and the Catholic Church, 1900–1965* (Notre Dame, IN: Notre Dame University Press, 1994); Vicki L. Ruiz and Miroslava Chávez-García, *Latina Lives, Latina Narratives: Influential Essays* (New York: Routledge, 2021); Vicki L. Ruiz, *From Out of the Shadows: Mexican Women in the Twentieth Century* (New York: Oxford University Press, 2008); Elizabeth R. Escobedo, *From Coveralls to Zoot Suits: The Lives of Mexican American Women on the World War II Homefront* (Chapel Hill: University of North Carolina Press, 2015); Jennifer R. Najera, *The Borderlands of Race: Mexican Segregation in a South Texas Town* (Austin: University of Texas Press, 2015); Monica Muñoz Martinez, *The Injustice Never Leaves You: Anti-Mexican Violence in Texas* (Cambridge, MA: Harvard University Press, 2018); Monica Perales, *Smeltertown: Making and Remembering a Southwest Border Community* (Chapel Hill: University of North Carolina Press, 2010);

Anthony Quiroz, *Claiming Citizenship: Mexican Americans in Victoria, Texas* (College Station: Texas A&M University Press, 2005); Rubén Orlando Martinez, *Latinos in the Midwest* (East Lansing: Michigan State University, 2011); Richard Baker, *Los Dos Mundos: Rural Mexican Americans, Another America* (Logan: Utah State University Press, 1995); George J. Sánchez, *Becoming Mexican American: Ethnicity, Culture and Identity in Chicano Los Angeles, 1900–1945* (New York City: Oxford University Press, 1995); and Jessica M. Vasquez, *Mexican Americans Across Generations: Immigrant Families, Racial Realities* (New York: New York University Press, 2011).

2 Alex Nuñez, "Switch-Hitting: Mexican Diaspora, Whiteness, and Tusconense Baseball, 1903–1954," *Journal of Arizona History*, 62, no. 4 (Winter 2021): 563–582.

3 Nuñez, "Switch-Hitting," 564.

4 Nuñez, "Switch-Hitting," 566.

5 Jorge Iber, "Mexico: Baseball's Humble Beginnings to Budding Competitor," in *Baseball Beyond Our Borders: An International Pastime*, ed. George Gmelch, 75–84 (Lincoln: University of Nebraska Press, 2017); quote from 76.

6 José M. Alamillo, "*Peloteros* in Paradise: Mexican American Baseball and Oppositional Politics in Southern California, 1930–1950," *Western Historical Quarterly* 34, no. 2 (2003): 191–211.

7 See Samuel O. Regalado, "Baseball in the Barrios: The Scene in East Los Angeles Since World War II," *Baseball History* 1, no. 2 (Summer 1986): 47–59; Richard Santillan and Francisco E. Balderrama, "Los Chorizeros: The New York Yankees of East Los Angeles and the Reclaiming of Mexican American Baseball History," Society for American Baseball Research (2011), accessed August 9, 2022, https://sabr.org/journal/article/los-chorizeros-the-new-york-yankees-of-east-los-angeles-and-the-reclaiming-of-mexican-american-baseball-history/.

8 Alberto Rodriguez, "Ponte El Guante! Baseball on the US-Mexican Border: The Game and Community Building, 1920s–1970s," in *Latinos and Latinas in American Sport: Stories Beyond Peloteros*, ed. Jorge Iber, 63–78 (Lubbock: Texas Tech University Press, 2020).

9 Jorge Iber, *Mike Torrez: A Baseball Biography* (Jefferson, NC: McFarland and Company, 2016).

10 Ben Chappell, *Mexican American Fastpitch: Identity at Play in a Vernacular Sport* (Palo Alto, CA: Stanford University Press, 2021).

11 Katherine M. Jamieson, "Advance at Your Own Risk: Latinas, Families and Collegiate Softball," in *Mexican Americans and Sport: A Reader on Athletics and Barrio Life*, ed. Jorge Iber and Samuel O. Regalado, 213–232 (College Station: Texas A&M University Press, 2007).

12 All of this information comes from Jorge Iber et al., *Latinos in U.S. Sports: A History of Isolation, Cultural Identity, and Acceptance* (Champaign, IL: Human Kinetics, 2011), 101–103, 177–181, 215–216, and 261–263.

13 Gregory S. Rodríguez, "Palaces of Pain—Arenas of Mexican American Dreams: Boxing and the Formation of Ethnic Mexican Identities in Twentieth Century Los Angeles" (PhD diss., University of California, San Diego, 1999).

14 Tom I. Romero II, "Wearing the Red, White, and Blue Trunks of Aztlan: Rodolfo 'Corky' Gonzales and the Convergence of American and Chicano Nationalism," in *Mexican Americans and Sport: A Reader on Athletics and Barrio Life*, ed. Jorge Iber and Samuel O. Regalado, 89–120 (College Station: Texas A&M University Press, 2007).

15 Fernando Delgado, "Golden but Not Brown: Oscar De La Hoya and the Complications of Culture, Manhood, and Boxing," *International Journal of the History of Sport* 22, no. 2 (March 2005): 196–211; Benita Heiskanen, *The Urban Geography of Boxing: Race, Class, and Gender in the Ring* (New York: Routledge, 2012).

16 Benita Heiskanen, "The *Latinization* of Boxing: A Texas Case Study," *Journal of Sport History*, 32, no. 1 (Spring 2005): 45–66. For basic information (popular literature) on some Mexican and Mexican American boxers, see Robert José Andrade Franco, "A History of Latino and Mexican Boxing," February 15, 2018, *Process: A Blog for American History*: https://www.processhistory.org/franco-latino-and-mexican-boxing/; and Ramses Sepulveda, "How Mexicans Came to Dominate the Sport of Boxing—A Brief History," March 25, 2021, https://www.linkedin.com/pulse/how-mexicans-came-dominate-sport-boxing-brief-sepulveda-m-p-a.

17 Troy Rondinone, *Friday Night Fighter: Gaspar "Indio" Ortega and the Golden Age of Television Boxing* (Urbana: University of Illinois Press, 2013), 22, 28, and 36.

18 Rondinone, *Friday Night Fighter*, 151–152.

19 The following two works are good primers on the rise of the sport, its early (collegiate) years, and what the game meant to Americans: John Sayle Watterson, *College Football: History, Spectacle, Controversy* (Baltimore, MD: Johns Hopkins University Press, 2000); and Michael Oriard, *Reading Football: How the Popular Press Created an American Spectacle* (Chapel Hill: University of North Carolina Press, 1993). Of course, there are many, many other works that detail the history of the sport.

20 Michael Oriard, *King Football: Sport and Spectacle in the Golden Age of Radio and Newsreels, Movies and Magazines, the Weekly and Daily Press* (Chapel Hill: University of North Carolina Press, 2001), 260.

21 Oriard, *King Football*, 206.

22 Mario Longoria and Jorge Iber, *Latinos in American Football: Pathbreakers on the Gridiron, 1927 to the Present* (Jefferson, NC: McFarland and Company, Inc., Publishers, 2020).

23 Jorge Iber, "On-Field Foes and Racial Misperceptions: The 1961 Donna Redskins and Their Drive to the Texas State Football Championship," in *Mexican Americans and Sport: A Reader on Athletics and Barrio Life*, ed. Jorge Iber and Samuel O. Regalado, 121–144 (College Station: Texas A&M University Press, 2007); quote from 131.

24 Iber, "On-Field Foes and Racial Misperceptions," 134.

25 Iber, "On-Field Foes and Racial Misperceptions," 136.

26 Jorge Iber, "Mexican Americans of South Texas Football: The Athletic and Coaching Careers of E. C. Lerma and Bobby Cavazos, 1932–1965," in *More than Just Peloteros: Sport and US Latino Communities*, ed. Jorge Iber, 184–205 (Lubbock: Texas Tech University Press, 2014); quote from 194.

27 Iber, "Mexican Americans of South Texas Football," 200.

28 Frederick Luis Aldama and Christopher González, *Latinos in the End Zone: Conversations on the Brown Color Line in the NFL* (New York City: Palgrave MacMillan, 2014). For the interviews, see chap. 5, 89–105.

29 Richard Lapchick, "The 2021 Racial and Gender Report Card: College Sports," annual report of the Institute for Diversity and Ethics in Sports (Orlando: University of Central Florida, 2021), 17.

30 USA Facts, "Our Changing Population: United States," accessed August 15, 2022, https://usafacts.org/data/topics/people-society/population-and-demographics/our-changing-population?utm_source=google&utm_medium=cpc&utm_campaign=&msclkid=dd75918f241c1c57598bf375a552970a.

31 Aldama and González, *Latinos in the End Zone*, 5 and 6.

32 Matthew Carey, "LA Film Festival: 'The Classic' Tells of East L.A. Football Rivalry with Much More at Stake than a Game," Non Fiction Film, June 21, 2017, accessed August 9, 2022, https://www.nonfictionfilm.com/news/la-film-festival-the-classic-tells-of-east-la-football-rivalry-with-much-more-at-stake-than-a-game.

33 Juan Javier Pescador, "Los Heroes del Domingo: Soccer, Borders, and Social Spaces in Great Lakes Mexican Communities, 1940–1970," in *Mexican Americans and Sport: A Reader on Athletics and Barrio Life*, ed, Jorge Iber and Samuel O. Regalado, 73–88 (College Station: Texas A&M University Press, 2007); quote from 73.

34 Paul Cuadros, " 'Fútbol Femenino' Comes to the New South: Latina Integration Through Soccer," in *Latinos and Latinas in American Sport: Stories Beyond Peloteros*, ed. Jorge Iber, 235–254 (Lubbock: Texas Tech University Press, 2020); quotes from 251 and 252.

35 David Trouille, *Fútbol in the Park: Immigrants, Soccer, and the Creation of Social Ties* (Chicago: University of Chicago Press, 2021); quote from 181.

36 Ignacio M. García, *When Mexicans Could Play Ball: Basketball, Race, and Identity in San Antonio, 1928–1945* (Austin: University of Texas Press, 2014). See also Ignacio M. Garcia, "William Carson 'Nemo' Herrera: Constructing a Mexican American Powerhouse While Remaining Colorblind," in *Latinos and Latinas in American Sport: Stories Beyond Peloteros*, ed. Jorge Iber, 33–46 (Lubbock: Texas Tech University Press, 2020); quote from 43.

37 Christine Marin, "Courting Success and Realizing the American Dream: Arizona's Mighty Miami High School Championship Basketball Team, 1951," in *More than Just Peloteros: Sport and US Latino Communities*, ed. Jorge Iber, 150–183 (Lubbock: Texas Tech University Press, 2020); quote from 157.

Chapter 3: The Sanchez Name Begins to Stand Out in State Wrestling Circles: 1956–1967

Portions of this chapter first appeared as Jorge Iber, "The Sanchezes of Cheyenne, Wyoming," *Annals of Wyoming* 92, no. 4 (Autumn 2020–Winter 2021): 2–17.

1 There is a substantial and growing literature on the role of Mexican Americans in the US military, particularly from World War II onward (this list is by no mean exhaustive); see the following: Maggie Rivas-Rodriguez, ed., *Mexican Americans and World War II* (Austin: University of Texas Press, 2005); Raul Morin, *Among the Valiant: Mexican Americans in WWII and Korea* (Los Angeles: Borden Publishing Company, 1963); Patrick J. Carroll, *Felix Longoria's Wake: Bereavement, Racism, and the Rise of*

Mexican American Activism (Austin: University of Texas Press, 2003); Ignacio M. García, *Hector P. García: In Relentless Pursuit of Justice* (Houston, TX: Arte Publico Press, 2002); and Juan David Coronado, *"I'm Not Gonna Die in This Damn Place": Manliness, Identity, and Survival of Mexican American Vietnam Prisoners of War* (East Lansing: Michigan State University Press, 2018).

2 This topic is covered in the Morin, Carroll, and García books mentioned in the previous note. Others that deal with such topics include (this list is by no means exhaustive): Ignacio M. Garcia, *White But Not Equal: Mexican Americans, Jury Discrimination and the Supreme Court* (Tucson: University of Arizona Press, 2009); Richard Griswold del Castillo, *World War II and Mexican American Civil Rights* (Austin: University of Texas Press, 2008); Michael A. Olivas, *"Colored Men" and "Hombres Aqui": Hernandez v. State of Texas and the Emergence of Mexican American Lawyering* (Houston, TX: Arte Publico Press, 2006); and Cynthia E. Orozco, *No Mexicans, Women, or Dogs Allowed: The Rise of the Mexican American Civil Rights Movement* (Austin: University of Texas Press, 2009).

3 Morin, *Among the Valiant*; Emily A. López, "Mexican American Veterans, Class and Identity During and After World War II" (MA thesis, University of Wyoming, Laramie, 2015).

4 For information on the life and contributions of Mr. Morin, see "Raul Morin, Author, Writer and Commercial Artist," accessed March 15, 2023, http://www.raulmorin.com/author_writer.html.

5 Morin, *Among the Valiant*, 285 of the Kindle edition.

6 Morin, *Among the Valiant*, 287 of the Kindle edition.

7 Morin, *Among the Valiant*, 287 of the Kindle edition.

8 López, "Mexican American Veterans, Class and Identity During and After World War II," 1.

9 López, "Mexican American Veterans," 2–3.

10 López, "Mexican American Veterans," 3.

11 López, "Mexican American Veterans," 5–6.

12 López, "Mexican American Veterans," 76–77.

13 López, "Mexican American Veterans," 78.

14 See "Freestyle vs. Greco-Roman Wrestling: What Are the Differences?," accessed March 27, 2023, https://grapplingschool.com/freestyle-vs-greco-roman-wrestling/#:~:text=The%20difference%20between%20Freestyle%20and%20Greco-Roman%20wrestling%20is,Freestyle%20is%20open%20for%20both%20males%20and%20females.

15 This information comes from the following website, accessed April 19, 2023, https://tackettjiujitsu.com/freestyle-vs-greco-roman-wrestling-what-are-the-differences/.

16 This information comes from the following website: "What Is Greco Roman Wrestling: From Rules to Olympic History," accessed April 19, 2023, https://olympics.com/en/news/what-how-greco-roman-wrestling-style-rules-scoring-techniques-olympics.

17 For information on Dick Delgado's legendary career at the University of Oklahoma, see Jorge Iber and Lee Maril, *Latino American Wrestling Experience: Over 100 Years of*

Wrestling Heritage in the United States, (Stillwater, OK: National Wrestling Hall of Fame, 2013), https://nwhof.org/latinowrestling, 15.

18 See the following for information on the Corr brothers: Iber, "The Sanchezes of Cheyenne, Wyoming," 9; "Edwin Corr," National Wrestling Hall of Fame page, accessed March 21, 2023, https://nwhof.org/hall_of_fame/bio/1988; "Dr. Bert L. Corr, PHS Alumni Honor Roll Member," accessed March 21, 2023, https://perryokalumni.com/?page_id=18325; and "Sooner Spotlight: The Corrs," no date, no author, accessed March 21, 2023, in author's possession.

19 José Leandro Montano, oral history interview, December 1981, for the La Cultura Hispanic Heritage Oral History Project, no. 832.

20 Henry Mascarenos, oral history interview, January 1983, for the La Cultura Hispanic Heritage Oral History Project, no. 889.

21 Leo Richard Sánchez, oral history interview, January 1983, for the La Cultura Hispanic Heritage Oral History Project, no. 877.

22 Victoriano Trujillo, oral history interview, January 1983, for the La Cultura Hispanic Heritage Oral History Project, no. 859

23 "Shelby Wilson Wrestles Jap," *Stillwater News-Press*, April 13, 1959; "State Matmen, Japs in Final NAAU Tuneup," *Tulsa Daily World*, April 14, 1959; Tom Lobaugh, "Foreign Recruits Shine as Cowboys Grab Mat Crown," *Tulsa Daily World*, April 16, 1959; "Returning Mat Kings Triumph," *Muskogee Daily Phoenix*, April 16, 1959; "Unsung OU Frosh Pins AAU Champ," *Tulsa Daily World*, April 17, 1959; "Here are Results of AAU Mat Meet," *Tulsa Daily World*, April 18, 1959.

24 Email from Gilbert Sanchez to author, March 28, 2023.

25 See the following: "Lamar J.C. Pins 21–8 Defeat on CSC 'B' Matmen," *Greeley Daily Tribune*, December 5, 1959; "2 Colo. Matmen Win AAU Titles," *Greeley Daily Tribune*, April 2, 1960; "Colo. Wrestler Is AAU Champ," *Greeley Daily Tribune*, April 4, 1960; "Colorado Boys in Wrestling Finals Trials," *Greeley Daily Tribune*, April 28, 1960; "Goltl Gains Third Round of Mat Trails," *Greeley Daily Tribune*, April 29, 1960; and "Goltl Wins 3rd Match in Mat Olympic Trials," *Greeley Daily Tribune*, April 30, 1960.

26 "Greco-Roman Trails Open," *Greeley Daily Tribune*, May 2, 1960; "Walt Goltl Wins Twice," *Greeley Daily Tribune*, May 3, 1960; "Top Wrestler Awarded CSU Scholarship," *Ft. Collins Coloradoan*, July 21, 1960.

27 Iber, "The Sanchezes of Cheyenne, Wyoming," 10. See also "CSU Wrestling Outlook Brighter," *Ft. Collins Coloradoan*, January 2, 1961.

28 Unless otherwise noted, all of these articles are from *Ft. Collins Coloradoan*: "CSU Wrestling Outlook Brighter," January 2, 1961; "Aggie Wrestlers Defeat Colorado," January 8, 1961; "C-State, Aggie Meet Figured to Be Donnybrook," *Greeley Daily Tribune*, January 19, 1961; "Ram Wrestlers Tackle Tough CSC Bears Here Tonight," January 20, 1961; "CSU's Undefeated Wrestlers Defeat CSC Bears, 14–11," January 22, 1961; "Ag Matmen to Face 2 Tough Iowa Foes," January 27, 1961; "Iowa State Rips CSU Wrestlers, 22–4," January 29, 1961; "Ram Wrestlers Entertain Cougars, Wyoming Next," February 2, 1961; "Aggie Wrestlers Defeat Washington State, 17–9," February 5, 1961; "Aggie Wrestlers Defeat Wyoming Pokes, 17–12," February 5, 1961.

29 All of these articles are from the *Ft. Collins Coloradoan*: "Ag Wrestling Improves Under Coach Woods' Coaching," February 9, 1961; "Ag Matmen Duel Western State, Utah This Weekend," February 10, 1961; "CSU Wrestlers Drop 2 on Road," February 12, 1961; "CSU Rams Rejoin Wrestling Race Saturday with Denver," February 24, 1961; "Ram Matmen Renew Wins Whipping Pioneers, 22–9," February 26, 1961.

30 Unless otherwise noted, all of these articles are from the *Ft. Collins Coloradoan*: "Skyline Meet Starts Friday," March 8, 1961; "CSU Ags, Wyoming Share Skyline Wrestling Crown," March 12, 1961; "Gonzales, Kohls Win Mat Titles," *Daily Sentinel*, March 12, 1961; "Four Ag Wrestlers Win Titles, Five Go to NCAA Finals Bouts," March 20, 1961.

31 Unless otherwise noted, all of these articles are from the *Ft. Collins Coloradoan*: Matt Kramer, "Oklahoma State Leads NCAA Wrestling Meet," March 24, 1961; "Lordino Reaches NCAA Mat Finals," *Greeley Daily Tribune*, March 25, 1961; "Sanchez to Wrestle," April 2, 1961; "NYAC Mat Hopes Suffer Big Blow," *Daily Sentinel*, April 6, 1961; and "Ag Grappler Gil Sanchez Defeated," April 7, 1961. See also 1961 NCAA Championship Brackets for the 31st NCAA Wrestling Tournament, Accessed March 30, 2023, http://www.wrestlingstats.com/ncaa/pdf/brackets/NCAA%201961.pdf; 1961 AAU Freestyle Championships, accessed March 30, 2023, https://image.aausports.org/sports/wrestling/results/past_results/freestyle.pdf; and AAU Greco-Roman National Championships, page 3, accessed March 30, 2023, https://image.aausports.org/sports/wrestling/results/past_results/greco_roman.pdf.

32 Unless otherwise noted, all of these articles are from the *Ft. Collins Coloradoan*: "Aggie Wrestlers Conduct Inter-Squad Test Tonight," December 8, 1961; "Ag Matmen Whip Mesa," December 10, 1961; "CSU Wrestlers Smother Western State, 20 to 12," January 7, 1962; "C-State Wrestlers Open '62 Campaign," *Greeley Daily Tribune*, January 10, 1962; "Aggie Wrestlers Battle Bears at Greeley Saturday," January 12, 1962; "Aggie Wrestlers Open Oklahoma Trip Tonight," January 19, 1962; "Okla. State Wrestlers Defeat CSU," *Greeley Daily Tribune*, January 20, 1962; "Oklahoma State Matmen Hand CSU First Loss," January 21, 1962; "OU Wrestlers Whip Rams," January 21, 1962; "Iowa State, CSU Aggies Wrestle to 13–13 Draw," February 4, 1962; "Aggie Wrestlers Whip Iowa Panthers," February 4, 1962; "Aggie Wrestlers Defeat Wyoming," February 11, 1962; "CSU Wrestlers Humble Denver," February 18, 1962; "CSU Wrestlers in Skyline Meet," March 9, 1962; and "Wyoming Grabs Skyline Wrestling Title; CSU 2nd," March 11, 1962.

33 Unless otherwise noted, all of these articles are from the *Ft. Collins Coloradoan*: "Eight Rams Enter NCAA Meet," March 21, 1962; "3 Ags Advance in NCAA Wrestling," March 23, 1962; "CSC's Flasche Wins Semi-Final Match," *Greeley Daily Tribune*, March 24, 1962; and "Oklahoma Ags Nab NCAA Wrestling; Rams Do Poorly," March 25, 1962. See also 1962 NCAA Wrestling Championship, accessed April 3, 2023, http://www.wrestlingstats.com/ncaa/pdf/brackets/NCAA%201962.pdf.

34 Lee Kjos, "More from Les," *Ft. Collins Coloradoan*, December 6, 1962.

35 Unless otherwise noted, all of these articles are from the *Ft. Collins Coloradoan*: "Aggie Wrestlers, Bears Wind Up in 12–12 Deadlock," January 13, 1963; "Bears, Rams Battle to 12–12 Mat Draw," *Greeley Daily Tribune*, January 14, 1963; "Sanchez's Victory Downs Panther Matmen," January 20, 1963; "Cowpokes Overpower CSU Grapplers, 26–8,"

January 27, 1963; "Aggie Wrestlers Bow to Western," January 27, 1963; "OU Grapplers Top Aggies in Dual Mat Meet," *Greeley Daily Tribune*, February 16, 1963; and "CSU Wrestlers Roll Over BYU," February 24, 1963.

36 Unless otherwise noted, all of these articles are from the *Ft. Collins Coloradoan*: "Tournament Next for Ag Grapplers," March 7, 1963; Bob Scales, "Bears Second in MIWA Tourney," *Greeley Daily Tribune*, March 11, 1963; "WSC Wins," March 11, 1963; "Ag Matmen Enter Meet," March 17, 1963; and "CSU Wrestlers to Enter National Championships," March 20, 1963.

37 Unless otherwise noted, all of these articles are from the *Ft. Collins Coloradoan*: "Hines, Sanchez Open Mat Meet with Wins; Ags 4th," March 22, 1963; "Oklahoma Races to Team Lead in NCAA Tourney," *Greeley Daily Tribune*, March 23, 1963; "Wrestling on TV," March 29, 1963; and "Cage Banquet Plans Ready," March 31, 1963. See also 1963 NCAA Wrestling Championship, accessed April 5, 2023, http://wrestlingstats.com/ncaa/pdf/brackets/NCAA%201963.pdf.

38 Iber, "The Sanchezes of Cheyenne, Wyoming," 11. See also "Five Residents Made Citizens," *Ft. Collins Coloradoan*, January 14, 1963.

39 "Sanchez to Seek Mat Team Bid," *Ft. Collins Coloradoan*, May 10, 1963.

40 "Tom Thompson Notched AAU Wrestling Victory," *Casper Morning Star*, March 24, 1964.

41 See the following: "AAU National Freestyle Championships, 1889–1982," accessed April 6, 2023, https://www.pawrsl.com/pa/AAU_1889-1982-Results.pdf; and AAU Greco-Roman National Championships, 1953–1982, accessed April 6, 2023, https://image.aausports.org/dnn/wrestling/Archive-Results/AAU-Greco-Roman-National-Championships/1953-1982-Results.pdf.

42 "Cheyenne Sending Sanchez Brothers to Olympic Trials," *Ft. Collins Coloradoan*, April 2, 1964. See also "Sanchez Brothers Eye Mat Regionals," *Casper Morning Star*, April 4, 1964. The information on Art's career will follow in this chapter, and Ray's accomplishments will be detailed in chapter 5.

43 Hal Brown, "Sanchez Makes Mat Return After Heart Murmur," *Lincoln Star*, December 8, 1966.

44 "Grapplers Vie For Olympics at Cheyenne," *Greeley Daily Tribune*, May 16, 1964; "CSC's Jim Innis Qualifies for Olympic Trials Finals," *Greeley Daily Tribune*, May 18, 1964; "AAU Wrestling Qualifiers Told," *Ft. Collins Coloradoan*, May 18, 1964; "Tom Thompson Is Qualifier For U.S. Olympic Mat Trial," *Casper Morning Star*, May 19, 1964; "1 Point in 7 Bouts but Auble 2nd," *Binghamton Press and Sun-Bulletin*, June 25, 1964; Dave Rossie, "Endicott-Style Olympic Trials," *Binghamton Press and Sun-Bulletin*, August 9, 1964; "Bush One of Tokyoish 3, but So is Gray," *Binghamton Press and Sun-Bulletin*, August 26, 1964; "Simon Finishes Undefeated in U.S. Olympic Free-Style Wrestling Trials: Army Man Wins Five Bouts Here; Takes 114.5-Pounds Laurels," *New York Times*, August 27, 1964; "Olympic Wrestlers Selected," *White Plains Daily Argus*, September 16, 1964. See also "Little Man with a Big Lock on Records," *Sports Illustrated*, March 26, 1962, accessed on April 6, 2023, https://vault.si.com/vault/1962/03/26/little-man-with-a-big-lock-on-records.

45 Hal Brown, "Sanchez Makes Mat Return After Heart Murmur," *Lincoln Star*, December 8, 1966; "Kelly Wants 'Outstanding' Title," *Lincoln Star*, December 9, 1966; "NU Grappler Wins Three Bouts," *Lincoln Star*, December 10, 1966.

46 Iber, "The Sanchezes of Cheyenne, Wyoming," 12; "Wrestling: A Sanchez Family Tradition," accessed March 18, 2019, https://sanchezwrestlinghistory.weeby.com/; "Driver Dies of Crash Injuries," *Casper Star-Tribune*, April 24, 1976.

47 Email from Art Sanchez to author, April 24, 2023.

48 Stan Wyman, "Mustang Wrestlers Beat Cheyenne in Close Match," *Casper Star-Tribune*, February 21, 1960; George Collier, "Lambkin Matmen Split 2 Matches," *Ft. Collins Coloradoan*, December 22, 1961.

49 "Mustangs Host Cheyenne Mat Clubs," *Casper Tribune-Herald*, January 5, 1962; "Central Grapplers Sneak by Mustangs In 28–24 Thriller," *Casper Star-Tribune*, January 7, 1962; "Landers Cops Mat Crown," *Casper Star-Tribune*, February 25, 1962; "Worland, Entering in All Classes, Rates as Pre-State Tourney Choice," *Casper Star-Tribune*, February 18, 1963; "Three Teams Favored," *Casper Star-Tribune*, February 21, 1963; "NCHS Wrestlers Competing in State Finals at Laramie," *Casper Morning Star*, February 22, 1963; "Worland Grabs Early Lead in State Wrestling Meet," *Casper Morning Star*, February 23, 1963; Stan Rowker, "Central's Ray Sanchez Unbeaten in Wrestling," *Casper Star-Tribune*, February 18, 1964; "HS Wrestlers Eye Regional Tourney," *Casper Morning Star*, February 19, 1964; "Tom Thompson Notched AAU Wrestling Victory," *Casper Morning Star*, March 24, 1964; "CSU Matmen Lose to Pokes," *Casper Star-Tribune*, February 11, 1966; "Cowboy Mat Chief Has His Problems," *Casper Star-Tribune*, February 18, 1966; "Oklahoma Routs Poke Grapplers," *Casper Star-Tribune*, February 22, 1966; "University Wrestlers Beat Utah," *Casper Star-Tribune*, March 1, 1966; "Gonzales Will Tighten Ties," *Casper Star-Tribune*, January 20, 1967; Emails from Mary Louise and Gil Sanchez to author, April 22 and April 7, 2020; email from Art Sanchez to author, April 26, 2020; Iber, "The Sanchezes of Cheyenne, Wyoming," 13; 36th NCAA Wrestling Tournament, accessed April 18, 2023, http://www.wrestlingstats.com/ncaa/pdf/brackets/NCAA%201966.pdf.

Chapter 4: Ray Sanchez Has a Brilliant Future: 1962–1981

1 Mike Christopulos, "Sports Scope," *Wyoming Eagle*, n.d., (Ray Sanchez's personal scrapbook).

2 Emails from Mary Louise Sanchez and Gil Sanchez to author, April 22 and April 7, 2020. See also "Mustangs Host Cheyenne Mat Clubs," *Casper Morning Star*, January 5, 1962.

3 All of the following articles are from the *Wyoming Eagle* and are part of Ray Sanchez's scrapbook collection: "Casper Edges Laramie for East Mat Honors," "Central Matmen Upset Blazers; Face Kimball," "Laramie Grapplers Pin Central," "Tribe, Bird Mat Teams Feud Today," "Tribe Beats East, 30–20." "Tribe Matmen Defeat Lingle," and "6 Central, 2 East Matmen in State Meet This Week." See also "Central Grapplers Face Tough Plainsmen Today," *Wyoming Eagle*, February 9, 1962.

4 "Tribe Close Third in Mat Meet," and "Central Second in Eastern Mat Tournament," *Wyoming Eagle*, February 24, 1962, and February 25, 1962.

5 Eric Lundberg, "Preps Head for Mat Meets," *Wyoming Eagle*, February 14, 1963; "Preps Eye Mat Finals," *Wyoming Eagle*, February 21, 1963; Gene Bryan, "Rugged Worland Takes Commanding Lead," *Laramie Daily Boomerang*, February 23, 1963. See also the following, all from the *Casper Star-Tribune*: "Wrestlers Deck Central Easily," February 3, 1963; "NCHS Wrestlers Competing in State Finals at Laramie," February 22, 1963; "Worland Grabs Early Lead in State Wrestling Meet," February 23, 1963; and "Warriors Ramble to Easy Mat Triumph," February 25, 1963.

6 See Joe Dowler resume, accessed June 21, 2023, https://wcaonline.net/download/hof_bios/JoeDowler.pdf.

7 For more information on specific meets prior to regionals this year, see the following (all are from the *Casper Star-Tribune*): "Wrestlers Host Central, East," January 30, 1964; "NCHS Wrestlers to Host Two Foes," January 31, 1963; "Wrestling Summary," February 1, 1964; "Mustang Wrestlers Thump Both Cheyenne Mat Team," February 2, 1964; and "HS Wrestlers Eye Regional Tourney," February 19, 1964.

8 Stan Bowker, "Central's Ray Sanchez Unbeaten in Wrestling," *Casper Star-Tribune*, February 18, 1964.

9 See the following (all are from the *Casper Star-Tribune*): Stan Bowker, "NCHS Wrestlers Enter Lusk Regional," February 20, 1964; "Wrestlers, Swimmers in State Meet: Four State Champion Lead Mat Qualifiers; Casper Sending Nine," February 27, 1964; Bill Herald, "Mustangs, Laramie Favored in Regional," February 21, 1964; "Nine Casper Wrestlers Qualify for State," February 23, 1964; Bill Herald, "State Wrestling, Swimming Meets Open Today," February 28, 1964; and "Mustangs Second in Wrestling Tournament," March 1, 1964.

10 Stan Bowker, "NCHS to Host Holiday Mat Tournament," *Casper Star-Tribune*, December 17, 1964; "Tournament Results," *Casper Star-Tribune*, December 19, 1964; and "NCHS Tournament Finals," *Casper Star-Tribune*, December 20, 1964.

11 For information on individual meets, see the following articles, all from the *Casper Star-Tribune*: Errol Genta, "NCHS Matmen to Wrestle East, Central," January 28, 1965; "NCHS Matmen Travel to Cheyenne," January 29, 1965; and "NCHS Matmen Defeat Cheyenne East, 22–20 to Keep Record Perfect," January 31, 1965.

12 All of these articles are from the *Casper Star-Tribune*: "Mat, Swim Tournaments Set for High Schools," February 24, 1965; Errol Genta, "Unbeaten Mustang Wrestlers Seek First State Mat Crown," February 25, 1965; Bill Herald, "Casper Picked in State Prep Wrestling," February 26, 1965; and "Cheyenne East Captures State Wrestling Title," February 28, 1965.

13 Max Jennings, "Ray Sanchez Has a Brilliant Future," *Casper Star-Tribune*, March 2, 1965. See also Iber, "The Sanchezes of Cheyenne, Wyoming," 14.

14 "1965 High School Honor Roll," *Amateur Wrestling News* 10, no. 16 (May 12, 1965): 6.

15 "Roshek Cops A.A.U. Title in Wrestling," *Casper Morning Star*, March 23, 1965.

16 Letter by Coach Dowler to unnamed individual, May 14, 1965. Copy of document in author's possession.

17 Letter by Coach Dowler to unnamed individual, May 14, 1965. See also "Sanchez Gets Win in First AAU Match," *Casper Morning Star*, April 17, 1965.

18 Letter by Coach Dowler to unnamed individual, May 14, 1965. See also "Sanchez Gets Win in First AAU Match," *Casper Morning Star*, April 17, 1965.

19 Letter by Coach Dowler to unnamed individual, May 14, 1965. See also "Sanchez Gets Win in First AAU Match," *Casper Morning Star*, April 17, 1965.

20 Various letters from these schools to Ray Sanchez are in his scrapbook.

21 "Wrestling: A Sanchez Family Tradition," accessed March 18, 2019, https://sanchezwrestlinghistory.weebly.com/.

22 See also "Cheyenne Hails Conquering Mat Hero," *Denver Post*, April 15, 1965.

23 Letter from Cecil M. Shaw, Ed.D. to Ray Sanchez, April 28, 1965. Letter from Governor Clifford Hansen to Ray Sanchez, April 23, 1965. Copy of these letters in author's possession.

24 "Ray Sanchez Not Picked for Team," *Casper Morning Star*, April 22, 1965; "Sanchez Not Picked for Team," *Casper Star-Tribune*, April 22, 1965. See also Richard Sanders page at the NWHF, accessed June 27, 2023, https://nwhof.org/hall_of_fame/bio/74.

25 Letter from Coach Joe Clark McDaniel to Ray Sanchez, June 7, 1965. Copy of letter in author's possession. See also "Distinguished Member Joe McDaniel Passed Away at 94 Years Old," accessed June 27, 2023, https://nwhof.org/news/distinguished-member-joe-mcdaniel-passed-away-at-94-years-old.

26 "Ray Sanchez Hurt in Wreck," *Billings Gazette*, August 3, 1965; "Prep Wrestler Recovering," *Casper Star-Tribune*, August 3, 1965.

27 "Great Plains Meet Results," *Lincoln Star*, December 12, 1965. At this time, the AAU rules called for no black marks to be given for a pin, one for a decision, two for a draw, three for being decisioned, and four for being pinned. Once a wrestler accumulated six black marks, they were eliminated from the competition.

28 Larry Dennis, "Douglas Selected Top Mat Entry," *Lincoln Star*, December 12, 1965; "Great Plains Results," *Lincoln Star*, December 12, 1965; Larry Dennis, "Mankind Is Ray's Concern, But Not on Wrestling Mat," *Lincoln Star*, March 20, 1966; "State Matmen Place in AAU," *Casper Star-Tribune*, March 23, 1966; Larry Dennis, "Mat Fun Turns to Serious Business," *Lincoln Star*, April 3, 1966; Barry Burkhart, "Defending Kings Fall," *Lincoln Star*, April 8, 1966; Larry Dennis, "Combs Wins Mat Honor," *Lincoln Star*, April 10, 1966; "AAU Mat Results," *Lincoln Star*, April 10, 1966.

29 "Ray Sanchez Hobbled by Injuries," *Casper Star-Tribune*, June 3, 1966.

30 Hal Brown, "Sanchez Makes Mat Return After Heart Murmur," *Lincoln Star*, December 8, 1966.

31 "Pokes Lose First Match," *Casper Star-Tribune*, January 31, 1967; "Cowboys to Meet CSU," *Casper Star-Tribune*, February 23, 1967.

32 "Worland Grappler Competes in WAC," *Casper Star-Tribune*, March 10, 1967. Information on Ray's record going into the NCAAs in 1967 comes from his vita. Copy in author's possession.

33 "37th NCAA Wrestling Tournament, 3/23/67 to 3/25/67 at Kent State," accessed June 28, 2023, http://www.wrestlingstats.com/ncaa/pdf/brackets/NCAA%201967.pdf. See also "2 Defenders Left in NCAA Wrestling," *Medina County Gazette*, March 25,

1967; "Wrestling Ends Today," *Daily Times* (New Philadelphia, Ohio), March 25, 1967; "Only One Title Pin," *Akron Beacon Journal*, March 26, 1967; and "McMinn Passed Up Basketball," *Lincoln Journal Star*, April 5, 1967.

34 Chuck Woodling, "Steak for Breakfast? Yes, indeed!" *Lincoln Star*, April 14, 1967.

35 "Libal Scores Upset," *Lincoln Star*, April 14, 1967; "Saturday's AAU Results," *Lincoln Star*, April 16, 1967. See also "AAU National Freestyle Championships, 1889–1982," accessed June 28, 2023, https://image.aausports.org/dnn/wrestling/Archive-Results/AAU-Freestyle-National-Championships/1889-1982-Results.pdf, page 13.

36 "Sanchez Slates Trial for U.S. Wrestling Team," *Casper Star-Tribune*, June 1, 1967.

37 "Cowboy Matmen Open Workouts," *Casper Star-Tribune*, October 13, 1967; "Godbe, Sanchez Are Sidelined," *Casper Star-Tribune*, December 1, 1967; Chuck Harkins, "Extra Points," *Casper Star-Tribune*, December 20, 1967.

38 Jeremiah Johnke, "Unrivaled: Ray Sanchez: Newest Inductee into Wyoming's Sports Hall of Fame," June 26, 2009, *Wyomingnews.com*.

39 All of these articles are from *Casper Star-Tribune*: "Ray Sanchez Out for Year," January 11, 1968; Chuck Harkins, "Extra Points," February 8, 1968; "Ray Sanchez Sets Return to Action," February 22, 1968; "Miller Still Unbeaten," March 6, 1968; "Miller in Quest of Clean Mark," February 29, 1968; "8 Mat Teams in CSU Meet," December 4, 1969; Chuck Harkins, "Extra Points," December 11, 1969; and "Extra Points," May 31, 1970. See also information from Johnke, "Unrivaled," and on Ray's record from 1968, which comes from his vita. Copy in author's possession.

40 All of these articles are from *Casper Star-Tribune*: Chuck Harkins, "Extra Points," May 31, 1970; "Extra Points," September 16, 1970; "Lander Loses Mat Mentor,"*Casper Star-Tribune*, April 22, 1972; "Sanchez is Mat Choice," May 11, 1973; Chuck Harkins, "Extra Points," August 26, 1973; "Soviet Squad Hard to Pin, Pronounce," May 26, 1974; and Chuck Harkins, "Extra Points," April 14, 1976.

41 Justin Williams, "In Their Blood," *Longmont Times-Caller*, n.d., Part of the Raymond Sanchez scrapbook.

42 University of Wyoming Athletics, "Where Are They Now," December 19, 2012, accessed July 5, 2023, https://gowyo.com/news/2016/6/29/5774118ee4b0bdd131ac993b_131479675724021602.

43 Irv Moss, "A Driven Wrestler Set Bar in Wyoming," *Denver Post*, June 30, 2009, accessed July 3, 2023, https://www.denverpost.com/2009/06/29/a-driven-wrestler-set-bar-for-wyoming/.

Chapter 5: The Next Generation of Sanchezes as Wrestlers and Coaches: 1979–2023

1 Joyce A. Surdam, "Political Attitudes of Mexican American and Anglo-American Students at Laramie Senior High School" (MA thesis, University of Wyoming, Laramie, 1970), 24–29.

2 Surdam, "Political Attitudes of Mexican American and Anglo-American Students," 45–52.

3 Esther De Herrera, oral history interview, June 1983, for the La Cultura Hispanic Heritage Oral History Project, OH 885.

4 Rafaela Rodriguez, oral history interview, March 1983, for the La Cultura Hispanic Heritage Oral History Project, OH 875.

5 Oralia Gómez-Mercado, oral history interview, July 1983, for the La Cultura Hispanic Heritage Oral History Project, OH 886.

6 Abe DeHerrera, oral history interview, June 1983, for the La Cultura Hispanic Heritage Oral History Project, OH 884. See also "DeHerrera Swearing-in Ceremony Friday," *Casper Star-Tribune*, January 17, 1996.

7 Bob Kearney, "Beach Will Host 17 Nations in Junior World Wrestling," *Miami Herald*, March 13, 1973; "AAU Picks 20 Wrestlers," *Miami Herald*, July 26, 1973; Bob Kearney, "Teams From 22 Nations Seek Junior World Wrestling Title," *Miami Herald*, July 29, 1973.

8 Bob Kearney, "U.S. Protests Mat Incident," *Miami Herald*, August 6, 1973.

9 Email from Jim Sanchez to author, May 4, 2023.

10 Email from Jim Sanchez to author, August 7, 2023.

11 Nuñez, "Switch-Hitting," 566.

12 "Matmen Picked," *Casper Star-Tribune*, July 14, 1979.

13 All of these articles are from *Casper Star-Tribune*: "Rock Springs Wrestlers Rated No. 1," December 5, 1979; Tom Bishop, "Wrestlers Head for Rapid City," December 13, 1979; Tom Bishop, "Green River Hosts Wrestling Tournament," January 25, 1980; Tom Bishop, "Rock Springs Leads Poll," February 13, 1980; Tom Bishop, "Rock Springs Hosts Top Wrestlers," February 22, 1980; Tom Bishop, "Mustang Grapplers Fall Short at R.S.," February 25, 1980.

14 All of these articles are from *Casper Star-Tribune*: Sean McMahon, "Natrona Wrestlers a Solid Choice; Green River Favored," February 19, 1981; Sean McMahon, "NC Grapplers Up for National Honor," April 16, 1981; Sean McMahon, "All-Star Prep Wrestling Squads Named," May 3, 1981; Bill Landen, "North Grapplers Meet South Tonight," July 11, 1981; "South Defeats North in Wrestling Match That Was Marred by a Forfeit," July 12, 1981.

15 See https://huskers.com/nebraskas-team-history; https://huskers.com/nebraskas-national-champions; and https://huskers.com/nebraskas-wrestling-all-american-honors—all three accessed August 28, 2023.

16 "Utah, Syracuse Challenge NU," *Lincoln Star*, January 5, 1983; "Know Debut Impressive as Husker Wrestlers Win," *Lincoln Journal Star*, January 22, 1983; Mike Babcock, "End Is Near, Push Is on for Nebraska Wrestlers," *Lincoln Journal Star*, January 26, 1983; Rod Henkel, "Nebraska-Penn State Matmen Matchup Set," *Lincoln Journal Star*, October 27, 1983.

17 "Nebraska Wrestling Coach Is Anxious to Start Season," *Omaha World-Herald*, October 26, 1983; Rod Henkel, "NU Wrestlers Open Season," *Lincoln Star*, October 28, 1983; "Husker Wrestlers Routed by 2nd-Ranked Cowboys," *Omaha World-Herald*, November 21, 1983; Rod Henkel, "NU Wrestlers Regroup for Pair of Rated Teams," *Lincoln Star*, November 23, 1983; Rod Henkel, "Slumping NU Wrestlers Set for Tournament," *Lincoln Star*, December 1, 1983; Rod Henkel, "NU Wrestlers Have Tough Job Against

ISU," *Lincoln Journal Star*, January 6, 1984; "Iowa State Wrestlers Crush Nebraska," *Lincoln Star*, January 8, 1984.

18 Unless otherwise noted, all of these articles are from the *Lincoln Star*: "Nebraska Wrestlers Defeat Bison, 31–15," January 15, 1984; Rod Henkel, "Saturday's Dual Special for NU Matman Sanchez," February 2, 1984; "3rd-Ranked OU Wrestlers at NU," *Lincoln Journal Star*, February 7, 1984; Rod Henkel, "'Murderers' Row' Key to NU's Chance in Big 8 Wrestling," February 25, 1984; Rod Henkel, "Huskers Advance Three Wrestlers to Finals," February 26, 1984.

19 Dave Sittler, "NU Faces 'Rebuilding' In Wrestling," *Omaha World-Herald*, October 26, 1984; "Mavericks to Hold 'Largest Wrestling Meet,'" *Omaha World-Herald*, November 17, 1984; "Pokes Claim Wrestle Title at UNO Meet," *Omaha World-Herald*, November 18, 1984; Mike Babcock, "Injuries Too Much to Overcome," *Lincoln Journal Star*, February 6, 1985; "Fifth-Ranked Iowa State Wrestlers Stymie Cornhuskers, 34–4," *Lincoln Star*, November 16, 1985; "NU Wrestler Marisette Leads Dual Sweep," *Lincoln Star*, December 8, 1985; "Wrestling: Nebraska 29, N. Dakota 9," *Lincoln Journal Star*, December 14, 1985; "Five Huskers Advance to Semifinals at Midwest Wrestling Championships," *Lincoln Journal Star*, December 30, 1985; "Wrestling: Nebraska 34, Tenn-Chattanooga 15," *Lincoln Journal Star*, January 6, 1986; "Wrestling: Nebraska 41, UNO 7," *Lincoln Journal Star*, January 16, 1986; "Albright Records 50th Career Pin," *Lincoln Star*, January 19, 1986; Mike Reilley, "Huskers' Albright Notches 100th Career Victory," *Lincoln Journal Star*, February 9, 1986; "Huskers Rally Past Drake," *Lincoln Journal Star*, February 20, 1986; "Huskers Wrestling Team Wins," *Lincoln Star*, February 23, 1986.

20 A technical fall occurs when one competitor achieves a fifteen-point margin over his opponent.

21 Unless otherwise noted, all of these articles are from the *Omaha World-Herald*: Lee Barfknecht, "Huskers' Goal at Big 8 Wrestling Tourney: Qualify 10 for Nationals," February 28, 1986; "Sooners Send 7 to Wrestle Finals," March 2, 1986; "OU Repeats as Mat Champ; Huskers Fourth," March 3, 1986; "Albright is 2nd Seed for NCAA Tourney," March 13, 1986; "Albright Advances in NCAA Wrestling," *Lincoln Journal Star*, March 14, 1986. See also "1986 NCAA Wrestling Championship," accessed August 28, 2023, http://www.wrestlingstats.com/ncaa/pdf/brackets/NCAA%201986.pdf.

22 "Four Husker Wrestlers Win at Wyoming Open." *Omaha World-Herald*, November 16, 1986; "Sanchez Earns Respect," *Beatrice Daily Sun*, November 21, 1986; "NU's Sanchez Earns Respect with Big Mat Win," *Columbus Telegram*, November 21, 1986; "NU Wrestler Sanchez Gets Tournament Honors," *Lincoln Star*, November 30, 1986.

23 "NU's Sanchez Tourney Honoree," *Lincoln Star*, December 7, 1986; Lee Barfknecht, "NU Wrestler 'Unstoppable' After Big Wins," *Omaha World-Herald*, December 9, 1986; Virgil Parker, "Huskers' Sanchez Continues Family's Wrestling Tradition," *Lincoln Star*, December 11, 1986; "NU Wrestlers Get Rare Win Over Sooners," *Omaha World-Herald*, February 7, 1987; Virgil Parker, "NU Wrestler Reaches Career Milestone," *Lincoln Star*, February 22, 1987.

24 Lee Barfknecht, "NU, Sooners to Wrestle for 3rd in Meet," *Omaha World-Herald*, March 5, 1987; "NU Wrestler Olson Earns Big 8 Title," *Lincoln Journal Star*, March 8,

1987; Virgil Parker, "Cornhusker Wrestler Had Change of Heart," *Lincoln Star*, March 11, 1987; "NU's Sanchez Seeded Second," *Lincoln Star*, March 19, 1987.

25 "State Sport Digest," *Lincoln Star*, March 20, 1987; 1987 NCAA Wrestling Championships, accessed on August 29, 2023, in author's possession.

26 "Huskers' Sanchez in Finals," *Lincoln Star*, March 21, 1987; "NU's Sanchez Set for NCAA Showdown," *Omaha World-Herald*, March 21, 1987; "NU's Sanchez, Iowa Wrestlers Settle for Second," *Lincoln Star*, March 22, 1987; "Stateshorts," *Lincoln Star*, April 8, 1987; "NU Wrestlers Excel," *Lincoln Star*, April 19, 1987; "Wrestling Clinic," *Chadron Record* and *Crawford Tribune*, June 5, 1987; "Sports Figures Set for Games,:" *Omaha World-Herald*, June 26, 1987; "Announcement: Wrestling Clinic," *Fremont Tribune*, July 2, 1987.

27 "Stateshorts," *Lincoln Journal Star*, March 22, 1989; "Husker Wrestlers Defeated in Mini Tournament," *Lincoln Star*, July 25, 1989; "NU Mat Aide Sanchez Competes," *Lincoln Journal Star*, April 9, 1991; "Husker Assistant Sanchez to Wrestle Soviet," *Lincoln Star*, April 9, 1991; "Clemson Names Wrestling Coach," *State*, July 4, 1992; "Clemson Names Ex-NU Wrestler Sanchez," *Lincoln Star*, July 4, 1992. See also "Clemson Wrestling: Going for More in 1994," p. 7, accessed August 30, 2023, http://www.scmat.com/Clemson%20Wrestling%201994-1995%20program.pdf.

28 Al Muskewitz, "Clemson's Recruiting Class Deviates from the Norm," *Anderson Independent-Mail*, February 12, 1993; Tom Layton, "Whitney's Hot Week Lands Him ACC Honor," *Greenville News*, March 3, 1993; "Henson Stays Perfect, Wins National Title," *Anderson Independent-Mail*, March 21, 1993; Tom Layton, "Henson Stands Tall on Wrestling Mat," *Greenville News*, February 1, 1994. See also "Clemson Wrestling: Going for More in 1994," p. 14.

29 "Clemson Swimmers May Face Last Meet," *Beaufort Gazette*, February 23, 1994; "Henson Becomes Coach," *Times and Democrat*, March 31, 1994; "College Notebook," *Anderson Independent-Mail*, June 30, 1994; Bob Cole, "Tiger Wresting Program Retools After Major Loses," *The State*, November 27, 1994; "Sport Briefing: Wrestling," *Anderson Independent-Mail*, February 5, 1995; "Clemson's Sanchez Resigns," *State*, February 15, 1995.

30 Tom Layton, "Tigers' Wrestling Coach Will Resign," *Greenville News*, February 15, 1995; "CU's Sanchez Quits," *Anderson Independent-Mail*, February 15, 1995; Josh Peter, "Source Says CU Broke Rules," *Anderson Independent-Mail*, February 23, 1995; "Clemson Wrestlers Allegedly Broke Rules," *Index-Journal*, February 23, 1995; Tom Layton, "Clemson Probes Whether Ineligible Wrestler Entered Tourney," *Greenville News*, February 24, 1995; Josh Peter, "Alleged Violation Concerns Sanchez," *Anderson Independent-Mail*, February 28, 1995.

31 Mark R. McCallum, "Clemson Wrestling Team Goes Down for the Count," *State*, March 17, 1995; "Wrestling: CU Close to Finishing NCAA Report," *Anderson Independent-Mail*, March 29, 1995; Tom Layton, "Clemson Reports NCAA Violations," *Greenville News*, April 5, 1995; "CU Wrestling Coach: Pressures Led to Violation," *Herald*, April 6, 1995; "Ex-Wrestling Coach Says Pressures of Job Led Him to Use Ineligible Wrestler," *Times and Democrat*, April 6, 1995; Tom Layton, "NCAA Clears Clemson Wrestling," *Greenville News*, September 30, 1995; "Sanchez Heads to Mizzou," *State*,

August 14, 1995; "MU Hires Sanchez as Wrestling Assistant," *Lincoln Journal Star*, August 16, 1995.

32 Joe Lyons, "Tiger Clinic to Feature Top Wrestler Sam Henson," *St. Louis Post-Dispatch*, November 10, 1995; Jeff Kidd and Mike McCombs, "Sanchez Would Come to BC Highly Recommended," *Beaufort Gazette*, August 10, 1998; Jeff Kidd and Mike McCombs, "Battery Creek Considering Former Clemson Wrestling Coach," *Island Packet*, August 11, 1998; "Sports at a Glance," *Times and Democrat*, August 14, 1998.

33 Jeff Kidd, "Gardner Visit Good as Gold," *Island Packet*, October 29, 2004.

34 Owen Driskill, "Dolphins' Backslide Continues," *Beaufort Gazette*, January 19, 1999; Jeff Kidd, "Sanchez: Dolphins on Rise." *Beaufort Gazette*, December 5, 1999; Worthy Evans, "BHS, BCHS Wrestling Season Begins," *Beaufort Gazette*, November 29, 2000; "School Contacts," *Island Packet*, August 5, 2004; Jeff Kidd, "Gardner Visit Good as Gold"; Ryan O'Connor, "Seahawks' New Coach Hopes Has His HHH Wrestlers Looking Up," *Island Packet*, November 27, 2004; Ryan O'Connor, "HHH's Murray Eyes State Title, Nationals," *Island Packet*, December 3, 2004; "Battery Creek High School," *Beaufort Gazette*, August 15, 2014. See also Gilbert Sanchez's LinkedIn page, accessed August 30, 2023, https://www.linkedin.com/in/gil-sanchez-47669844.

35 Gary Schoene, "Jim Sanchez Chosen for World Matches," *Wyoming State Tribune*, July 21, 1982; "Jim Sanchez Wins World Wrestling Title," *Wyoming State Tribune*, August 1982.

36 Email from Jim Sanchez to author, September 12, 2023.

37 During these years, the criterion in case of a tie was the wrestler with the highest scoring move won the match. For example, if wrestler "A" had three one-point moves and wrestler "B" had one three-point move, wrestler B would be declared the winner.

38 "Japan Wrestlers Defeat Wyoming Team, 7–1," *Casper Star-Tribune*, January 10, 1984; Mark LaPedus, " 'Photo Finish' 4-A Mat Race on Tap," *Casper Star-Tribune*, February 24, 1984; Mark LaPedus, "Central, Douglas Top Pack," *Casper Star-Tribune*, February 25, 1984; Mark LaPedus, "Natrona Bags State Mat Title," *Casper Star-Tribune*, February 26, 1984; "Classic Wrestler from Iowa Knows How to Survive," *Pittsburgh Press*, March 11, 1984; "3 State Stars Have 137–1 Record," *Pittsburgh Press*, March 23, 1984; Rick Emert, "Pennsylvania Stars Rip Up U.S., 31–15," *Pittsburgh Press*, April 1, 1984. See also "5 Iowa Preps Are Wrestling All-Americans," *Des Moines Register*, April 15, 1984; and *All-American Wrestling*, "1984 All-American High School Wrestling Team," n.d., copy in author's possession.

39 Email from Jim Sanchez to author, September 12, 2023. See also Cynthia Placek, "U.S. Takes Second in Stockholm," *Amateur Wrestling News*, 1985.

40 "Freshman Leads NU Wrestlers," *Lincoln Journal Star*, December 4, 1986; "Husker Wrestlers Tip Drake," *Lincoln Journal Star*, February 28, 1987; "NU Wrestlers Excel," *Lincoln Journal Star*, April 19, 1987; "NU Wrestler Jim Sanchez Goes 1–1," *Lincoln Journal Star*, July 15, 1987; Virgil Parker, "Cornhusker Wrestlers Vent Their Frustrations," *Lincoln Journal Star*, February 16, 1988; "Wrestling," *Lincoln Journal Star*, December 18, 1988; Michael Larsen, "Depleted NU Wrestling Team Triumphs," *Lincoln Star*, February 16, 1989; Michael Larsen, "NU Wrestlers Pin No, 12 Minnesota," *Lincoln Journal Star*, Feb-

ruary 16, 1989; "National Open Freestyle," *Amateur Wrestling News* 32, no. 13. See also email from Jim Sanchez to author, September 12, 2023.

41 Jim Sanchez's resume, copy in author's possession. See also email from Jim Sanchez to author, August 31, 2023.

42 Unless otherwise noted, the quotes by Frank Sanchez come from an interview conducted by me in January 2021 with Dr. Sanchez.

43 Frank Sanchez, interview with author, January 2021. See also the following articles from the *Casper Star-Tribune*: Greg Livovich, "Mustang Sit Atop Wrestling Ranks," February 15, 1985; "No Individual Champs, but Green River Wins," February 24, 1985; "Natrona Coach Thinks Pride Lifted Wolves to 4-A Victory," February 25, 1985; "State Grapplers Head Overseas," June 14, 1985; Dennis Durband, "A Great Time for Fun, Learning Other Cultures," February 21, 1986 (contains Candelaria quote).

44 Frank Sanchez, interview with author, January 2021. For introductory information on the Mexican American experience in the state of Nebraska, see Roger P. Davis, "Latinos Along the Platte: The Hispanic Experience in Central Nebraska," *Great Plains Research* 12 (Spring 2001): 27–50; and Bryan Winston, "Mexican Community Formation in Nebraska, 1910–1950," *Nebraska History* 100, no. 1 (2019): 3–19. For information on Jason Kelber, see "JASON KELBER: 2013 Iowa Wrestling Hall of Fame Inductee," accessed on September 7, 2023, https://www.iowawrestlinghalloffame.com/inductee/jason-kelber.

45 Frank Sanchez, interview with author, January 2021.

46 Frank Sanchez, interview with author, January 2021. See also Claudine McCarthy, "Learn What It Takes to Become a College President," *Dean and Provost* 19, no. 8 (February 2018): 12; and "Dr. Frank Sanchez Named President of Manhattanville College," June 27, 2023, accessed on September 8, 2023, see https://www.mville.edu/news/dr-frank-sanchez-named-president-of-manhattanville-college.php.

47 Email from Glenn Sanchez to author, September 12, 2023; interview with Glenn Sanchez, September 22, 2023.

48 Emails from Greg Sanchez to author, August 10, 2023, and September 15, 2023. See also these articles from *The Daily Sentinel*: "On the Scoreboard," February 12, 1990; "On the Scoreboard," February 16, 1990; and "Wrestlers Begin Action in Prep All-State Games," February 20, 1990.

49 Email from Phil Sanchez to author, September 7, 2023.

50 Email from Phil Sanchez to author, September 15, 2023

51 Email from Phil Sanchez to author, September 15, 2023. See also Sanchez Sports Academy, accessed September 12, 2023, https://mrsanchezsportsacademy.weebly.com; "Palm Springs Grant Recipients Hit a Bullseye on Behalf of Their Middle School Physical Education Students," *California Teachers Association Institute for Teaching: CTA Board Report*, May 2016; and Joan L. Boiko, "Palm Springs Archery Program Target's Student Behavior," *Desert Sun*, May 9, 2016.

52 "3A Brackets," *Daily Sentinel*, February 16, 1987; "On the Scoreboard: Prep Wrestling," *Daily Sentinel*, February 21, 1987.

53 See "Wrestling: A Sanchez Family Tradition," accessed on September 21, 2023, https://sanchezwrestlinghistory.weebly.com/; Ray Sanchez Facebook page,

https://www.facebook.com/raymond.sanchez.39; and Raymond Sanchez, interview with author, October 3, 2023.

54 Britt Sanchez, interview with author, September 30, 2023.

55 Britt Sanchez, interview with author, September 30, 2023.

56 All of the following articles are from the *Casper Star-Tribune*: "Rawlins 49, Torrington 9," December 23, 1991; "Rawlins 38, Douglas 23," January 4, 1992; "Cheyenne East 32, Rawlins 30," February 17, 1992; "1992 Wyoming State High School Wrestling Qualifiers," February 28, 1992; "Wyoming State High School Wrestling Championships Results," February 29, 1992; "State Wrestling Champions," March 1, 1992; "Wrestling," March 2, 1992; "Prep All-Conference," April 2, 1992; "Wyoming State High School Wrestling Championships Results," February 28, 1993; and "State Wrestling Champions," March 1, 1993.

57 Pat Rooney, "Wrestling: Niwot Mourns Passing of Former Coach Gary Daum," Boulder County High School Sports (BOCOPreps.com), September 24, 2012, accessed September 15, 2023, https://www.bocopreps.com/2012/09/24/wrestling-niwot-mourns-passing-of-former-coach-gary-daum/.

58 Pat Rooney, "Wrestling: Niwot Mourns Passing"; Pat Rooney, "Wrestling: Coaching Shuffle Underway at Niwot, Longmont," Boulder County High School Sports (BOCOPreps.com), May 20, 2014, accessed September 15, 2023, https://www.bocopreps.com/2014/05/20/wrestling-coaching-shuffle-underway-at-niwot-longmont/. See also interview with Scott Sanchez, September 25, 2023.

Conclusion: The Most Recent Generation of Sanchezes on the Mat and the Significance of Sport in Latino/Hispanic History and Life

1 Interview with Scott Sanchez, September 25, 2023.

2 Interview with Scott Sanchez, September 25, 2023. See also "Wrestling," *Casper Star-Tribune*, January 9, 2023; "Wrestling," *Casper Star-Tribune*, January 19, 2023; Jeremiah Johnke, "East Sammy Sanchez Adding to Family Legacy," *WyoSports*, February 18, 2023, https://www.wyomingnews.com/wyosports/high_school/cheyenne_east/easts-sammy-sanchez-adding-to-family-legacy/article_6299eb38-af37-11ed-a13d-afb068f49ad3.html; "Regional Wrestling," *Casper Star-Tribune*, February 19, 2023; and "State Wrestling Roundup," *Casper Star-Tribune*, February 26, 2023.

3 Interview with Ray Sanchez, October 3, 2023. See also "Wrestling: A Sanchez Family Tradition," https://sanchezwrestlinghistory.weeby.com/.

4 "4- and 3-Time Champions," *Casper Star-Tribune*, February 27, 2010.

5 Spencer Condie, email to author, January 11, 2022.

6 See "Wrestling: Wyoming State Champions, Individual," accessed October 16, 2023, https://champlists.com/wrestling/individual/. For a review of the role of Latinos in collegiate wrestling, see Jorge Iber and Lee Maril, *Latino American Wrestling Experience: Over 100 Years of Wrestling Heritage in the United States* (Stillwater, OK: National Wrestling Hall of Fame 2014), https://nwhof.org/latinowrestling.

7 Joe Ramirez Jr. oral history interview, January 1983 for the La Cultura Hispanic Heritage Oral History Project, OH 854. See also Joe Ramirez Jr. obituary, accessed on April 18, 2024, Obituary for Joe Ramirez Jr., Gorman Funeral Homes (gormanfh.com).

8 For an examination of wrestling and a Mexican American athlete for a popular audience, see Henry Cejudo and Bill Plaschke, *American Victory: Wrestling, Dreams, and a Journey Toward Home* (New York: CELEBRA, 2011).

9 John M. Barron et al., "The Effects of High School Athletic Participation on Education and Labor Market Outcomes," *Review of Economics and Statistics*, 82, no. 3 (2000): 409–421; quotes from pages 409 and 420; Bradley T. Ewing, "The Labor Market Effects of High School Athletic Participation: Evidence from Wage and Fringe Benefit Differentials," *Journal of Sport Economics* 8, no. 3 (June 2007): 255–265; quotes from 262 and 263.

10 Lindsey Darvin et al., "¿Por Qué Jugar? Sport Socialization Among Hispanic/Latina Female Division I Student Athletes," *Journal of Amateur Sport*, 3, no. 2 (2017): 27–54.

11 Darvin et al., "¿Por Qué Jugar?," 31.

12 Darvin et al., "¿Por Qué Jugar?," 37, 38, and 39.

13 Darvin et al., "¿Por Qué Jugar?," 37, 38, and 39.

14 Juan M. Hinojosa, "The Effects of Athletic Sport Teams Participation on Hispanic High School Student Academic Achievement" (PhD diss., Texas A&M University–Kingsville, 2018).

15 Hinojosa, "The Effects of Athletic Sport Teams Participation," 56 and 57.

16 Hinojosa, "The Effects of Athletic Sport Teams Participation," 60, 61, 63, and 66.

17 Luis A. Inoa, "Latino Males in the U.S. and the Effect of High School Sports Participation on a Multi-Dimensional Construct of Academic Achievement" (PhD diss., State University of New York at Albany, 2018), 1–2.

18 Inoa, "Latino Males in the U.S.," 61.

19 Inoa, "Latino Males in the U.S.," 93 and 157.

20 Inoa, "Latino Males in the U.S.," 145 and 157.

21 Sylvia Martinez and Evan Mickey, "The Effects of Participation in Interscholastic Sports on Latino Students' Academic Achievement," *Journal for the Study of Sports and Athletes in Education* 7, no. 2 (August 2013): 97–114.

22 Martinez and Mickey, "Effects of Participation in Interscholastic Sports," 103.

23 Martinez and Mickey, "Effects of Participation in Interscholastic Sports," 108–109.

24 Martinez and Mickey, "Effects of Participation in Interscholastic Sports," 112.

25 See Manuel Silva, "Factors That Influence the Participation of Latinos in Intercollegiate Athletics" (PhD diss., Claremont Graduate School, Claremont, CA, 2014); and Guillermo Ortega, "Understanding Experiences, Engagement, and Persistence for Latina/o Student-Athletes" (PhD diss., University of Houston, 2020). For specific research on why Latino college-level athletes tend to be overlooked, see Azadeh F. Osanloo et al., "'Los Olvidados': An Integrative Review of the Extant Literature Review on the Forgotten Ones in Intercollegiate Athletics," *Journal for the Study of Sports and Athletes in Education* 12, no. 1 (2018): 53–74.

26 Silva, "Factors That Influence the Participation of Latinos in Intercollegiate Athletics," 67.

27 Brett Thomas Olmsted, "Los Mexicanos de Michigan: Claiming Space and Creating Community Through Leisure and Labor, 1920–1970" (PhD diss., University of Houston, 2017).

28 Silva, "Factors That Influence the Participation of Latinos in Intercollegiate Athletics," 70.

29 Silva, "Factors That Influence the Participation of Latinos in Intercollegiate Athletics," 88.

30 Ortega, "Understanding Experiences, Engagement, and Persistence for Latina/o Student-Athletes," 34, 46, and 72.

31 Snellman et al., "The Engagement Gap: Social Mobility and Extracurricular Participation Among American Youth," *Annals of the Academy of American Political and Social Science* 657 (January 2015): 194–207; quote from 204.

32 Emails from Mary Louise Sanchez and Gil Sanchez Sr. to author, April 7 and 22, 2020.

Bibliography

Alamillo, José M. "*Peloteros* in Paradise: Mexican American Baseball and Oppositional Politics in Southern California, 1930–1950." *Western Historical Quarterly* 34, no. 2 (2003): 191–211.

Alanís Enciso, Fernando Saúl. *They Should Stay There: The Story of Mexican Migration and Repatriation During the Great Depression*. Chapel Hill: University of North Carolina Press, 2017.

Aldama, Frederick Luis, and Christopher González. *Latinos in the End Zone: Conversations on the Brown Color Line in the NFL*. New York: Palgrave MacMillan, 2014.

Anderson, Marc C. "What's to Be Done with 'Em'? Images of Cultural Backwardness, Racial Limitations, and Moral Decrepitude in the United States Press, 1913–1915." *Mexican Studies / Estudios Mexicanos* (Winter 1998): 23–70.

Arnold, Peg. "Wyoming's Hispanic Sheepherders." *Annals of Wyoming* 69 (Winter 1997): 29–42.

Barron, John M., Bradley T. Ewing, and Glenn R. Waddell. "The Effects of High School Athletic Participation on Education and Labor Market Outcomes." *Review of Economics and Statistics* 82, no. 3 (2000): 409–421.

Bortz, Jeffrey, and Marcos Aguila. "Earning a Living: A History of Real Wage Studies in Twentieth Century Mexico." *Latin American Research Review* 41, no. 2 (2006): 112–138.

Carey, Matthew. "LA Film Festival: 'The Classic' Tells of East L.A. Football Rivalry with Much More at Stake than a Game." *Non Fiction Film*, June 21, 2017. Accessed August 9,

https://doi.org/10.5876/9781646427529.c007

2022, https://www.nonfictionfilm.com/news/la-film-festival-the-classic-tells-of-east-la-football-rivalry-with-much-more-at-stake-than-a-game.

Carlson, Lewis H. *Remembered Prisoners of a Forgotten War: An Oral History of Korean War POWs*. New York: St. Martin's Press, 2002.

Cejudo, Henry, and Bill Plaschke. *American Victory: Wrestling, Dreams, and a Journey Toward Home*. New York: CELEBRA, 2011.

Chappell, Ben. *Mexican American Fastpitch: Identity at Play in a Vernacular Sport*. Palo Alto, CA: Stanford University Press, 2021.

Chavez, David Julian. "Civic Education of the Spanish-American." MA thesis, University of Texas, Austin, 1923.

Cheyenne, Wyoming, 1940–1955: WWII National Defense Work Shortage of Living Quarters Justifying the Construction of Federal Housing Projects. Thousand Oaks, CA: UBuildABook, 2016.

Cohen, Robert W. *The 50 Greatest Players in Green Bay Packers History*. Guilford, CT: Lyons Press, 2018.

Cuadros, Paul. "'Fútbol Femenino' Comes to the New South: Latina Integration Through Soccer." In *Latinos and Latinas in American Sport: Stories Beyond Peloteros*, edited by Jorge Iber, 235–254. Lubbock: Texas Tech University Press, 2020.

Darvin, Lindsey, Alicia Cintron, and Meg Hancock. "¿Por Qué Jugar? Sport Socialization Among Hispanic/Latina Female Division I Student Athletes." *Journal of Amateur Sport* 3, no. 2 (2017): 27–54.

De León, Arnoldo. "Our Gringo Amigos: Anglo Americans and the Tejano Experience." *East Texas Historical Journal* 31, no. 2 (1993): 72–79.

De León, Arnoldo. *They Called Them Greasers: Anglo Attitudes Toward Mexicans in Texas, 1836–1900*. Austin: University of Texas Press, 1983.

Delgado, Fernando. "Golden but Not Brown: Oscar De La Hoya and the Complications of Culture, Manhood, and Boxing." *International Journal of the History of Sport* 22, no. 2 (March 2005): 196–211.

Dupre, Florie S. "Play as a Factor in the Education of Children." PhD dissertation, University of Texas, Austin, 1925.

Early, Gerald. "Birdland: Two Observations on the Cultural Significance of Baseball." *American Poetry Review* (July/August 1996): 9–10. Accessed March 16, 2022, https://www.writing.upenn.edu/~afilreis/50s/baseball.html.

Ewing, Bradley T. "The Labor Market Effects of High School Athletic Participation: Evidence from Wage and Fringe Benefit Differentials." *Journal of Sport Economics* 8, no. 3 (June 2007): 255–265.

Folsom-Cobb. "Comparative Study of Athletic Ability of Latin American and Anglo-American Boys on a Junior High School Level." MA thesis, University of Texas, Austin, 1952.

Fonseca, Vanessa. "'Donde mi amor se ha quedado': Narratives of Sheepherding and *Querencia* Along the Wyoming Manito Trail." *Annals of Wyoming* 89, nos. 2–3 (Spring–Summer 2017): 6–12.

Freedman, Lew. *Jump Shot: Kenny Sailors, Basketball Innovator and Alaskan Outfitter*. Portland, OR: Westwind Press, 2015.

García, Alephonso. "Beet Seasons in Wyoming: Mexican American Family Life on a Sugar Beet Farm near Wheatland During World War II." *Annals of Wyoming* 73, no. 2 (Spring 2001): 14–17.

García, Ignacio M. *When Mexicans Could Play Ball: Basketball, Race, and Identity in San Antonio, 1928–1945*. Austin: University of Texas Press, 2014.

Garcia, Ignacio. "William Carson 'Nemo' Herrera: Constructing a Mexican American Powerhouse While Remaining Colorblind." In *Latinos and Latinas in American Sport: Stories Beyond Peloteros*, edited by Jorge Iber, 33–46. Lubbock: Texas Tech University Press, 2020.

Gmelch, George, ed. *Baseball Beyond Our Borders: An International Pastime*. Lincoln: University of Nebraska Press, 2017.

Gomberg-Muñoz, Ruth. "Not Just Mexico's Problem: Migration from Mexico to the United States, 1900–2000." *Journal of Latino/Latin American Studies* 3, no. 3 (Spring 2009): 2–18.

Gonzales, Manuel G. *Mexicanos: A History of Mexicans in the United States*. 3rd ed. Bloomington: Indiana University Press, 2019.

Grenardo, David A. "It's Worth a Shot: Can Sports Combat Racism in the United States?" *Journal of Sports and Entertainment Law* 12 (2021): 237–318.

Guzmán, Gonzalo. "Education for a New Race: White Schools, Child Labor, and Creating the Mexican in the Equality State, 1917–1941." PhD dissertation, University of Washington, Seattle, 2018.

Guzmán, Gonzalo. "'This Change You Know': Schools as the Architects of the Mexican Race in Depression-Era Wyoming." *History of Education Quarterly* 61 (2021): 392–422.

Halberstam, David. *The Coldest Winter: America and the Korean War*. New York: Hyperion, 2007.

Hastings, Max. *The Korean War*. New York: Touchstone Books, published by Simon and Schuster, 1987.

Heiskanen, Benita. "The *Latinization* of Boxing: A Texas Case Study." *Journal of Sport History* 32, no. 1 (Spring 2005): 45–66.

Heiskanen, Benita. *The Urban Geography of Boxing: Race, Class, and Gender in the Ring*. New York: Routledge, 2012.

Hewitt, William L. "Mexican Workers in Wyoming During World War II: Necessity, Discrimination, and Protest." *Annals of Wyoming* 54, no. 2 (1982): 20–34.

Hinojosa, Juan M. "The Effects of Athletic Sport Teams Participation on Hispanic High School Student Academic Achievement." PhD dissertation, Texas A&M University–Kingsville, 2018.

Huginnie, Andrea Yvette. "'Strikitos': Race, Class, and Work in the Arizona Copper Industry, 1870–1930." PhD dissertation, Yale University, New Haven, CT, 1991.

Iber, Jorge, ed. *Latinos and Latinas in American Sport: Stories Beyond Peloteros*. Lubbock: Texas Tech University Press, 2020.

Iber, Jorge. "Mexican Americans of South Texas Football: The Athletic and Coaching Careers of E. C. Lerma and Bobby Cavazos, 1932–1965." In *More than Just Peloteros: Sport and US Latino Communities*, edited by Jorge Iber, 184–205. Lubbock: Texas Tech University Press, 2014.

Iber, Jorge. "Mexico: Baseball's Humble Beginnings to Budding Competitor." In *Baseball Beyond Our Borders: An International Pastime*, edited by George Gmelch, 75–84. Lincoln: University of Nebraska Press, 2017.

Iber, Jorge. *Mike Torrez: A Baseball Biography*. Jefferson, NC: McFarland and Company Inc., Publishers, 2016.Iber, Jorge. "On-Field Foes and Racial Misperceptions: The 1961 Donna Redskins and Their Drive to the Texas State Football Championship." In *Mexican Americans and Sport: A Reader on Athletics and Barrio Life*, edited by Jorge Iber and Samuel O. Regalado, 121–144. College Station: Texas A&M University Press, 2007.

Iber, Jorge. "The Sanchezes of Cheyenne, Wyoming: The First Generation of a Family of Wrestlers at the Local, State, and National Stage." *Annals of Wyoming* 92, no. 4 (Autumn 2020–Winter 2021): 2–17.

Iber, Jorge, and Lee Maril. *Latino American Wrestling Experience: Over 100 Years of Wrestling Heritage in the United States*. Stillwater, OK: National Wrestling Hall of Fame, 2013. https://nwhof.org/latinowrestling.

Iber, Jorge, and Samuel O. Regalado. *Mexican Americans and Sport: A Reader on Athletics and Barrio Life*. College Station: Texas A&M University Press, 2007.

Iber, Jorge, Samuel O. Regalado, Jose M. Alamillo, and Arnoldo De Leon. *Latinos in U.S. Sports: A History of Isolation, Cultural Identity, and Acceptance*. Champaign, IL: Human Kinetics, 2011.

Inoa, Luis A. "Latino Males in the U.S. and the Effect of High School Sports Participation on a Multi-Dimensional Construct of Academic Achievement." PhD dissertation, University of Albany, State University of New York, 2018.

Jamieson, Katherine M. "Advance at Your Own Risk: Latinas, Families and Collegiate Softball." In *Mexican Americans and Sport: A Reader on Athletics and Barrio Life*, edited by Jorge Iber and Samuel O. Regalado, 213–232. College Station: Texas A&M University Press, 2007.

Jewitt, Keith. "The Spanish-Speaking Students in Laramie High School, 1940–1950." MA thesis, University of Wyoming, Laramie, 1950.

King, Genevieve. "The Psychology of a Mexican American Community in San Antonio, Texas." MA thesis, University of Texas, Austin, 1936.

Knight, Alan. *The Mexican Revolution*, vol. 1: *Porfirians, Liberals, and Peasants*. Lincoln: University of Nebraska Press, 1986.

Lapchick, Richard. "The 2021 Racial and Gender Report Card: College Sports." Annual report of the Institute for Diversity and Ethics in Sports. Orlando: University of Central Florida, 2021.

Longoria, Mario, and Jorge Iber. *Latinos in American Football: Pathbreakers on the Gridiron, 1927 to the Present*. Jefferson, NC: McFarland and Company Inc, Publishers, 2020.

López, Emily A. "Mexican American Veterans, Class and Identity During and After World War II." MA thesis, University of Wyoming, Laramie, 2015.

López-Alonso, Moramay. "Growth with Inequality: Living Standards in Mexico, 1850–1950." *Journal of Latin American Studies* 39, no. 1 (February 2007): 81–105.

Macias, Jennifer. "The Years After World War II: Latinx Families in Wyoming." *Annals of Wyoming* 89, nos. 2–3 (Spring–Summer 2017): 25–31.

Marin, Christine. "Courting Success and Realizing the American Dream: Arizona's Mighty Miami High School Championship Basketball Team, 1951." In *More than Just Peloteros: Sport and US Latino Communities*, edited by Jorge Iber, 150–183. Lubbock: Texas Tech University Press, 2014.

Martinez, Sylvia, and Evan Mickey. "The Effects of Participation in Interscholastic Sports on Latino Students' Academic Achievement." *Journal for the Study of Sports and Athletes in Education* 7, no. 2 (August 2013): 97–114.

Martinez, Trisha Venisa-Alicia. "Living the Manito Trail: Maintaining Self, Culture, and Community." PhD dissertation, University of New Mexico, Albuquerque, 2019.

Mitchell, Elmer. "Racial Traits in Athletics." *American Physical Education Review* 27, no. 3 (March 1922): 93–99.

Mitchell, Elmer. "Racial Traits in Athletics." *American Physical Education Review* 27, no. 4, (April 1922): 147–152.

Mitchell, Elmer. "Racial Traits in Athletics." *American Physical Education Review* 27, no. 5, (May 1922): 197–206.

Molina, Natalia. *Fit to Be Citizens? Public Health and Race in Los Angeles, 1879–1939*. Berkeley: University of California Press, 2006.

Molina, Natalia. *How Race Is Made in America: Immigration, Citizenship, and the Historical Power of Racial Scripts*. Berkeley: University of California Press, 2014.

Montoya, Camila. "Not a Sweet Deal: Mexican Migrant Workers in the Sugar Beet Farms of the Midwest and Mountain States, 1900–1930." MA thesis, Michigan State University, East Lansing, 2000.

Morin, Raul. *Among the Valiant: Mexican Americans in WWII and Korea*. Los Angeles: Borden Publishing Company, 1963.

Nuñez, Alex. "Switch-Hitting: Mexican Diaspora, Whiteness, and Tusconense Baseball, 1903–1954." *Journal of Arizona History* 62, no. 4 (Winter 2021): 563–582.

Olmsted, Brett Thomas. "Los Mexicanos de Michigan: Claiming Space and Creating Community Through Leisure and Labor, 1920–1970." PhD dissertation, University of Houston, 2017.

Oriard, Michael. *King Football: Sport and Spectacle in the Golden Age of Radio and Newsreels, Movies and Magazines, the Weekly and Daily Press*. Chapel Hill: University of North Carolina Press, 2001.

Oriard, Michael. *Reading Football: How the Popular Press Created an American Spectacle*. Chapel Hill: University of North Carolina Press, 1993.

Ortega, Guillermo. "Understanding Experiences, Engagement, and Persistence for Latina/o Student-Athletes." PhD dissertation, University of Houston, 2020.

Osanloo, Azadeh F., Julia L. Parra, and Chadrhyn A. A. Pedraza. "'Los Olvidados': An Integrative Review of the Extant Literature Review on the Forgotten Ones in Intercollegiate Athletics." *Journal for the Study of Sports and Athletes in Education* 12, no. 1 (2018): 53–74.

Overstreet, Daphne. "ON STRIKE! The 1917 Walkout at Globe, Arizona." *Journal of Arizona History* 18, no. 2 (Summer 1977): 197–218.

Park, Joseph F. "The 1903 'Mexican Affair' at Clifton." *Journal of Arizona History* 18, no. 2 (Summer 1977): 119–148.

Pescador, Juan Javier. "Los Heroes del Domingo: Soccer, Borders, and Social Spaces in Great Lakes Mexican Communities, 1940–1970." In *Mexican Americans and Sport: A Reader on Athletics and Barrio Life*, edited by Jorge Iber and Samuel O. Regalado, 73–88. College Station: Texas A&M University Press, 2007.

Rankine, Margaret E. "The Mexican Mining Industry in the Nineteenth Century with Special Reference to Guanajuato." *Bulletin of Latin American Research* 11, no. 1 (January 1992): 29–48.

Regalado, Samuel O. "Baseball in the Barrios: The Scene in East Los Angeles Since World War II." *Baseball History* 1, no. 2 (Summer 1986): 47–59.

Rodriguez, Alberto. "Ponte El Guante! Baseball on the US-Mexican Border: The Game and Community Building, 1920s–1970s." In *Latinos and Latinas in American Sport: Stories Beyond Peloteros*, edited by Jorge Iber, 63–78. Lubbock: Texas Tech University Press, 2020.

Rodríguez, Gregory S. "Palaces of Pain—Arenas of Mexican American Dreams: Boxing and the Formation of Ethnic Mexican Identities in Twentieth Century Los Angeles." PhD dissertation, University of California–San Diego, 1999.

Romero, Tom I., II. "Wearing the Red, White, and Blue Trunks of Aztlan: Rodolfo 'Corky' Gonzales and the Convergence of American and Chicano Nationalism." In *Latinos and Latinas in American Sport: Stories Beyond Peloteros*, edited by Jorge Iber, 89–120. Lubbock: Texas Tech University Press, 2020.

Rondinone, Troy. *Friday Night Fighter: Gaspar "Indio" Ortega and the Golden Age of Television Boxing*. Urbana: University of Illinois Press, 2013.

Rosales, Miguel A. "A Mexican Railroad Family in Wyoming" *Annals of Wyoming* 73, no. 2 (2001): 28–32.

Sanchez, George J. *Boyle Heights: How a Los Angeles Neighborhood Became the Future of American Democracy*. Oakland: University of California Press, 2021.

Sanchez, Virginia. "Pal Norte: The Sanchez and Espinoza 1940s Family Migration from Mora County, New Mexico to Cheyenne, Wyoming." *Annals of Wyoming* 89, nos. 2–3 (Spring–Summer 2017): 16–24.

Sandoval, T. Joe. "A Study of Some Aspects of the Spanish-Speaking Population in Selected Communities in Wyoming." MA thesis, University of Wyoming, Laramie, 1946.

Santillan, Richard, and Francisco E. Balderrama. "Los Chorizeros: The New York Yankees of East Los Angeles and the Reclaiming of Mexican American Baseball History." Society for American Baseball Research (2011). Accessed August 9, 2022, https://sabr.org/journal/article/los-chorizeros-the-new-york-yankees-of-east-los-angeles-and-the-reclaiming-of-mexican-american-baseball-history/.

Schoening-Aiken, Ellen. "The United Mine Workers of America Move West: Race, Working Class Formation, and the Discourse on Cultural Diversity in the Union Pacific Coal Towns of Southern Wyoming, 1870–1930." PhD dissertation, University of Colorado, Boulder, 2002.

Silva, Manuel. "Factors That Influence the Participation of Latinos in Intercollegiate Athletics." PhD dissertation, Claremont Graduate School, Claremont, CA, 2014.

Snellman, Kaisa, Jennifer M. Silva, Carl B. Frederick, and Robert D. Putnam. "The Engagement Gap: Social Mobility and Extracurricular Participation Among American

Youth." *Annals of the Academy of American Political and Social Science* 657 (January 2015): 194–207.

Standish, Peter. *The States of Mexico: A Reference Guide to History and Culture*. Westport, CT: Greenwood Press, 2009.

Surdam, Joyce A. "Political Attitudes of Mexican American and Anglo-American Students at Laramie Senior High School." MA thesis, University of Wyoming, Laramie, 1970.

Thompson, Merrell E., and Chuck D. Dove. "A Comparison of Physical Achievement of Anglo and Spanish American Boys in Junior High School." *Research Quarterly* 13 (October 1942): 341–346.

Trouille, David. *Fútbol in the Park: Immigrants, Soccer, and the Creation of Social Ties*. Chicago: University of Chicago Press, 2021.

Walsh-Shaw, Bruce. "Sociometric Status and Athletic Ability in Anglo American and Latin American Boys in a San Antonio Junior High School." MA thesis, University of Texas, Austin, 1951.

Watterson, John Sayle. *College Football: History, Spectacle, Controversy*. Baltimore, MD: Johns Hopkins University Press, 2000.

Wylie, Philip. *Generation of Vipers*. 2nd ed. London: Dalkey Archive Press, 1986.

La Cultura Hispanic Heritage Oral History Project Interviews

Archuleta, Frances and Bernardo, January 1983, OH 844
Arias, Nellie, no date listed, OH 904D
Bustos, Catherine, July 1982, OH 824
DeHerrera, Abe, June 1983, OH 884
DeHerrera, Esther, June 1983, OH 885
Fuentes, Jose C., January 1982, OH 868
Gómez-Mercado, Oralia, July 1983, OH 886
Mascarenos, Henry, January 1983, OH 889
Montano, José Leandro, December 1981, OH 832
Palma-Sandoval, Celso, May 1983, OH 903
Ramirez, Joe, Jr., January 1983, OH 854
Rodriguez, Rafaela, March 1983, OH 875
Sanchez, Alicia, August 1982, OH 842
Sanchez, Leo Richard, January 1983, OH 877
Sanchez, Paul, December 1981, OH 858
Trujillo, Victoriano, January 1983, OH 859

Sanchez Family Materials and Interviews (in Author's Possession)

Interview with Britt Sanchez, September 30, 2023
Interview with Frank Sanchez, January 2021
Interview with Glenn Sanchez, September 22, 2023

Interview with Ray Sanchez, October 3, 2023
Interview with Scott Sanchez, September 25, 2023
Ray Sanchez's personal scrapbook
"Wrestling: A Sanchez Family Tradition," https://sanchezwrestling.weebly.com

Emails from Sanchez Family Members and Others (in Author's Possession)

Arthur Sanchez to author, February 15, 2023
Arthur Sanchez to author, March 14, 2023
Arthur Sanchez to author, April 24, 2023
Arthur and Mary Louise Sanchez to author, April 26, 2020
Gilbert Sanchez to author, April 7, 2020
Gilbert Sanchez to author, March 28, 2023
Glenn Sanchez to author, September 12, 2023
Greg Sanchez to author, August 10, 2023
Greg Sanchez to author, September 20, 2023
Jim Sanchez to author, April 26, 2020
Jim Sanchez to author, May 4, 2023
Jim Sanchez to author, August 7, 2023
Jim Sanchez to author, August 31, 2023
Jim Sanchez to author, September 12, 2023
Mary Louise Sanchez to author, April 7, 2020
Mary Louise Sanchez to author, April 22, 2020
Phil Sanchez to author, September 7, 2023
Phil Sanchez to author, September 15, 2023
Spencer Condie to author, January 11, 2022

Newspapers/Magazines

Akron Beacon Journal
Amateur Wrestling News
Anderson Independent-Mail
Associated Press
Beatrice Daily Sun
Beaufort Gazette
Billings Gazette
Binghamton Press and Sun-Bulletin
Casper Morning Star
Casper Star-Tribune
Casper Tribune-Herald
Chadron Record
Columbus Telegram

Crawford Tribune
Daily Sentinel
Daily Times
Denver Post
Desert Sun
Des Moines Register
Ft. Collins Coloradoan
Fremont Tribune
Greeley Daily Tribune
Greenville News
Index-Journal
Island Packet
Laramie Daily Boomerang
Lincoln Journal Star
Lincoln Star
Longmont Times-Caller
Medina County Gazette
Miami Herald
Muskogee Daily Phoenix
New York Times
Omaha World-Herald
Pittsburgh Press
St. Louis Post-Dispatch
Sports Illustrated
The State
Stillwater News-Press
Times and Democrat
Tulsa Daily World
White Plains Daily Argus
Wyoming Eagle
Wyoming News
Wyoming State Tribune
Wyoming Tribune Eagle
WyoSports

Index

AAU Rocky Mountain meet, 71
Abeyta, Jesse, 131
Abrams, Dan, 78
Aguila, Marcos, 18–19
Alamillo, José M., 7, 8–9, 46, 47
Aldama, Frederick Luis, 52, 54–55
Alirez, Andrew Jr., 124
Alirez, Andrew Sr., 117, 124
All-Wyoming Cultural Exchange team, 113, 114
Alvarez, Luis, 46, 47
Amateur Athletic Union (AAU), 66, 68, 71, 84–88, 89, 91
American GI Forum (AGIF), 62
American Physical Education Review (Mitchell), 9–11
Among the Valiant (Morin), 60–61
Anderson, Chris, 106
Anderson, Jim, 90
Antrev, Miazbeh, 109
Aoki, Hiroaka ("Rocky"), 65, 66, 68, 74
Aragón, Art, 49
archery, 124–25
Archuleta, Bernardo, 30
Archuleta, Frances, 30
Arias, Nellie, 34
Arnold, Peg, 22
Asher-Wyoming Company, 31
ASU Invitational, 92
Atlantic Coast Conference (ACC), 110
Aullman, Lee, 127

Babka, Richard, 4
Bailey, Leo, 106
Barnes, David, 77–78
Barrera, Lefty, 49
Barron, John M., 133
Barzun, Jacques, 142*n12*
baseball, 46–48
basketball, 56–57
Battery Creek High, 113
Battle of Unsan (1950), 32

beet farming, 22–23, 24
Benavides High School, 53–54
Bengston, Gene, 83
Big 8, 102–3, 106, 108–9
bilingualism, 39
Bingham, Mike, 70
Blaha, Buddy, 108
Borquez, Bryan, 125
borregueros, 22
Bortz, Jeffrey, 18–19
Bowker, Stan, 82
boxing, 48–51
Brown, Larry, 37, 42, 138
Burgener, Scott, 127
Bush, Bill, 85
Bustos, Catherine, 33–34

Campbell, Matt, 103
Campos, Ray, 78
Candelaria, Don, 118
Carey Junior High School, 98, 128, 129–30
Carr, Joe, 99
Casper Star-Tribune, 131
Castillo, Fernando, 53
Cavanaugh, Steve, 90
Cavazos, Bobby, 54
Chappell, Ben, 48
Chavez, Cesar, 119
Chavez, David Julian, 9
Chávez, Julio César, 49
Chávez, Rafael, 131
Cherry, Jack, 108
Cheyenne Central High School (CCHS): Art wrestles for, 77–78; Frank wrestles for, 117–18; Gil Jr. wrestles for, 102; Jim wrestles for, 113–15; Ray wrestles for, 81–88; Scott teaches at, 128
Cheyenne East High School, 129
Cheyenne High School (CHS), 4, 37, 42–43, 99
Cheyenne Wrestling Club, 117, 129
Christopulos, Mike, 81
Cisneros, John, 131
Cisneros family, 131
Clark, Paul, 109
Classic, The (2017), 55
Clemson University, 110–12
Cobb, Albert Folsom, 11
Colina, Bert, 48–49
Colorado High School All-State Games, 122
Colorado State College, 68
Colorado State University (CSU), 69–74, 119–20, 137
Condie, Spencer, 131
Córdova, Jake, 131–32
Corr, Bert Jr., 65
Corr, Ed, 65
counterscripts, 8, 44, 45, 64, 95
Cuadros, Paul, 56
cultural exchanges, 113, 114, 118
Curtis, Wally, 71, 72, 73
Cuvo, Jack, 116

Darkus, Kevin, 104
Darvin, Lindsey, 134
Daum, Gary, 127
Davis, Barry, 107
DeAno, John, 72
DeHerrera, Abe, 97–98
De Herrera, Esther, 96
De La Hoya, Oscar, 49, 50
De León, Arnoldo, 7, 8–9, 42
Delgado, Dick, 65, 69
Delgado, Fernando, 49, 50
Dickenson, Lonnie, 83
discrimination: confronted by veterans, 62–63; experienced by Mexican American women, 34–35; experienced by Sanchezes, 137; experienced by Victoriano Trujillo, 68; against Mexican Americans, 4, 6–12, 34–35, 37–38; sports as combatting, 13–14. *See also* segregation
Division I (D-I) NCAAs, 116
Donna High School, 53
Doughty, Van, 72
Douglas, Bill, 83
Dove, Claude C., 11
Dowler, Boyd, 4
Dowler, Joe, 4–5, 82, 84–85, 86, 88
Dupre, Florrie S., 9

"Earning a Living: A History of Real Wage Studies in Twentieth Century Mexico" (Bortz and Aguila), 18–19

Eaton, Aileen, 51
Eddy, Ivan, 81
education: as barrier to Mexican Americans' entry into football pipeline, 55; of Mexican Americans, 37, 38; scholarship on, of minority students, 38–42, 95–97; sports' impact on academic achievement, 133, 135–37
Eighth Cavalry Regiment, 32
employment: educational circumstances and move toward better, 96–98; in Guanajuato, 18–19; and ill treatment of Spanish-surnamed workers, 23–24; of Marcelino Sanchez, 31, 60, 63; of Mexican Americans, 95; and migration to Wyoming, 20–23, 24–26; sports' impact on future, 133–34; of Susan Sanchez, 33; treatment and relations by race, 27–28
Espior World Championships, 114–15
Evanoff, Steve, 98, 99
Ewing, Bradley T., 133–34

Facinelli, Joe, 113–14
family values, 137–38
Fehrs, Bob, 78, 103, 104, 106
Fernández, Bob, 131
Fife, David, 122
"fitness for citizenship," 45–46, 101, 119
Fit to Be Citizens? (Molina), 7
Fitzpatrick, Tim, 107
Flores, Tom, 54
Focke, Jackson, 130
Fonseca, Vanessa, 21
football, 51–55
Fort Collins High School, 77–78
Freestyle wrestling, 64, 142*n6*
Frías, Oscar, 131
Frick, Jim, 109
Friday Night Fighter (Rondinone), 50–51
Frontier Villa, 35
Fuentes, Jose C., 29
Fujikawa, Wright, 81, 84, 90
fútbol, 55–56
"'Fútbol Femenino' Comes to the New South" (Cuadros), 56
Fútbol in the Park (Trouille), 56

Gable, Dan, 98
García, Alephonso, 24
García, Hector, 60
García, Ignacio M., 56–57
García Smith, Solomón, 48
Gardner, Rulon, 112
Gatorade All American, 114
Gator Bowl (1954), 54
Geidel, Jeremy, 122
gender identity, 50
Gibbons, Jeff, 105
GI Bill, 60, 63
Gómez Mercado, Oralia, 97
Gonzales, Claude, 72, 73
Gonzales, Justin, 131
Gonzales, Rodolfo "Corky," 49–50
González, Christopher, 52, 54–55
Graff, Tyler, 117
Grandstaff, Mike, 69
Grappling School, 64
Graven, Ricky, 73
Great Plains AAU Tournament, 76–77
Great Plains Wrestling Tournament, 89
Greco-Roman wrestling, 64–65, 142*n6*
Greeley West High School, 125
Grenardo, David A., 13–14, 133
Gribben, Joe, 108
Griffin, Eddie, 110
Grub, Warren, 74
Guadian, Manuel, 17, 29
Guadian, Mary, 29
Guadian, Michael, 29
Guadian, Olga, 29
Guadian, Rosemary, 29
Guadian, Valina Bonilla, 17, 29
Guanajuato, circumstances motivating migration from, 17–20
Gutiérrez, Dan, 81
Gutiérrez, Tony, 57
Guzmán, Gonzalo, 40–41, 95–96

Hansen, Clifford, 87
Hanson, Dave, 70
Hartman, Rick, 83
Heiskanen, Benita, 49, 50
Henjyoji, Grant, 91
Henjyoji, Rich, 85–86, 89
Henson, Sam, 110, 111, 112

Hernández, Ray, 81
Hernández family, 131
"Heroes del Domingo, Los" (Pescador), 55–56
Herrera, Nemo, 56–57
Hewitt, William L., 24, 26–27
Hilton Head Island Middle School, 112–13
Hines, Ken, 72, 73
Hinojosa, Juan M., 135
Hitoshi, Mayutama, 114
Horizon High School, 123
Howell, Kurt, 114
How Race Is Made (Molina), 7–8
Hughes, Bill, 73
Huginnie, Andrea Yvette, 27, 28

Iber, Jorge, 7, 8–9, 46, 48, 52–54
identity, *mexicano*, 118–19
immigration: circumstances motivating, 17–23; and employment, 24–26
industrialization, 18, 19
Inoa, Luis A., 135–36
Iowa State Teachers College, 70

James Workman Middle School, 124–25
Jamieson, Katherine M., 48
Jennings, Max, 84
Jewitt, Keith, 38–40
Johansen, Steve, 85
Johnson, Chad, 127
Johnson, Floyd, 77
Johnson, Greg, 91
Johnson, Rob, 109
Johnson Junior High School, 81, 98
Jordan, John, 66
Junior National Wrestling Championships, 114
Junior World Wrestling Championships, 98–99, 115

Kanno, Kenichi, 89
Kapp, Joe, 54–55
Kelber, Jason, 119
Keller, Dwayne, 86, 89
Kennedy, Bridgette, 124
Kestle, Dale, 86
King, Genevieve, 11
King Football (Oriard), 51–52
Knight, Alan, 18, 19–20
Knight, Dan, 114
Korean War, 31–33, 60–63
Krauder, Eil, 39
Kreimier, Josh, 117
Kuczewski, Len, 81
Kuh, George D., 120
Kujah, Dale, 92

Lage, Kurt, 106
Lamar Junior College, 68
Lander Valley High School, 93
Lane, Scott, 106
Laramie High Plainsmen, 43
Laramie High School, 96
Latinos in the End Zone (Aldama and González), 54–55
Latinos in U.S. Sports: A History of Isolation, Cultural Identity, and Acceptance (Iber et al.), 7, 8–9
League of United Latin American Citizens (LULAC), 62
Lee Williams High School, 126, 130
Lenz, Aaron, 122
Lerma, Everardo Carlos "E. C.," 53–54
Lewis, Randy, 109
Liams, Sam, 82
Little League, 45–46
living standards, in Mexico during late nineteenth and early twentieth centuries, 18–19
Lobof, Rod, 84
Logan, Noel, 110
Longoria, Mario, 52
López, Emily A., 60, 62–63
Lopez-Alonso, Moramay, 19
Lucas, Rick, 78
Lundberg, Eric, 81

Macias, Jennifer, 24, 27
Magafas, Alex, 106
Magomedkhan, Aratsilov, 99
Mantauch, Dan, 109
Manual High School, 100
Marin, Christine, 57
Marisette, Chris, 104
Martin, Jim, 114
Martínez, Jerry, 90

Martínez, Nolan, 131
Martínez, Sylvia, 136–37
Martínez, Trisha Venisa-Alicia, 21
MASA (Mexican American Student Association), 119
Mascarenas, Henry, 67
Maughan, Arthur, 74
Maughan, Bucky, 104
Maughan, Jack, 104, 106, 124
McCollum, Dan, 111
McCracken, Mark, 72
McDaniel, Joe C., 88, 92
McMillin, Billy, 55
McMinn, Glen, 75, 76, 90
Medbery, Connor, 117
Medina, Rudy, 82
Melchoir, Ken, 90
Mexican Americans: discrimination against, 4, 6–12, 34–35, 37–38; perception of, by educators, 40–41, 95–97; political awareness and activity of, 96; scholarship on majority-population perceptions of, 6, 7–8; transformation of aspirations of, 60–63
"Mexican Americans of South Texas Football" (Iber), 52, 53–54
"Mexican American Veterans, Class and Identity During and After World War II" (López), 60, 62–63
"Mexican labor," 28
mexicano identity, 118–19
"Mexicanos de Michigan, Los" (Olmsted), 12–13
Mexico, circumstances motivating migration from, 17–23
Meyer, Greg, 127
Miami High School Vandals, 57
Michelson, Leon, 92
Mickey, Evan, 136–37
Midlands Invitational, 103, 104
Miller, Andre, 108–9
Miller, Don, 92
mining, 24–25, 27–28
Mitchell, Elmer D., 9–11
Molina, Natalia, 6, 7–8
Montano, José, 66
Montoya, Camila, 22–24
Morgan, Alfred, 104
Morin, Raul, 60–61
Mountain Intercollegiate Wrestling Association, 73
Mueller, Ollney, 66
Mullison, Don "Tuffy," 73
Muro, Javier, 127
Murray, Calvin, 112–13

National Sports Festival, 102
Navarro, Cándido, 20
NCAA Nationals, 71, 73–74, 78, 90–91
Nedialho, Georgien, 114
Neff, John, 71
Nelson, Tim, 103
Nelson Land and Livestock Company, 22
Neumann, Tim, 106, 107, 108, 109
Neville, Nick, 106
Niwot High School, 127
North Dakota State University (NDSU), 104
Northern Iowa Open, 107
Northern Open Wrestling Tournament, 107
North High School, 98, 99
Norton, Tom, 72
Nuñez, Alex, 45–46, 48, 101, 119
Nuñez, Tommy, 45

"official racism," 62
Oldfield, Joe, 70
Oliver, Don, 54
Oliver, Greg, 112
Olmsted, Brett Thomas, 12–13
Olsen, Steve, 72
Olson, Anthony, 78
Olympic Training Center, 124
Olympic trials, 68–69, 74–76, 89
"On-Field Foes and Racial Misperceptions" (Iber), 52–53
Ontiveros, Milton, 4
Orester, Steve, 84
Oriard, Michael, 51–52
Ortega, Gaspar "Indio," 50–51
Ortega, Guillermo, 137, 138
Our Lady of San Juan Shrine (Pharr), 53

Palomino, Carlos, 49
Patterson, George, 104

"*Peloteros* in Paradise" (Alamillo), 47
Perry, Mark, 107
Pescador, Juan Javier, 55–56
Piper, Bob, 72
Pipher, Clint, 122
Pitman, Troy, 127
Pittsburgh Press–Dapper Dan Classic, 114
Plunkett, Jim, 54
Pollard, Gary, 72
Powell High School, 43
prisoners of war (POWs), 32–33, 63

racial scripts, 7–8, 12
racism. *See* discrimination
railroad work, 25–27, 29–30
Ramirez, Harold, 132
Ramirez, Joe Jr., 132
Ramirez, Sally, 132
Ramos, Armando "Mando," 49
Ramos family, 131
Rawlins High School, 93, 96, 97, 127
Reeves, Orville, 78
Regalado, Samuel O., 7, 8–9, 46, 47
Reinhart, Steve, 81
Rhodes, Dell, 90
Rhodes, Ron, 91
Rice, Bryce, 90
Ríos, Julius, 131
Risha, Ed, 102
Rivers, Joe (José Ybarra), 48
Robertson, Port, 65
Robinson, Terry, 70
Rocky Mountain AAU Wrestling Tournament, 74
Rodriguez, Alberto, 46, 47–48
Rodríguez, Gregory S., 49
Rodriguez, Gus, 131
Rodríguez, Rafaela, 96–97
Rokha, Tim, 109
Romero, Tom L., 49–50
Romine, Done, 72
Rondinone, Troy, 49, 50–51
Rosales, Miguel A., 24, 25–26
Rozel, Tom, 77

Sailors, Kenny, 3–4
Saint Joseph Orphanage, 36
Salas, Joe, 48
Sanchez, Albert, 28
Sanchez, Alicia, 34–35
Sanchez, Arthur: on childhood neighborhoods, 35–36; collegiate wrestling career of, 78; competes at Olympic trials, 74, 75–76; high school wrestling career of, 77–78; marriage of, 78; on marriage of Marcelino and Susan, 31; military service of, 100; postathletic career of, 100, 123; as wrestler, 5
Sanchez, Britt, 126–27
Sanchez, David, 5, 77
Sanchez, Dora Alice, 74, 76
Sanchez, Elijio, 17, 27, 28–29
Sanchez, Ernest, 28
Sanchez, Frank, 117–21, 138
Sánchez, George, 117–18, 120
Sanchez, George J., 8
Sanchez, Gilbert Jr., 102–13
Sanchez, Gilbert Sr.: childhood of, 35–37; Coach Brown's influence on, 42; coaches son, 102; collegiate wrestling career of, 69–74; comeback of, 76; competes at Olympic trials, 68–69, 74–76; competes in Great Plains AAU Tournament, 76–77; diagnosed with heart murmur, 76; Frank on, 117; high school wrestling career of, 42–43; on importance of athletics to Sanchez family, 139–40; influences and connections in wrestling career of, 65–66, 68, 69; as Junior World coach, 101*f*; military service of, 59–60, 62, 63–64; postathletic career of, 98–100; and social and economic mobility of Sanchez family, 134; treatment of, 137; wins USMC title, 75; as wrestler, 5
Sanchez, Glenn, 100, 121–22
Sanchez, Greg, 100, 122–23
Sanchez, Guadalupe, 25–26
Sanchez, Jeanie Gonzalez, 78
Sanchez, Jesús, 25–26
Sanchez, Jim, 86, 113–17
Sanchez, Leo Richard, 67
Sanchez, Lillian, 28
Sanchez, Lynn, 94
Sánchez, Manuel, 81
Sanchez, Marcelino, 28, 30–33, 36, 60, 63

Sanchez, María Romo, 17, 28
Sanchez, Mary, 28
Sanchez, Mary Louise Gonzalez, 78, 100
Sanchez, Natalie, 100
Sanchez, Paul, 29–30
Sanchez, Philip, 100, 123–25
Sanchez, Raymond Jr., 125–26
Sanchez, Raymond Sr.: collegiate wrestling career of, 88–93; competes at Olympic trials, 74–76; competes in Great Plains AAU Tournament, 76–77; injuries of, 89, 90, 91, 92, 94; junior high and high school wrestling career of, 81–88; marriage of, 78; as National Freestyle wrestling champion, 3–5; notoriety of, 79, 80; physical stature of, 3–4; recognition for, 92, 93; teaching career of, 93–94
Sanchez, Sammy, 128, 129–30
Sanchez, Scott, 93, 127–28, 129
Sanchez, Susan Guadian, 29, 30–31, 33, 63
Sanchez, Vic, 85
Sanchez, Virginia, 21–22
Sanchez, Zachary, 129, 130
Sanchez family, homes of, 35–36
Sanders, Richard, 87–88, 90
Sandoval, Celso Palma, 30
Sandoval, Junior, 73
Sandoval, Ray, 68
Sandoval, T. Joe, 37
Santana, Carlos, 51
Scales, Bob, 73
Scherr, Bill, 104
Scherr, Jim, 104
Schoener, Carey, 112
Schoening-Aiken, Ellen, 24–25
Schoolboy World Cadet Festival, 113
Scott, Earl, 53
Scott, Hiram, 92
Seely, Jerry, 72
segregation: in Douglas and Casper, 68; and education of Mexican Americans, 38, 40–41. *See also* discrimination
Seim, Paul, 111
sharecropping, 18
Sharpe, Luke, 78
Shaw, Cecil M., 87
sheepherding, 21–22
Silva, Manuel, 137–38
Simons, Gray, 76
Sinclair Refinery, 66
Skyline Conference, 69–72, 78
Smiley Junior High / Middle School, 100
Smith, Bill, 87–88
Smith, John, 103, 106–7, 108, 109, 113
Sniff, Dan, 68, 69
soccer, 55–56
"social racism," 62–63
Sociedad de Obreros Libres, La (The Society of Free Laborers), 23
softball, 48
Sorenson, Dylan, 130
Spanish-surnamed athletes: interaction with broader campus community, 138; scholarship on American beliefs regarding, 6–14; in Wyoming, 131–32
sports: impact on academic achievement, 135–37; impact on future success, 133–34; impact on Latinos / Hispanics, 132–33; reduction in low-income and minority students' participation in, 139; role in lives of Latino/as, 44–58; scholarship on Latino/as in, 132–39; as tied to work ethic, 120
Standish, Peter, 17–18
States of Mexico, The (Standish), 17–18
Stevenson, Dave, 70
Stewart, Lowell, 71, 73
Stockholm Open, 114
Surdam, Joyce A., 96
Swendlund, Kent, 72, 73
"Switch-Hitting: Mexican Diaspora, Whiteness, and Tusconense Baseball, 1903–1954" (Nuñez), 45–46, 101, 119
Sydney Lanier High School, 56–57

Tamura, Mitsy, 66
Taylor, Chad, 108
Texas Tech Red Raiders, 54
Thomas Jefferson High, 100
Thompson, Merrell E., 11
Thornton High School (THS), 100, 122, 123–24
Tolan, Bill, 81
Topeka, Kansas, 48
Torrez, John ("Johnny Boy"), 48

Torrez, Mike, 46, 48
Torrington, 41
Tromble, Tristen, 130
Trouille, David, 56
Trujillo, Thad, 130
Trujillo, Victoriano, 67–68
Trujillo family, 131

Umezawa, Jyo, 71, 72
United Mine Workers of America (UMWA), 24–25
United States Marine Corps (USMC), 59, 62, 65, 68
United States Military Academy (USMA), 74
United States' World Games (1966), 89
University of Missouri, 112
University of Nebraska, 103–9, 111, 115–16, 118–19
University of Nebraska Omaha Open, 104–6
University of Northern Colorado, 122–23, 124
University of Wyoming, 70, 78, 88–93
University of Wyoming Sports Hall of Fame, 93
US Olympic Festival mini tournament, 109
US Open, 116
US World Championship Tournament, 74
US Wrestling Federation Senior Open, 109

veterans, 60–63
Vietnam War, 100
Virginia Duals, 111–12

wages: differences in, in 1900, 28; in Mexico during late nineteenth and early twentieth centuries, 18–19; sports' impact on future, 133–34
Wahl, David, 70
Walsh-Shaw, Bruce, 11–12
Washakie County High School, 97
Washington State University (WSU) Cougars, 70
Weaver, Darl, 89
Webster, Don, 70, 71
Western Athletic Conference (WAC) Championships, 90
When Mexicans Could Play Ball (García), 56–57
Wide World of Sports, 74
Willett, Mike, 83
Williams, Jim, 102
Williams, Roy, 72
Wilson, Dick, 66, 71
Wolf, Paul, 69
Wood, Cache, 130
Woodling, Chuck, 91
Woods, Ollie, 69, 70, 72
work ethic, 120, 122
World War II, 60–63
wrestling, styles of, 64–65, 142*n*6
Wright, Kelly, 103
Wyoming Open, 106–7
Wyoming Sports Hall of Fame, 92
Wyoming state wrestling tournament (1956), 42–43

Ybarra, José (Joe Rivers), 48

Zúñiga, David, 131

About the Author

JORGE IBER is professor of history and vice president of Campus Access and Engagement at Texas Tech University. He is author or coauthor of several books on the role of sport in the lives/history of Latinos/Hispanics in the United States, including *Mike Torrez: A Baseball Biography*, *Señor Sack: The Life of Gabe Rivera*, and *Béisbol on the Air: Essays on Major League Spanish-Language Broadcasters*.